'Ne regarde pas en arrière!
A quinze pas fixe les yeux!
Ami, pense à la terre.
Elle nous attend tous les deux.'
(*'Don't look back! Fix your gaze five yards ahead!*
Friend, think of the earth that waits for both of us.')

Orphée aux enfers—Jacques Offenbach

Little drops of water, little grains of sand,
Lots and lots of buckets, standing close at hand,
Yards and yards of hosepipe ready in the hall—
That's the stuff to give 'em when incendiaries fall!

Children's book, 1940

I

OUT WITH A BANG

It really was a hell of a blast.

The explosion occurred at daybreak on the second Tuesday morning of September, its shock waves rippling through the beer-stained streets of Mornington Crescent. It detonated car alarms, hurled house bricks across the street, blew a chimney stack forty feet into the sky, ruptured the eardrums of several tramps, denuded over two dozen pigeons, catapulted a surprised ginger tom through the window of a kebab shop and fired several roofing tiles into the forehead of the Pope, who was featured on a poster for condoms opposite the tube station.

As the dissonance pulsed the atmosphere it fractured the city's fragile caul of civilization, recalling another time of London bombs. Then, as now, dust and debris had speckled down through the clear cool air between the buildings, whitening the roads and drifting in the morning sunlight like dandelion seeds. For a split second, the past and the present melted together.

It was a miracle that no one was seriously injured.

Or so it seemed at first.

When Detective Sergeant Janice Longbright received the phone call, her first thought was that she had overslept and missed the start of her shift. Then she remembered that she had just celebrated her retirement from the police force. Years of being woken at odd hours had taught her to focus her attention within three rings of the bedside telephone. Rubbing dreams from her head, she glanced at the clock and listened to the urgent voice in her ear. She rose from the side of her future husband, made her way quietly (as quietly as she could; she was heavy-footed and far from graceful) through the flat, dressed and drove to the offices above Mornington Crescent tube station.

Or rather, she drove to what was left of them, because the North London Peculiar Crimes Unit had, to all intents and purposes, been obliterated. The narrow maze of rooms that had existed in the old Edwardian house above the station was gone, and in its place wavered fragments of burning lath-and-plaster alcoves. The station below was untouched, but nothing remained of the department that had been Longbright's working home.

She made her way between the fire engines, stepping across spit-sprays from snaked hosepipes, and tried to discern the extent of the damage. It was one of those closed-in mornings that would barely bother to grow light. Grey cloud fitted as tightly over the surrounding terraces as a saucepan lid, and the rain that dampened the churning smoke obscured her view. The steel-reinforced door at the entrance to the unit had been blown out. Firemen were picking their way back down the smouldering stairs as she approached. She recognized several of the officers who were taping off the pavement and road beyond, but there was no sign of the unit's most familiar faces.

An ominous coolness crept into the pit of her stomach as she watched the yellow-jacketed salvage team clearing a path through the debris. She dug into the pocket of her overcoat, withdrew her mobile and speed-dialled the first of the two numbers that headed her list. Eight rings, twelve rings, no answer.

Arthur Bryant had no voicemail system at home. Longbright had ceased encouraging him to record messages after his 'static surge' experiments had magnetized the staff of a British Telecom call centre in Rugby. She tried the second number. After six rings, John May's voice told her to leave a message. She was about to reply when she heard him behind her.

'Janice, you're here.' May's black coat emphasized his wide shoulders and made him appear younger than his age (he was somewhere in his eighties—no one was quite sure where). His white hair was hidden under a grey woollen hat. Streaks of charcoal smeared his face and hands, as though he was preparing to commit an act of guerrilla warfare.

'John, I was just calling you.' Longbright was relieved to see someone she recognized. 'What on earth happened?'

The elderly detective looked shaken but uninjured, a thankfully late arrival at the blast scene. 'I have absolutely no idea. The City of London Anti-terrorist Unit has already discounted political groups. There were no call signs of any sort.' He looked back at the ruined building. 'I left the office at about ten last night. Arthur wanted to stay on. Arthur...' May widened his eyes at the blasted building as if seeing it for the first time. 'He always says he doesn't need to sleep.'

'You mean he's inside?' asked Longbright.

'I'm afraid so.'

'Are you sure he was still there when you left?'

'No question about it. I rang him when I got home. He told me he was going to work right through the night. Said he wasn't tired and wanted to clear the backlog. You know how he is after a big case, he opens a bottle of Courvoisier and keeps going until dawn. His way of celebrating. Mad at his age. There was something in his voice...'

'What do you mean?'

May shook his head. 'I don't know. As though he wanted to talk to me but changed his mind, that weird hesitation thing he does on the phone. Some officers in an ARV from the Holmes Road division saw him standing at the window at around four thirty. They made fun of him, just as they always do. He opened the window and told them to bugger off, threw a paperweight at them. I should have stayed with him.'

'Then we would have lost both of you,' said Longbright. She looked up at the splintered plaster and collapsed brickwork. 'I mean, he can't still be alive.'

'I wouldn't hold out too much hope.'

A tall young man in a yellow nylon jacket came over. Liberty DuCaine was third-generation Caribbean, currently attached to the unit in a forensic team with two young Indian women, the brightest students from their year. Liberty hated his name, but his brother Fraternity, who was also in the force, hated his more. Longbright raised her hand.

'Hey, Liberty. Do they have any idea why—'

'An incendiary device of some kind, compact but very powerful. You can see from here how clean the blast pattern is. Very neat. It destroyed the offices but hasn't even singed the roof of the station.' The boy's impatience to explain his ideas resulted in a staccato manner of speech that May had trouble keeping up with. 'There are some journalists sniffing around, but they won't get anything. You OK?'

'Arthur couldn't have got out in time.'

'I know that. They'll find him, but we're waiting for a JCB to start moving some of the rafters. They haven't picked up anything on the sound detectors and I don't think they will, 'cos the place came down like a pack of cards. There's not a lot holding these old houses in one piece, see.' Liberty looked away, embarrassed to be causing further discomfort.

Longbright started walking towards the site, but May gently held her back. 'Let me take you home, Janice,' he offered.

She shrugged aside the proffered hand. 'I'm all right, I just didn't think it would end like this. It *is* the end, isn't it?' Longbright was already sure of the answer. Arthur Bryant and John May were men fashioned by routines and habits. They had closed a case and stayed on to analyse the results, catching up, enjoying each other's company. It was what they always did, their way of starting afresh. Everyone knew that. John had left the building first, abandoning his insomniac partner.

'Who's conducting the search? They'll have to verify—'

'The fire department's first priority is to make sure it's safe,' said Liberty. 'Of course they'll report their findings as quickly as possible. Anything I hear, you'll know. John's right, you should go home, there's nothing you can do.'

May stared up at the building, suddenly unsure of himself.

Longbright watched the column of rusty smoke rising fast in the still grey air. She felt disconnected from the events surrounding her. It was the termination of a special partnership; their names had been inextricably linked, Bryant, May, Longbright. Now she had left and Bryant was gone, leaving May alone. She had spent so much time in their company that the detectives were more familiar than her closest relatives, like friendly monochrome faces in old films. They had been, and would always be, her family.

Longbright realized she was crying even before she registered the shout, as though time had folded back on itself. A fireman was calling from the blackened apex of the building. She couldn't hear what he was saying, would not allow herself to hear it. As she ran towards the ruins with the fire officers at her heels, the familiar codes started passing through the rescue group.

A single body, an elderly white male, had been located in the wreckage. For Arthur Bryant and John May, an unorthodox alliance had come to a violent end. They were her colleagues, her mentors, her closest friends. She would not allow herself to believe that Bryant was dead.

An immolation had joined the end to the beginning, past and present blown together. John May had always sensed that a routine demise would not be enough for his partner. They had just closed a sad, cruel case, their last together. There were no more outstanding enemies. Bryant had finally started thinking about retirement as the unit headed for a period of radical change, sanctioned by new Home Office policies. He and May had been discussing them only the Friday before, during their customary evening walk to the river. May thought back to their conversation, trying to recall whether they had spoken of anything unusual. They had strolled to Waterloo Bridge at sunset, arguing, joking, at ease in each other's company.

John and Arthur, inseparable, locked together by proximity to death, improbable friends for life.

2

CRIMINAL PAST

'You mean to tell me that amateurs are being invited to solve murders?' asked Arthur Bryant with some surprise. 'Have a pear drop.'

'Is that all you've got?' May rattled the paper bag disappointedly. 'They kill my mouth. A study published by the Scarman Centre had apparently found that trained investigators are no better than non-professionals at telling whether a suspected criminal is lying.' The centre was a leading crime-research institute based at Leicester University. Politicians took its findings very seriously.

'Surely the Home Office and the Association of Chief Police Officers won't endorse the scheme?' Bryant squinted into the bag. 'I thought there was some Winter Mixture left.'

'I don't know where you get those sweets. I'm sure they don't make them any more. HO's already endorsed the plan. They reckon any respected person with common sense and an analytical mind can be recruited. Civilians are going to be given unlimited access to evidence and records. I thought you'd be pleased. You suggested the same thing years ago.'

'Well, the general public have a distinct advantage over us.' Plastic carrier bags floated around the traffic lights at the end of the Strand like predatory jellyfish. The hum of traffic around them was like the drone of bombers. The air was acrid with exhausts. Bryant leaned on his walking stick to catch his breath. The stick was a sore point; May had bought it for his partner's birthday the previous year, but Bryant had been horrified by the suggestion that he was facing mobility difficulties. It had remained in his conservatory for several months, where it had supported a diseased nasturtium, but now the elderly detective found himself discreetly using it. 'Civilians aren't limited by knowledge of the law. I've been employing members of the public ever since the unit opened in nineteen thirty-nine.'

'Looks like HO has finally come around to your way of thinking,' May remarked. 'They've got a new police liaison officer there, Sam Biddle.'

'No relation?'

'His grandson, I believe.'

'How odd. I was thinking about old Sidney Biddle only the other day. So sensible, solid and efficient. I wonder why we all hated him? Do you remember, I once tricked him into shaving his head by telling him that German bomber pilots could spot ginger people in the blackout. I was terrible in those days.'

'The grandson is forwarding candidates to us. We could do with more recruits like DuCaine. It'll be a fresh start for the unit. I rang you last night to discuss the matter, but your mobile was switched off.'

'I think it broke when I dropped it. Now it keeps picking up old radio programmes. Is that possible? Anyway, there's no point in having it turned on when I'm playing at the Freemason's Arms.' They stepped through the scuffed gloom of the buildings hemming Waterloo Bridge. 'I once took a call while I was going through the Gates of Hell, hit one of the pit-stickers and nearly broke his leg. The cheeses weigh about twelve pounds.'

'Am I supposed to have any idea what you're talking about?' May asked.

'Skittles,' the detective explained. 'I'm on the team. We play in the basement of a pub in Hampstead. The discus is called a cheese.'

'Playing children's games with a bunch of horrible old drunks isn't my idea of fun.' He tended to forget that he was only three years younger than his partner.

'There aren't many players left,' Bryant complained.

'I'm not surprised,' replied May. 'Can't you do something more productive with your evenings? I thought you were going to tackle your memoirs.'

'Oh, I've made a healthy start on the book.' Bryant paused at the centre of the bridge to regain his wind. The pale stone balustrades were dusted with orange shadows in the dying sunlight. Even here the air was musty with vans. There was a time when the stale damp of the river permeated one's clothes. Now the smell only persisted at the shoreline and beneath the bridges. 'They say there are fish in the river again. I heard another human torso was washed up by Blackfriars Bridge, but there was nothing about salmon. I'm looking up old contacts. It's rather fun, you should try it. Go round and see that granddaughter of yours, get her out of the house.'

'April had a breakdown. She can't bear crowds, can't relax. The city gets her down.'

'You have to make the best of things, fight back, that's what Londoners are supposed to be good at. You really should go and see her, encourage her to develop some outside interests.' Bryant looked for his pipe but only managed to find the stem. 'I wonder what I've done with the rest of this,' he muttered. 'I've just finished writing up our first case. Did I tell you I went back to the Palace to look over the files? They were still where I'd left them in the archive room, under tons of old photographs. The place is exactly as I remember it.'

'Surely not,' exclaimed May, amazed.

'Oh, theatres don't change as fast as other buildings.'

'I thought some of the finest halls were destroyed in the sixties.'

'Indeed they were, music halls mostly, but the remaining sites are listed. I watched as they put a wrecking ball through the Deptford Hippodrome.'

'How many other files have you got tucked away?'

'You'd be surprised. That business with the tontine and the Bengal tiger, all documented. The runic curses that brought London to a standstill. The corpse covered in butterflies. I've got all our best cases, and a register of every useful fringe group in the capital.'

'You should upgrade your database. You've still got members of the Camden Town Coven listed as reliable contacts. And do I need to mention the Leicester Square Vampire?'

'Anyone can make a mistake,' said Bryant. 'Look at that, a touch of old Shanghai in London.' He pointed as a fleet of bright yellow tricycles pedalled past, dragging bored-looking tourists around the sights. 'Do you want to buy me a cup of tea at Somerset House?'

'It's your turn to pay.'

'I didn't think you'd remember.' Bryant squinted at the fading sun that was slipping behind the roof of the Savoy, as pale as a supermarket egg. 'Not only were the files on the Palace Phantom still in the archives, but I discovered something interesting about our murderer. I've often thought of him over the years, poor old bugger.' Ahead, the Embankment was picked out in neon, fierce reds and blues, part of a Thamesside festival. It looked like a child's drawing of the river finished in crayons.

'What did you find out?'

'I was thinking of paying a visit to the Wetherby tomorrow morning,' Bryant announced, not quite answering the question. The Wetherby was a sister clinic to the Maudsley on Southwark's Denmark Hill, and housed a number of patients suffering from senile dementia.

'Are you finally going to have yourself checked over? I'd love to join you, but I'm having lunch with an attractive lady, and nothing you say will persuade me to do otherwise.'

Bryant made a face. 'Please don't tell me that you're entertaining the notion of *relations*.'

'I have every hope.'

'I must say I find it rather grotesque that you still have a sex drive at your age. Can't you just use Internet porn? How old is this one? She must be younger because you don't fancy women as old as you, which makes her, let me guess, late fifties, a post-war child with a name like Daphne, Wendy or Susan, a divorcée or a widow, a brunette if your track record is anything to go by. She probably considers you the older child she never had, in which case she'll be mooning over you, wanting to cook you meals and so on, and won't mind waiting a little longer for the pleasure of finding one of your vulgar off-the-peg suits hanging in the other side of her wardrobe.'

Irritated by the accuracy of his partner's predictions, May dug out his lighter and lit a cigarette, which he wasn't supposed to have.

'What I do in my free time is no concern of yours. I'm not getting any younger. My cholesterol's through the roof. This might be my last chance to have sex.'

'Don't be revolting,' snapped Bryant. 'You should pack it in, a man of your age, you're liable to pull something in the pelvic region. You're better off taking up something productive like wood carving. Women cost a fortune, running up restaurant bills and trawling shops for a particularly elusive style of sandal.'

'They still find me attractive. They might even consider you if you smartened up your act a bit.'

'I stopped buying shirts after they went over six quid. Besides, I like the trousers they sell at Laurence Corner, very racy, some of them.'

'They sell ex-military wear, Arthur. That's the lower half of a demob suit you're wearing. Look at those turn-ups. You could park a bike in them.'

'It's all right for you, you've always been able to impress women,' Bryant complained. 'You don't have the demeanour of a bad-tempered tortoise.'

May's modern appearance matched the freshness of his outlook. Despite his advanced age, there were still women who found his attentiveness appealing. His technoliteracy and his keen awareness of the modern world complemented Bryant's strange psychological take on the human race, and their symbiotic teamwork dealt them an advantage over less experienced officers. But it still didn't stop them from arguing like an old married couple. Their partnership had just commenced its seventh decade.

Those who didn't know him well considered Arthur Bryant to have outlived his usefulness. It didn't help that he was incapable of politeness, frowning through his wrinkles and forever buried beneath scarves and cardigans, always cold, always complaining, living only for his work. He was the oldest active member of the London police force. But May saw the other side of him, the restless soul, the gleam of frustrated intellect in his rheumy eye, the hidden capacity for compassion and empathy.

'Fine,' said Bryant. 'You go off with your bit of fluff, and I'll go to the clinic by myself. There's something I want to clear up before I close my first volume. But don't blame me if I get into trouble.'

'What sort of trouble could you possibly get into?' asked May, dreading to think. 'Just make sure you wear something that distinguishes you from the patients, otherwise they might keep you in. I'll see you on Sunday, how's that?'

'No, I'll be in the office on Sunday.'

'You could take some time off. I'll even come and watch you play skittles.'

'Now you're being patronizing. But you can come to the unit and help me close the reports. That's if you can tear yourself away from ... let's see, Daphne, isn't it?'

'It is, as it happens,' admitted May, much annoyed.

'Hm. I thought it would be. Well, don't overdo things.' Bryant stumped off across the bridge, waving a brisk farewell with his stick.

That had been on Friday evening. May had no idea that Sunday would be their last day together in Mornington Crescent.

3

FULL CIRCLE

Five days later, Longbright stood in a private, neglected section of Highgate Cemetery, watching as a simple service placed a public seal on Arthur Bryant's life. Behind them, journalists and Japanese tourists took photographs through the railings. Arthur had no surviving relatives. His landlady Alma was the only non-official in attendance. She had threatened to talk to the press if she wasn't allowed at the graveside. Alma was privy to most of the unit's secrets, via her indiscreet tenant.

Longbright remained beside the wet rose plot containing her colleague's urn as members of the unit trooped by, awkwardly pausing to offer their condolences. Liberty DuCaine led the new generation of unit employees. It felt like the passing of an era.

Longbright was strong. She preferred to stand alone, and refused to cry. Her fiancé offered to drive her home, but she told him to wait in the car. The cemetery grounds were still waterlogged from the recent torrential rain. Briars and nettles drooped over fungus-stained stone, nature anxious to hide all signs of earthly disturbance. Arthur Bryant had arranged to be buried here sixty years earlier, after the death of his greatest love. The retired detective sergeant found it hard to appreciate that a man of such peculiar energy could be so totally obliterated: the forensic lab had identified his body by the melted set of false teeth Bryant had been fitted with during the year Margaret Thatcher came to power.

Some kind of songbird was making a fuss in the tree behind her. Longbright turned towards it, and found May standing silently in her shadow. 'I guess that should be a symbol of hope,' she said, 'but I wish I had a gun.'

'I know how you feel,' admitted May. 'I don't know what to do without him, how to begin going on. What's the point? It's as though someone tore up the world.'

'Oh, John, I'm so sorry.' She took his hands in hers. She felt angry, not sorry. She wanted to accuse someone and blame them for the loss of their friend. She had seen more of life's unfairness than most people, but it did not stop her from wanting revenge. Alma Sorrowbridge came over and stood quietly with them. The West Indian landlady wore a large silver cross on her black-lace bosom. She was very old now, and shrinking fast.

'John, I wanted to speak to you earlier, but they'—she pointed back at the journalists—'they were watching me. I have something for you.' She pulled a newspaper-covered oblong from beneath her coat. 'I found this in Mr Bryant's flat. It's addressed to you. Not that I've been touching his things, you understand.'

May accepted the slim folder and tore off the wrapping. His breath condensed around the cream linen cover as he studied it. 'This is Arthur's handwriting,' he said, tracing an ink indentation with his finger. 'Has anyone else looked at it?'

'I showed it to Detective Sergeant Longbright earlier.'

'I took a section of the binding for forensic testing,' Longbright explained. 'Just to make sure it was his.'

May examined the gilt edge of the paper. 'I've certainly never seen it before. Might be the first chapter of his book.'

'It was stuck down the back of the wardrobe,' said Alma. 'I moved it to hoover. He told me he was going to write his memoirs, and wanted to borrow my old fountain pen because it had a broad italic nib.'

'Why would he want to write with that?'

'You know how he had these funny ideas. Never let me clean under his bed in sixty years. He had things growing.'

'I'm not surprised.'

'No, in round glass pots.'

'Ah, Petri dishes, yes, he did that sort of thing all the time. Thank you for this, Alma.'

Bryant's landlady made her painful way out of the cemetery. May wondered how long she would cope without her tenant. He watched her go before returning his attention to the book. His numb fingers carefully parted the pages. Inside was a single loose sheet covered in dense scrawl. 'He never kept case notes like this,' he told Longbright. 'Arthur wasn't organized enough. He couldn't even find his dry-cleaning tickets.' Despite Bryant's lack of proficiency with laundry collection, it appeared that he had indeed written something in the last weeks of his life. Unfortunately, it wasn't readable.

'It's in shorthand,' explained Oswald Finch when May talked to him later. The unit's staff had been temporarily rehoused in storage rooms on the top floor of Kentish Town police station. Finch was, strictly speaking, a retired forensic pathologist but knew a thing or two about indecipherable writing, as anyone who had seen his own handwriting could testify. 'Definitely shorthand. Not the most recent kind either, an older version. This is tachygraphy of the type that Samuel Pepys used in his diaries. Before the nineteenth century it was popular among lawyers and naval officers. Hopelessly arcane now, of course. Be interesting to see how he copes with modern vocabulary. Analogous nouns and phonetic spelling, probably. That's why he wanted the broad nib, to place emphases.'

'But can you transcribe it?' May asked impatiently.

'Good heavens, no. But I might be able to download a program that can. Could you leave it with me for a few days?'

'I'd rather read it myself. Can you forward the program to me?'

Finch had almost forgotten that May had once trained as a codebreaker. 'I don't see why not. It won't be very user-friendly, though.'

'How typical of him not to write it in plain English. I'll call you with a new e-mail address and security reference. I'm going to be on leave for a while. I have to get out of London.'

Finch understood. Arthur Bryant was virtually a symbol of the city. There were memories of the man and his cases almost everywhere you looked.

A few days later John May drove down into the Sussex country-side, and it was there, on the rich green downs above Brighton, seated in the attic room he had rented above an unpropitious pub called the Seventh Engineer, that he downloaded the translation program and set to work.

At the start of the document was a note from Finch:

John—I've tried to give you a head start by programming substitutions for the most frequently used words, but some of it's still a bit wonky. Bryant appears to have used a very peculiar writing style. It's rather rambling and all very indiscreet, the only good thing being that many of the people in his account are presumably dead and therefore unavailable to pursue lawsuits. I hope it throws some light on what has happened. Perhaps DS Longbright can help you fill in the gaps. From the way Arthur hid it, he seems to have anticipated that something disastrous might occur. If you think this has any bearing on the blast, we'd better put together a report for RL.

RL was Raymond Land, the unit's impatient and unforgiving new acting head. May's eye was drawn to the postscript: *'By the way, you might be interested to know that Longbright's mother features in the case. I'd forgotten she once worked at the unit. I think Arthur had a crush on her.'*

May set about copying the pages of the notebook into his laptop. After typing in a few hundred words, impatience got the better of him, and he ran the translation program. His fingers idled against the keyboard as he tried to make sense of what he read.

He was looking at an account of their first case, the start of a memoir. Through the fractured text he began to hear Bryant's voice. Pouring himself a gin, he began typing again. He transcribed the single loose sheet and ran the translation program, watching as the letters unscrambled themselves.

An uncomfortable sensation began to take hold of him. The loose page was a fresh addendum, a confidence not intended for publication. Its final line acknowledged a failing: *'I know I will go back, because I cannot leave the past alone...'* May was suddenly sure that Bryant had done something to cause his own death. You didn't work with a man for sixty years without gaining an insight into his behaviour. Arthur had disturbed the past, and somehow it had killed him. The idea was preposterous, but stuck fast.

He stared at the words on the screen and thought back to their first meeting in the Blitz. That strange, exhilarating time had also ended with a consignment to flames. It was as though events had somehow come full circle. Bryant had known that his actions could place him at risk. Why else would he encode the memoir and hide it?

The elliptical translation wasn't enough to provide an explanation. May knew he would have to rely on his own elusive memories in order to appreciate what had happened. As the sun slipped below the trees and the shadows became scented with damp earth, he closed his eyes and allowed his thoughts to drift across over half a century, to a time when London's character was put to a test few other cities could have hoped to survive.

He tried to remember how the seeds of their future had been sown. It was 1940. It was November. A nation was at war, and the world had blundered into darkness.

4

SKY ON FIRE

Viewed from the far perspective of world terrorism, the wartime bombing of London now seems unimaginably distant. But the blossoming white dust clouds, debris bursting through them like the stamens of poisoned flowers, contained the same moment of horror common to all such events.

The conflict had been so long anticipated that in some perverse way its arrival was a relief. The people of Britain had methodically prepared their defences. This time the island did not wait to recruit its forces. Conscription created armies, and attacks were launched by sea and sky. For those who remained behind, daily life took strange new forms. Children carried their gas masks to school. Public information leaflets explained the rules of the blackout. Rationing made the nation healthier. An aura of orderly common sense settled across the city of London.

As the fittest men were conscripted, the streets grew quieter, and an air of becalmed expectancy prevailed. It felt as though a great change was drawing near. More civilians found a purpose in war than in peace. Nothing could be taken for granted, not even an extra day of life. For those who were as old as the century, it was the second time to fight.

In 1939, London was the largest city in the world. The riches of the British empire still poured through its financial institutions. Memories of the Depression had faded. Good times, boom times, had arrived. Despite the false celebration of 'peace in our time', rearmament paved the way to prosperity. One still saw reminders of the Great War on the streets: one-armed liftmen, blinded match-sellers, men who stuttered and shook when you spoke to them. During that earlier conflict, German airships had bombed the city but managed to kill only 670 people. Surely, everyone said, it would not happen again.

Even so, the Committee of Imperial Defence had begun a study into air-raid precautions as early as 1924. They calculated how many bombs could be dropped by Germany should hostilities recommence, and how many people they would kill. Every ton of explosive would cause fifty casualties, a third of them fatal. Three thousand five hundred bombs would fall on London in the first twenty-four hours. It would be essential to maintain public order, to prevent the city from descending into a living hell. For the first time in a war, the reinforcement of morale at home became a priority.

The first bomb to explode in London was not dropped by the Germans but planted by the IRA, and aimed at the most prosaic of targets—Whiteley's emporium in Bayswater. German bombers could not reach their target, and the city had become an impregnable citadel. The country's prime minister had seen active military service, and was experienced in the way of warfare. The King remained in Buckingham Palace. The government, the monarchy, the people were seen to be moving in one direction. The shops remained open. The deckchairs were set out in Hyde Park, and the band played on.

But by November 1940, the uneasy anticlimax of the Twilight War had been over for six months, and the Blitz had become a way of life. After the fall of France, the nation was braced for imminent invasion, and Londoners were so used to living under the constant threat of air attack that they simply went on with their business. 'Taking it' became part of the fight, as important as attacking.

Bombs were particularly devastating when they hit crowded stations. One hundred and eleven people were crushed and blown apart at Bank station. Sixty-four were drowned in cascading mud at Balham. Everyone knew someone who had died, or who had narrowly escaped death. The thin newspapers were filled with vague news of victories, but personal experience suggested only misery and endurance.

Images etched themselves in John May's mind and remained there throughout his life: a bus standing on its end, a warden hugging a silent, terrified child, a bright blue hat at the edge of a blood-spattered crater. One night, audiences emerged from *Faust* at Sadler's Wells to find the sky on fire. If London was the centre of the world, the world was burning. It was a violent place in which to discover a purpose. It was a good place to forge a friendship.

5

SANDWICHES ON THE BRIDGE

On the morning of Monday, 11 November 1940, after a weekend of sirens, booming anti-aircraft guns, distant bombs and droning aircraft, nineteen-year-old John May was most concerned about getting to work early, because it was his first day in a new job and he was anxious to make a good impression.

He jumped from the rear platform of the bus as it slowed on its turn from the Aldwych, and searched the ashen pavements of the Strand, wondering if he had somehow missed an air-raid warning. It was still quite dark, too early for a daylight assault. The blackout ended half an hour before sunrise, when the greatest danger to commuters was the 'silent peril', trolley buses that glided by with a whisper of sheened steel. The clear weather of the last two days had allowed heavier bombing raids than usual, but the morning was mild and overcast, a healthy sign; German bombers were unable to follow the river into London's heart when the cloud base was so low.

May wasn't sure where the nearest shelter was, and had yet to make his way to Bow Street. He kept his shirt-tail hanging out below the hem of his jacket as a white flag to motorists; over four thousand people had been killed in blackout accidents during the first few months of the war. It was safer to take an overseas posting with the British Expeditionary Force.

The shops and restaurants of the Strand had been boarded up

from the Kardomah to the Coal Hole, but a sign nailed beneath a shirtmaker's 'Business As Usual' banner pointed the way to a shelter. May made a mental note of it. The street lamps were off, and only strips of white paint on the kerbs marked out his route. He passed a large branch of Boots fortified with sandbags and, near the top, when those had run out, old telephone directories.

May wondered if he was over-keen, turning up so early on his first day. There had been several raids the previous night and few Londoners had managed more than four hours' sleep, despite the protestations of patriots who insisted that their slumber was undisturbed by falling bombs. This morning it seemed as if the entire city had decided on a late start. He passed a pair of sleepy-eyed girls walking arm in arm, their matching homemade hats pinned with luminous brooches. An ARP warden paused in a shop doorway to draw guiltily on a thin roll-up. An elderly man in a cap and a heavy wool coat checked the gutter for dog-ends. The grey street smelled of rolling tobacco and charred wood.

Sixty years later, John May would amble along the same route and see more people sleeping rough than he had during the war, but at the moment, on this anaemic Monday, all he cared about was reaching his office before someone decided that they had made a terrible mistake and didn't actually need a new recruit to work in an experimental police department, especially not a kid who had been prematurely thrust into his profession by the outbreak of war.

He found the police station at Bow Street with ease—he'd spent enough mornings in Covent Garden with his father to know his way around—but could not locate the entrance he had been instructed to use. Carfax, the bulldog-faced desk sergeant, sent him out of the front door, past the hand-printed sign to the public that read: 'Be Good—We're Still Open', and into a side alley where he discovered the unmarked blue door. Failing to find a bell, he was about to knock when it suddenly opened.

'Are you the new chap?' asked a statuesque young woman whose cockney accent emerged through carmine lips. 'Blimey, you're a bit eager, aren't you?' She opened the door wider. 'You'd better come in, you're making the street untidy.'

May pulled off his cap and stepped into a narrow corridor. The young woman's protuberant bust was alarmingly close to his face in the darkness, but she didn't seem to notice. 'Go up the top of them stairs and take the first right. Mind you don't trip on the treads, some of the rods are gone, and there's textbooks everywhere. We only just moved in.'

May reached the linoleumed landing and found himself standing before a faintly lit office door. Radio music played inside. On the panel in front of him was tacked a sheet of paper reading: 'KNOCK AND WAIT'. He did so, lightly, and when nothing occurred, more heavily.

'You don't have to bash the thing in,' called an irritated voice. 'Just open it.'

May entered a cluttered sepia room with a sloping floor. A pair of green glass desk lamps threw cones of light against the blackout curtains, where a young man with chestnut hair and a purple scarf knotted round his throat was trying to see something through a magnifying glass. 'The Home Office insists on the "Knock and Wait" signs,' he explained, not looking up. 'They're meant to give us time to clear away sensitive papers. As if we had any in the first place. Here.' He thrust the glass at May, together with a sheet of butcher's paper covered in hand-drawn illustrations of butterflies. 'See if you can spot a hidden message on that.'

Taken aback, May turned his attention to the drawing and studied it carefully. 'They all have the same pattern, red admirals,' he said, 'but the colours are wrong. They rather look like naval code. You know, signal flags. Admirals, I suppose that's the tip-off. I think I can read it.' He squinted at the page. 'W-E-R-E-O-U-T-O-F-T-E-A.'

'I see.' The young man snatched the sheet of paper back from him. 'It'll be from the tailors downstairs. They were both in the navy. We have to share the kettle and the gas ring. Bit of a smartarse, are you?'

'N-No,' stammered May.

'Jolly good,' said the young man, holding out his hand. 'I'm Arthur Bryant.' He tugged his fawn cardigan over a pudgy stomach and smiled conspiratorially. 'You must be Mr May. What should I call you?'

'John, sir.'

'Don't call me "sir", I've not been knighted yet. You look fairly sturdy. We could do with someone like you.' Bryant was the indoor type, shorter and fleshier than his counterpart. May boxed and played football. He had a long reach, wide shoulders and thick thighs, a look women liked. In decades to come, the difference in their heights became more noticeable as Bryant shrank and May's posture stayed firm.

'Did you meet our glamorous DS?'

'Rather.' May nodded enthusiastically.

'She's a hoot, isn't she?' Bryant's smile unclouded into a grin. 'One of the first female detective sergeants in the country, thanks to this mess.' May assumed he was referring to the war and not the room. 'Idolizes American film stars, wears make-up and high heels to work against the rules, not at all frightened of looking like a tart. Gladys Forthright. She's engaged to a sergeant called Harris Longbright. Do you think she's just doing it for the assonance?' Bryant barked an extraordinary laugh. 'I must say I thought they were going to send me someone older. You're what, twenty?'

'Nineteen.'

'Nineteen, eh?' Bryant rolled his pale blue eyes. 'That's a bit young for this lark.'

'Not at all,' May bridled. 'There were lads younger than me lost at Scapa Flow.'

'You're right, of course. Eight hundred on the *Royal Oak*. It makes one doubt the existence of a grand plan. Still, all hands to the pumps at home, eh? I hope we'll be able to do something useful together. I hear they're making you a detective.'

'Apparently.' May tried to sound nonchalant. 'I was on a one-year intensive but I wasn't able to finish the course. It's impossible to get into Hendon, and our place was closed down. They've run out of instructors.'

'So they just bumped you up? Very decent of them. I'm twenty-two and absolutely forbidden from participating in investigations unaided because they think I'm irresponsible, but there's no one else available to head the unit, ha ha. They probably sent you here because you look sensible. Good trick, that.' Bryant peered round the edge of the blackouts, saw that the street was growing light and opened the curtains, hastily switching off the desk lamps. 'We can't afford to get fined again,' he explained, looking down through the X-taped windows. 'I'm hopeless at remembering to turn things off.'

'You didn't get called up?'

'Well, I did, but I've a bit of a dicky pump.' He gave his chest an exploratory tap. 'And there were other factors that prevented me from going,' he added mysteriously. Years later, May found out that Bryant's brother had died on a Thames barge, and because their mother lived alone in Bethnal Green without financial support, the Port of London Authority had arranged a special dispensation for her surviving son. There was another mitigating circumstance that protected Bryant from conscription, but it was not something he felt comfortable speaking of. 'What about you?'

'Essential industry. I'm waiting for a post to come up. I've been recommended for cypher-breaking. Shortlisted for a special unit intercepting codes coming from the Atlantic.'

'They're putting something together in Hertfordshire, aren't they? If they don't get a move on it'll all be over. Do you want a pipe? We've still got some tobacco, but it's a bit ropy.' Bryant waved a wallet of foul-smelling shag past him and dropped it into the chaos of the desk.

'I don't, thanks,' said May, removing his coat and looking for somewhere clean to put it. 'There's a very good code station already running, but they're stocking it with the best of the Oxford grads. I'll just have to wait my turn.'

'You probably want to know what this is all about,' said Bryant, pushing a chair at him. 'Sorry no one could tell you much, but the MoI and the Home Office are very big on public morale at the moment.'

'I've noticed,' said May. 'The block on information is a bit stiff. Part of Hyde Park near Marble Arch was roped off at the weekend. They reckon an underground shelter was blown to bits, heads and arms and legs everywhere. The only way they could tell the girls from the men was by their hair. But I didn't see anything about it in the papers.'

'No, you wouldn't. I can understand that, but some of the other directives are driving us barmy.' Bryant sucked noisily at his pipe. 'This business with lifts having to be kept at the bottom of shafts during raids, except in tube stations, where they have to be kept at the top. I suppose it's sensible, but all transgressions have to be reported, and it makes so much paperwork. Not that you'll have had any paperwork on us.'

'No, they wouldn't even tell me what PCU stood for.'

'Peculiar Crimes Unit, isn't it frightful? I think their perception of the word "peculiar" and mine differ somewhat. I've got some bumph here you can read through.' He rooted around among his papers, sending several overstuffed folders to the floor, but failed to locate anything specific.

Thinking about his first impression of Arthur Bryant some years later, May was reminded of a young Alec Guinness, bright-eyed and restless, distracted and a little awkward, filled to exhaustion with ideas. May was less excitable, and his habit of keeping a rein on the more excessive reaches of his imagination pegged him to others as the reserved, serious one. After their deaths, it was said by their biographer that 'Bryant said what he meant and May meant what he said'. May was the diplomat, Bryant the iconoclast, a decent combination as it turned out.

'They meant "peculiar" in the sense of "particular", but the damage is done, and the name is attracting some very odd cases. We had a report last month of a man sucking blood out of a Wren in Leicester Square. It's hopeless. The Heavy Rescue Squads are busy trying to locate people who've been buried alive under tons of rubble, most of the central London constabulary remaining at home have left to join the ARP, the ATS and the AFS, and we're expected to go chasing around after Bela Lugosi. Morale again, you see. They don't want people to think there's a bogeyman roaming around in the blackouts, otherwise they won't head to the shelters. Panic in the streets; it's an image that scares the hell out of them. You'd think we were more of a propaganda unit than a proper detective squad.'

'How many of us are there?' asked May, moving a stack of handwritten music scores from a chair and seating himself.

'Half a dozen, including you. Superintendent Davenport's the most senior DI, spends all of his time haunting the HO and the Met, or playing billiards with Sergeant Carfax, who's married to his ghastly sister. She comes creeping around here on the scrounge for salvage donations, got a face like a witch doctor's rattle. No, we don't see too much of Davenport, luckily. Then there's Dr Runcorn, rather ancient and not much cop but the only forensics wallah they could spare us. We have a young pathologist called Oswald Finch, tragically born without a sense of humour, we use him for the serious stuff. DS Forthright is also a part-time member of the WVS. Then there's us two, and finally a couple of utterly vacant PCs, Crowhurst and Atherton. Crowhurst has something wrong with his depth perception and falls over a lot, and Atherton used to be a greengrocer.'

'My father is a greengrocer,' said May indignantly.

'No offence, old man,' apologized Bryant, whose own father had abandoned his family to earn drink money in Petticoat Lane peddling rings for blackout curtains at a shilling a dozen, 'but poor old Atherton really would be better employed shifting sprouts. Oh, and we're getting one more today, a former copper called Sidney Biddle. I've got his details around here somewhere. Davenport was very keen about taking him on. I get the feeling he's coming in as a bit of a spy, though I'm not sure what he'll find to report on. We're rather a dead-letter office. To date we've had a hand in a couple of prosecutions, but nothing that can be made public.'

'Why not?'

Bryant rubbed his nose ruminatively. 'The sort of cases that pass through here are a bit of an embarrassment for everyone concerned. The regular force can't handle them, so they end up on these desks.' He indicated the overflowing surfaces of the two desks that had been shoved back to back beside the window. 'I'll have a clear-up while you get settled. Have Forthright find you a tea mug, and hang on to it. You never know when there'll be a shortage. We can get most things, but you hear rumours and everyone goes mad.'

May knew what he meant. With each passing week, a household item, so taken for granted before the war, would vanish from the list of available home comforts. Last week there was a run on toothbrushes. The smallest rumour was enough to spark panic buying. Foods were fast disappearing from the daily menu. Oddly, the commonest items seemed to cease first, so that sugar, butter and bacon were rationed while milk chocolate remained available.

At lunchtime, Bryant took his new partner for a walk down to the Thames. The city was turning itself into a fortress, barricaded, sandbagged and patrolled in imminent expectation of invasion.

'What topsy-turvy times we live in,' laughed Bryant, striding across the windy reach of Waterloo Bridge, his scarf flapping about his prominent ears. 'I've stood here after the alert has sounded and watched the German bombers flying low along the river, dropping their loads on the docks, then I've gone back to the unit to investigate a theft of cufflinks from some diplomat's quarters in Regent's Park as if it was the most important thing in the world.'

'What's your speciality?' asked May, pacing beside him.

'Mine? Academic studies, really. Classics. Abstruse thought. The HO thought the war might throw up a few cases that need sensitive handling, and realized that there were no brainboxes in the field of detection.'

'Who decides which cases we get?'

'Well, Davenport likes to pretend he does, but the orders come from higher up. He's not a total dunderhead, of course, just ineffectual. I think being placed in charge of this unit is a bit beyond him. He's rather straitlaced. The RAF wouldn't have him because he's short-sighted, and he's still miffed. My word, I don't like the look of that.'

In the distance white clouds were breaking, and shafts of sunlight glowed above patches of oily water.

'They're trying to restrict movement around the city, putting up a lot of barricades, something about not wanting too many people out on the streets, but I managed to flannel a couple of passes out of Davenport that should get us anywhere we want to go. Where do you live?'

'I'm staying with an aunt in Oakley Square,' May explained, leaning on the white stone balustrade and looking down into the water. 'Camden Town. I'll be able to walk in if the services are disrupted. I was born in Vauxhall, not a very salubrious area, but my mother managed to get me into a decent school.' He laughed. 'They've shifted all the children from our local Mixed Infants down to Kent for the duration. Poor people of Kent.'

'I heard a country woman on the wireless say that she would rather take a savage from Fiji than a child from Birmingham,' said

Bryant. 'Those kids will probably give the countryside a good shaking up.'

'I take it you're a town man, then.'

'Lord, yes. I went on a hop-picking holiday once and was never so miserable in my entire life, although I did learn how to poach rabbits. I'd hate to be out of the city and miss all this. Everyone's so friendly all of a sudden. I think it's because we're part of something at last, not pulling in different directions. Can't you feel it? Things are shaking up instead of sticking where they've always been. Remember how everyone used to hate the ARP wardens before Christmas, going on about how they did nothing except play darts and cards all day? Look at them now, being treated like heroes. I think some good will come of it. The old sangfroid is starting to melt, don't you think? Lords and layabouts sharing the same misfortunes.'

'Spoken like a communist,' joked May.

'I believe in liberty but I'd fight for it, I'm not a conchie,' said Bryant hastily. The wind was watering his pale eyes. 'I'd like to have fought in the Spanish Civil War but I didn't know anyone else who was going. There aren't too many people in Whitechapel who've heard of Franco. I think it's mostly the upper classes who can afford to support their ideologies, not us proles. And you don't have to be politically astute to know that Neville Chamberlain behaved like an arse. I was sixteen when I saw newsreel footage of Hitler's Congress of Unity and Strength, and I remember thinking, nothing good will come of this. All those fervent torchlight parades. If I could see it, why couldn't politicians? Are you a Catholic?'

May was taken aback. 'No, C of E. Why?'

'You have the unperplexed attitude of a boy raised by priests. Practising?'

'Not terribly regular.'

'So what's your take on all this?'

May looked gloomily into the shadows beneath the bridge. 'I suppose we're being tested.'

'Think you'll come out of it with your faith intact?'

'I'm not too sure about that.' He shook his head sadly. 'Very possibly not.'

'Interesting. A war to shake the faith of the Church. Combat is

supposed to strengthen one's resolve. Well, we'd better be getting
back. There's not much on at the moment, but I'm expecting Sidney
Biddle after luncheon. Davenport wants me to make him feel welcome.'

'I've got some sandwiches,' said May, pulling a square of grease-
proof paper from his jacket pocket. 'Egg and mustard cress, do you
want one?'

'I've got ham and beetroot, we can have half each. Let's eat them
here. We might see a plane come down.'

'It's a deal.'

The two young men stood in the middle of the bridge exchanging
sandwiches as the first of the Luftwaffe's bombers appeared low
over the Thames estuary.

6

ACTS OF VIOLENCE

May closed the transcribed files on the laptop and shut its lid. Beyond the bedroom window above the pub, a car stereo was playing hip-hop at a deafening volume, the bass notes shaking the glass in its casement. The elderly detective rose and watched the vehicle fishtail rubber streaks on tarmac. His partner Bryant had always liked noise, thriving in the dirt and chaos of the city streets.

May's instinct, when away from Bryant but thinking of him, was to pick up the telephone and call for a chat. The day before the funeral he had absently done just that, and had been disconcerted to hear Bryant speaking—in that confused tone he adopted with all technological devices—on his office voicemail line.

Now he rang the unit and asked to be put through to Liberty DuCaine.

'We've got no incendiary evidence matching the blast pattern yet,' Liberty told him. 'It's hard to say what sort of device caused it. There was a piece of shell casing found in the next street, but it's still being analysed.' He sounded harassed and distracted. There was a lot of noise in the background.

'But you have a team on the case, don't you?' asked May.

'Sort of. There's a lot going on here at the moment.'

'This was a bomb attack that killed a senior police officer, for God's sake. It should receive the highest priority.'

'I'm aware of that, Mr May.' Liberty's voice was filled with patience. 'But right now we have a full-scale drug war on our hands. Two gangs of fifteen-year-old wannabe Yardies running around the streets of Lambeth armed with AR-15 laser-sighted armour-piercing rifles that fire nine hundred and fifty rounds a minute. Damned things are accurate to six hundred yards, not that any of them can shoot straight. The little bastards are buying them from American websites. We've got two civilians dead and one of our men down. You must have seen the newspapers.'

'Forgive me, no, I haven't picked up a copy. The unit's not supposed to get involved with stuff like that.'

'Under these conditions everyone has to help out. I'm sorry, Mr May, I understand how upset you are, but things are bad here. I promise we'll have someone call you as soon as there's any news.'

May thanked him and hung up. He felt obsolete. The new crimes infecting the crowded city streets were almost beyond his comprehension. People were being shot—shot!—for the most trivial reasons: a jumped traffic light, an altercation in McDonald's, simply being in the wrong place at the wrong time. When had it started to go so wrong?

May thought back to the war, and his first meeting with Arthur, and that led him to the murder. The first one, his first sight of a dead body. That had changed everything. A fall from innocence, and the start of a lifelong fascination with violent crime.

7

FINAL STEPS

The lights. The wings. The devil's face. She saw them again and again, until she was dizzy, until she felt sick. The slender woman, her arms raised tightly above her head, spun on the empty stage until she began to fall.

Tanya realized how tired she was when her pirouette nearly toppled her into the orchestra pit. It was Sunday, 10 November 1940, and she had been rehearsing the whole of the afternoon. Angry with the failure of her limbs, she continued to work on her solo long after the rest of the company had grown tired of competing with her. Now the cast had gone across to the Spice of Life pub, hoping that an air raid would force them all down to the cellar, where they could stay, hurricane-lit and vintage-fed, for the remainder of the evening. They had left her alone with her restless energy, a solitary figure marking out her steps in the penumbral auditorium.

This time she had only just managed to stop at the edge of the stage. As she walked off into the wings to collect her towel, the muscles in her calves trembled with exertion. Stan Lowe, the stage doorkeeper, was supposed to wait for her to leave, but even he had gone off to the Spice. Her stomach was unsettled. She found a foil-wrapped chunk of marzipan chocolate in her bag, and chewed it. London theatres were beautiful but claustrophobic, designed to present the tableaux of traditional plays, and although the stage of the Palace was deep, it was not wide enough to be occupied by a cast of their size. Choreography had to be reined in, grand gestures expunged from Tanya's repertoire of movement.

This was not to be a late-nineteenth-century production of the kind usually associated with Jacques Offenbach; there were no monobosoms, trains, boned corsets and fans to restrict the movement of the dancers, leaving them with only the jumps and lifts of a traditional ballet corps. Instead their gestures were to be free and unrestricted, but this created problems in the finite space, especially now that the wings had been deepened. Tanya wondered how she could augment her moves without antagonizing everyone. The wings, necessary to hide the ranks of dancers from the audience's view while they were queuing to go on, ate into the performance space, reducing the area in which they could operate.

It was while she was sponging the sweat from her long neck that she heard the noise. It sounded like someone coughing, or barking hoarsely. The pitch was low and indistinct, emanating from the chest, like the racketing of the homeless man who bedded down behind the protective canopy of the theatre after it closed. He always arrived as the last of the players left, and scrunched himself up behind a section of board in the corner of the main entrance, beyond the reach of the ARP patrols. He was not like the young men she used to see sleeping rough in Soho Square before the war. He reeked of the night's dark recesses, reminding her that the lost and the lonely were easy prey in a time of hostilities. He smelled, she noticed, how the whole of London was starting to smell, of uncleanliness, of fatigue, of death.

Tanya allowed her towel to fall and tilted her head. The sound was usually deadened in here, but tonight she sensed something else. The house lights were down and only the stage remained illuminated, a miasma of emerald and crimson. She wondered if the homeless man had managed to find his way in somehow, and was waiting for her to leave the warmth and safety of the set.

It came again, the strange coughing noise. A muttered phrase, a warning. She could almost make out words, but where were they coming from? The triple-decked theatre was a whispering gallery; you could tell where sounds originated because the air was so dead and echoless.

'Who's there?' she called at last. 'Geoffrey, if that's you it's not amusing.'

She knew most of the others didn't like her. There was very little dancing in this production, and of the three classically trained ballerinas featured, only she had a solo. The others watched her working hard, thinking that she was trying to steal the limelight, and resentment accumulated like stormclouds; she was used to that. She was damned good and she had the solo, and if the rest of them didn't like it they could go to hell.

She realized that she had been rehearsing alone for over three hours, only breaking for half a sandwich. Like all dancers, so much of her body fat had been converted to muscle that she needed to eat regularly. Tanya enjoyed the solitude of practice, but now her body was resisting her commands.

She left from the upstage right exit. One part of the set was fixed, the carmine cretonne mask of a gigantic demon, its lips arched wide in the rictus of a satanic scream. The mouth was so large that several dancers could enter through it at once. The designs were too grotesque for her tastes, inappropriate to the times. People were scared enough. The artist was newly exiled from Eastern Europe, and it showed.

Tanya was dressed in a sweat-soaked blouse and slacks, but decided not to suffer the cold water of the dressing room. Most of the backstage corridor lights had been turned off hours ago in order to comply with government restrictions on electricity, and she didn't want to stay any longer than necessary. She felt even queasier now, and wondered if she had eaten something that disagreed with her.

As she looked up at the darkened tiers, she felt the building closing in. Something about its shape induced a sensation of claustrophobia. Although the corridors burrowing through its brickwork had been repainted a cheerful yellow, they were still cramped and confining after the expanse of the stage. The sides and understage areas were a nightmarish maze of columns and tunnels, with wiring strapped in loose bundles along the ceilings and walls. There was nowhere to store anything. It was all too elaborate, even for the grand opera it had been built to contain. The electricians were forever leaving boxes and cables lying around. Her supple limbs were her greatest asset, and needed to be protected from such dangers. It would take only one fall to end her career. She wasn't getting any younger. Who knew how many seasons she had left?

At least the Palace was still open. Other theatres were going dark. Bombs were keeping the audiences away. Hardly any of the central playhouses had adequate emergency exits. If the war lasted much longer she doubted there would be a play left running in the entire West End.

As she made her way up the centre aisle she heard the voice again. This time it was more distinct. A stream of muttered non-sense, like the rambling of a fever. It could only be coming from the back of the stalls. The rear seats were arranged beneath the dark saucer-shaped overhang of the dress circle. To reach the exit she had to pass through to the back. No other door on this level was open.

Tanya was not easily intimidated. She was fit and strong, and more than a match for any crazy drunk who had wandered in from the street. But suppose it wasn't a drunk? What if someone meant her harm? She had enemies. All successful people did, it was the underside of victory. Some of the adulatory fan mail she received bordered on obsessive. Suppose she had a secret admirer who turned out to be mad, like that girl she had worked with in Milan?

Tanya paused at the shadowed edge of the centre aisle, unsure what to do.

But there was really no choice. She had to leave through the rear stalls doors or remain in the building, retracing her steps and pass-ing through the labyrinth of unlit corridors that led to the dress-ing rooms. It was time to remember who she was, the star of the only big production to be opening in the West End since war broke out, the show's number one dancer, not some gutless chorine. She marched forward into the red plush darkness, and found the rear doors padlocked.

Her nerve did not fail. She returned to the proscenium and climbed up into the wings, making her way around the slip and fol-lowing the few lights which, oddly, appeared to have been left on for her. They provided her with a runway, a direction back into the building.

If there was another exit apart from the stage door, which Stan always locked as he left, Tanya had yet to discover it. She'd heard that there was a separate side entrance especially reserved for roy-alty, but was not sure how to reach it. The air grew colder the fur-ther she ventured from the stage, and the trickle of sweat between her shoulder blades dried like a sliver of frost. She could no longer hear the voice, and began to wonder if she had imagined it. This part of the building ran below ground level, but a goods lift waited just ahead of her. The cage was up above, and as she summoned it she fancied she heard a fresh movement in the flies, like the dragging of a sandbag.

The cable wheel trundled into action. The lift creaked and started to descend.

Darkened theatres did not usually frighten Tanya. She had spent half of her life in them, and the stories of ghosts walking across balconies after the audience filed out were just colourful fables that enhanced the reputations of their houses. Even so, tonight seemed different. Her stomach was tinged with the poisonous acidity she usually experienced before the first public performance of a new piece.

It was then that she felt the touch, cold fingers on her right shoulder, a light tap that caused her to cry out in alarm. But there was no one to be seen. From somewhere above her came a distinct footfall—thump—then silence. Tanya pulled back the trellis door and jumped into the lift cage. She had just managed to shut it when the muscles in her legs stopped holding her up, and she fell heavily forward.

Her head brushed against the wooden side wall as she dropped onto her knees. She wondered why she was having such difficulty moving. She felt too tired to reach up and press the ground-floor button. Trying to control the tic of a rogue nerve in her calf, she lay sprawled across the floor of the lift, her mind pitched into panicked possibilities. Suppose it was a stroke, like the one her mother had suffered? Her career would be obliterated in a heartbeat. She forced herself to consider her options. Could she crawl over to the brass button panel and find the alarm?

Her legs were insensate, as if they had been injected with cocaine. What now? It became hard to think, or to feel anything at all, just numbness, blessed numbness. Someone was touching her useless limbs. She could definitely feel something cold gripping her ankles, but what was it? How could anyone touch her without opening the trellis door? She listened to the rasping breath and longed to turn her head, but her muscles failed to respond. Something was clutching her hard now, pulling at her feet. A feeling came at last, cold metal scraping her toes. Her legs were being moved, her body pulled and twisted so that her head slid onto the floor, forcing her to look up at the ceiling. What the hell was wrong with her feet?

They were sticking out of the cage. Whatever it was that had taken hold of her had pulled her feet between the staves of the trellis, so that her ankles were resting on the crossbars. She was alone now, left in this graceless position, trying to imagine a way out of an absurd predicament.

This is how people die, she thought. A bomb falls on the building, the bricks close in around you and you're trapped until someone can dig you out. This is my worst fear made real. My mother alone in her kitchen, trying to call for the maid, attempting to reach the telephone in the hall. I should have been there for her instead of rehearsing, always rehearsing. Now it is too late.

She heard a new noise.

The click of a button being pushed was followed by the familiar whirring of oiled gears. The lift was being summoned on the floor above. She forced her head up and watched in horror as the concrete level of the floor descended to her sightline, down to her ankles, brushing, then touching, then pressing, then crushing.

The audiences of the Palace Theatre, Cambridge Circus, had delighted in a thousand lingering kisses, a thousand cruel deaths, a thousand emotional farewells. But there was no audience here tonight to witness the end of a dancer, to see the terrible cleaving of bone and flesh, the stream of blood, not lurid Kensington Gore but something real and dark and intimate, to hear the agonized screams of a woman in mourning for the end of her career as much as the loss of her feet.

8

THE ARRIVAL OF THE CUCKOO

Sidney Biddle had never been in trouble with the police, so he joined them, and then the trouble began. At the outbreak of war, he entered training with a determination to be the scourge of the criminal world, anxious to change the ways of people he considered corrupt, stupid, lazy and weak. Any officer will tell you that a person entering the force with such a mentality is doomed to a lifetime of disappointment. Triumphs are transitory, failures painful, gratitude rare and grudging. Policemen and nurses are yoked together under the category of social services, but nurses bond with their patients. Policemen get no thanks from those they arrest.

Not that Biddle expected appreciation, but he had been hoping for more concrete results from his zealous approach to the law. At school he had been hardworking and humourless, possessed with a religious fire. His parents were at a loss to understand him, and blamed themselves for having produced a child so determined to be a model citizen that they were forced to hide newspapers from him, in case he discovered new enemies within their pages.

After police college, Biddle found himself inexplicably on the beat. He had expected to start in a position of greater responsibility, but his attitude had bothered his seniors, who wisely decided to drum a little humility into him before allowing their star pupil to turn his searching gaze on a sinning populace.

Biddle hated life in the constabulary, manning inquiry desks to deal with old ladies who had lost their dogs, walking freezing patrols, scouring the rough parts of Islington for troublemakers, assigned the gaslit thieves' walks that no one else would touch. It appeared to him that the police were fighting a losing battle. Recruitment standards were in freefall. The police were taking whoever they could get, and they couldn't get much.

In his eyes, there was a far deeper malaise eating into modern society, a moral turpitude that allowed slum children to die in squalor and innocents to be coshed in the streets. He considered most of his colleagues to be more stupid than the lads they were trying to catch. What kind of a world was it that allowed thieving to become more of a vocation than policing? He hated the lapel-thumbing swaggers, the beery airing of prejudices, the backslapping arrogance, the barely veiled contempt for civvies.

Displaying an excessive devotion to duty is no way to make friends. Biddle's colleagues singled him out for all the worst tasks. When he finally managed to get a transfer, it was to a unit so invisible to the rest of the force that he felt sure he would be safe at last. Nobody seemed to know what the new job would entail, but Biddle figured it had to be better than staying where he was.

He was told that the new unit operated under independent financial status, and was answerable only to the Home Office. He had heard rumours: that a series of special squads was being set up to deal with crimes of terrorism, treason and misconduct, acts that were likely to cause social unrest, panic and the loss of that indefinable but essential wartime quality—public spirit. There were already the best part of a dozen services in place to cope with the physical needs of a nation at war. One unit was studying the psychological aspects of propaganda and misinformation, and another was to gauge the effect of continuous bombing on public morale.

The PCU did not publicly recruit and had very few permanent staff. No one inside it was allowed to mix with regular members of the force for reasons of security. There were other stories: of an ongoing feud between the unit and the City of London police, and of a row with the Home Office over the cost of hiring a group of white witches to help with an investigation.

Not since the country's civil war had the rumour-mongering machine worked so adroitly. Adolf Hitler, many said, was consulting an astrologer called Karl Ossietz to help him formulate his invasion plans. There was a belief among shop girls in the north of England that German paratroopers were landing in Norway disguised as parsons, that they were coming for healthy English girls and would force them into German baby farms. When sensible folk started believing nonsense like this, clearly something had to be done, but solid information was hard to come by. Mail was censored. All sensitive details were excised. No weather forecasts were issued. Every time an offensive was launched the newspapers sold out in minutes, and you had to find yourself a wireless.

Biddle expressed his views to Superintendent Farley Davenport at a lecture on law enforcement, and was invited to apply to the unit. A few days later, he was notified that his application had been accepted. He couldn't stay where he was because his colleagues were making his life hell, and the PCU seemed to be the only other place left for him. He was exempt from conscription because the police recognized his zealotry as a useful tool in troubled times, so long as it could be controlled. And Davenport aimed to control it well.

Which was how Biddle found himself in the chaotic offices above the tailor's, in the alley beside Bow Street station one murky Monday afternoon in November 1940. He felt uneasy from the moment DS Forthright invited him to step inside. The unit didn't appear to be attached to the police station, or anywhere else where real officers gathered. There were no incident, briefing or custody rooms, no communal areas of any kind. There appeared to be a secure property room and some kind of makeshift crime lab, which was odd, because they were usually tucked away in separate offices far from public view, or buried inside much larger buildings where protection could be assured. Such places were primed with red steel alarm bells because tons of evidence, including cash, jewellery, guns and narcotics, passed through them. This unit was beside a busy police station, right on a crowded public thoroughfare, and didn't appear to be protected in any way that he could see.

'You won't have seen a place like this before because we're an experimental unit,' Forthright explained, reading his mind, 'and at the moment it's a one-off. We're a bit short of space but at least we've still got a roof over our heads. I'd take you to your office, duckie, but it's full of tea chests.'

The detective sergeant seated herself on the edge of Bryant's battered desk and studied Davenport's latest recruit. Tough-looking, sturdy, hair cropped too close to the head. It gave him the appearance of being carved from solid bone. She'd heard a lot about this young chap. He sounded too good to be true, or at least, too good for the unit. He didn't say much but his small grey eyes took everything in, and he was already starting to unnerve her.

'I'm sure your mates have warned you about Mr Bryant,' she said, more to break the silence than for any purpose of imparting information. 'He's the unit's big thinker. You've probably heard he's a bit potty.'

'Is he?'

She paused to consider the idea. 'Well, I suppose it depends upon your attitude towards clairvoyants, spiritualists, table-tappers and the like.'

'Cranks and crackpots, society's wastrels,' said Biddle without hesitation.

'Then yes, I reckon you'll find he is a bit eccentric.' Forthright sighed and looked at the floor, wondering if Bryant was on his way back yet.

'I'm told he works long hours.' Biddle crossed to the mantelpiece and studied the books piled there. *Common Folk Remedies. A Comprehensive History of Occult Practices. The Complete Mythology of the British Isles. The Everyman Book of Wartime First Aid.* The last one had several pages place-marked with playing cards, and in one case a haddock bone. He looked further along the shelf. *Unnatural Vices—Their Causes and Cures. The Third Sex. Fifty Thrifty Cheese Recipes. Nachtkultur and Metatropism. How to Spot German and Italian Aircraft.* A picture of a beautiful, melancholy woman looking out across the Thames at sunset, and a sepia print of a crazy-looking old lady, possibly Bryant's grandmother, were balanced on top of a copy of *Whither Wicca? The Future of Pagan Cults.* What kind of madman read stuff like this?

'He's young, Mr Biddle. He doesn't sleep much because he has a lot of energy and doesn't want to miss anything.'

'How old is he?'

'Twenty-two, but don't let his age fool you. When he's awake and at the office he expects everyone else to be as well. You'll soon get used to his funny ways.'

'I was employed directly by Mr Davenport and ultimately report to him.' Biddle looked around the shabby room and sniffed. Stale tobacco and something unhealthily perfumed. He sniffed again.

'Incense,' Forthright explained. 'He reckons it helps him to concentrate.' She folded her arms across her ample bosom. 'If you think this is a step up to promotion, Mr Biddle, you can forget it. It's a bleeding dead-end job.'

'I'm not looking to make my name. I just want to see results achieved,' Biddle told her.

'Well, we all want to do our bit, I'm sure,' Forthright agreed. 'But if you keep an open mind, you can learn a lot.'

'And Mr Bryant's new partner is starting today? I'm surprised not to see him here.'

Forthright found herself not wanting to volunteer any more information. She already liked John May. He looked logical and uncomplicated. Arthur was hoping he would handle the technical side of assignments, deal with the labs, tests, collation of evidence, procedural work. The DS raised her head at the sound of footsteps in the corridor.

The door opened to reveal Bryant, wrapped in a huge, partially unravelled brown scarf, with his new partner in tow.

'Stone the crows, Gladys, are you still here?' Bryant pulled ineffectually at the scarf. 'I thought you'd be gone by now.' It was Forthright's afternoon for working for the WVS in the Aldwych.

'I was settling in your new colleague.' Forthright rose from the desk corner and straightened her serge jacket.

'Not ours, surely?' asked Bryant, glancing vaguely at Biddle. 'This can't be the fellow. He's as fit as a butcher's dog. I thought we only got the halt and the lame. Welcome to the unit, Mr Biddle.' Bryant held out his hand. 'I hear you've proven a bit too smart for your local constabulary. This is another new teammate, Mr John May.' Bryant peered down into his scarf to find the knot, then glanced up at Biddle, studying his colleague with undisguised interest. 'We're certainly getting some young blood today. How old are you?'

'Twenty-one, sir.'

'We'd better find you a place to hang your hat,' said Bryant airily. 'I understand you're Davenport's man.'

'I report to him.'

'So am I right in assuming you're here to keep an eye on us?'

'I wouldn't put it like that, sir.'

'Really?' Bryant smiled cheerfully. 'How would you put it?'

Biddle had never taken such an instant dislike to anyone in his life. There was something about Arthur Bryant that made him want to punch him in the face. The other, taller man had not yet said a word. Perhaps he felt the same way.

'Mr Biddle will need to be released for his forensic course,' Forthright reminded him.

'Oh yes? What are you studying?'

'Blood and tissue typing, gas chromatography, perishable evidence,' Biddle replied.

'Hm. Anything more—intuitive?'

'Sir?'

'Interested in forensic psychology at all? Like to get inside the perpetrator's mind rather than studying the mud he leaves behind on his boots?'

'Not sure about that, sir.'

Bryant grunted disapprovingly. 'Well, with Mr Davenport's permission, we'll have to see if we can whip you into shape. I suppose you've been hearing a lot of rubbish about the unit.'

'No, sir.' Biddle stared blank-eyed at him. He appeared to be studying a point on the wall somewhere above Bryant's head.

'Don't worry, I've heard the rumours too. All I ask is that you're here when I'm here. If your classes clash, we'll have to work something out.'

'I'd prefer to let Mr Davenport decide my priorities, sir.'

'Oh, I see,' said Bryant, seeing all too well. He thought for a moment, then brightened up. 'In that case, you can start by making us all some tea. Sweet and strong. I won't ask where you get the sugar from although there's a shifty-looking chap on the corner of the alley who does a nice line in demerara, and use my mug, not a cup, they're for visitors. Make one for Mr May as well. Do you take sugar, Mr May?'

Biddle glared more fiercely than ever at the spot on the wall. 'That's not a duty covered in my job, sir.'

'Nor's cleaning the lavatories, but that's what you'll be doing if you don't learn to make decent tea. I'm timing you. Tick tock, tick tock. Off you go.'

Biddle reluctantly retreated, and Bryant booted the door shut behind him.

'So, it seems we have a cuckoo in the nest,' said Bryant with a sigh. 'He looks a bit of a Jerry, don't you think? It must be the haircut. Oh, bugger.' A siren had begun to wail in the street, rising in tone, then dropping. 'We have to go down to the cells next door. Biddle can bring our teas over, but he'd better not spill any.'

9

PECULIAR CRIMES

'I wouldn't make too many jokes about Davenport in here if I were you, Arthur,' warned Gladys. She glanced at John May hovering awkwardly beside them in the cell, anxious not to appear to be listening. 'I won't always be around to protect you.'

The green and cream corridor of the underground cell sheltered the entire staff of Bow Street. The PCU personnel were granted their own cell during air raids, either out of respect for their privacy or because Sergeant Carfax had been saying unpleasant things to the others about them. The lights were off, and the acrid stench of the hurricane lamps made everyone's eyes water.

'You're not talking about marrying old Longbright again, are you?' asked Bryant with a grin. 'I thought you'd put your wedding plans off until after the war.'

'Not wishing to sound morbid, Arthur, I could be an old maid or a widow by then. Eight years I've been at Bow Street, eight years of late nights and ruined weekend plans, and what happens? Hitler invades Denmark and all leave is cancelled. Not only do I have to do my job, but I also get to be your nursemaid, placate your landlady, arrange for your laundry to be collected, fend off reporters and lie to everyone who's trying to have this place closed down. Now I've been given one weekend in which to get married and sort out the rest of my life. Is it too much to want a little happiness before we're all blown to smithereens?'

'Perhaps you have a point,' Bryant admitted. 'I wish you a long and happy marriage to the bounder Longbright. Listen.' From somewhere above them came the muffled thump of a bomb. The next one would reveal whether bombers were heading towards them or away, like the forking of thunderstorms. 'We may emerge from here to find the unit gone. Give us a cuddle.'

'I most certainly will not, you dreadful man.'

Bryant was going to miss DS Forthright. He had felt a passion for her from the morning he had seen her standing in the queue of the Strand Lyons, adjusting her stockings in plain view of the staff. As she hitched up the hem of her skirt, he had become so distracted by her shiny dark thighs that he had emptied a jug of milk down the front of his trousers. When Gladys looked up and saw Bryant staring at her she seemed genuinely surprised. 'What?' she had asked loudly in Bow Bells elocution. In the manner of British gentlemen across the centuries, everyone had looked away, embarrassed.

There was something peculiarly unselfconscious about Gladys. She didn't seem to care what anyone thought of her. Bryant was aware of other people every second of his life. What women thought of him mattered to a punitive degree. It was to do with being young, of course. After he adjusted to the idea of being undesirable, life became easier. By the time he hit forty, he no longer cared about the effects of what he said or did, which was good for him and bad for everyone else.

Forthright had put a highly promising pathology career on hold in order to gain field experience in the unit, and planned to continue her studies at night, but the war had come along and changed everything. The last thing she had wanted was to have some lovesick young man mooning over her, especially one as callow as Bryant. She knew it was only infatuation, and told him so. Worse was to follow when it became apparent that she was in love with a much older man. Utterly fed up, Bryant had allowed work to fill his waking hours, and tried not to think about Forthright and her fiancé spending their weekends locked away in some bedroom retreat, at it like knives while bombs fell around them. Now she was going, to hearth and husband and probably loads of children, leaving them stuck with the ghastly sneak Biddle. Was it any wonder he felt frustrated?

'I can't imagine why Longbright wants to get married at his age,' complained Bryant. 'Harris is old enough to be your father.'

'Not in the legal sense. Thirteen years, if you must know. We can still have children.'

'Vile thought. I'm surprised he still has the ability after working in the radiography department for so long. They all get tired sperm. And you'll be working for him, which won't be healthy.'

'I've worked for him before. He's the best there is.'

Bryant pulled his scarf over his ears and threw it onto the bunk by the door. Atherton, Crowhurst and Runcorn were seated glumly beside one another, reminding May of a Victorian souvenir brought back from an unfashionable resort. 'Do sit down and relax, John. You're going to be seeing a lot of this place.' Bryant turned to Forthright. 'You'll have no one to take you to the flicks, old sausage. I hear Longbright hates picture palaces.'

'You might as well face the fact,' she ran a crimson fingernail over the permanently windswept tufts of Bryant's hair, 'you've run out of ways to stop me leaving.'

'You're the only one who knows how I like things,' Bryant wheedled.

'Mr May will soon learn to cope with your foibles. He can be the other half of your brain from now on, can't you, Mr May?' She patted a smudge of soot from Bryant's collar. There was a dull smokiness to the afternoon air of London that hung in the clothes these days, as though someone was constantly lighting bonfires. 'It's about time you treated yourself to some new shirt cuffs. I'd have sent you a formal invitation to the wedding, but it's in a register office and I know you don't approve.' Forthright's eyes twinkled. 'It's a pity. There wouldn't have been anything nicer than to see your funny little face peering over the top of a hired morning suit.'

Bryant flopped back his hair and gave her a helpless look.

'He's all yours, Mr May.' Forthright pulled off her police sweater, and nearly took their eyes out. 'I have to get changed. That's the all-clear. Arthur, why don't you go and keep an eye on your other new recruit?'

Bryant brightened a little. 'Making his life a living hell might cheer me up. He's taking a long time with that tea. You don't suppose he's been flattened? This is for you, by the way.' He produced a badly wrapped package from his coat and passed it to her. The red ribbon slipped from the brown paper the moment Forthright touched it.

'Oh, Arthur.' She looked down at the dog-eared copy of *Bleak House*. He had brought it with him from the office, the only item he felt was worth protecting. It was Bryant's favourite book, the ancient edition his father had bought for him in Paternoster Row, the one he always kept above his desk. She knew how much it meant to him. Curling the ribbon round her fingers, she slipped the roll into a pocket without thinking. 'I am going to miss you, you know.' She reached over and tugged the top of his ear.

Atherton had a camera with a flashbulb, and suddenly took a picture. Everyone looked surprised.

'Go on now, bugger off,' said Bryant, reaching for his pipe as the others started to file out. 'Mr May and I have a lot to discuss. Someone has to explain what's expected of him.'

Forthright went to her WVS meeting. Biddle sullenly reappeared with mugs of tea just as they were leaving the cell. Back in the unit, the young detectives settled themselves in chairs opposite one another. Bryant opened a window and tamped down his pipe.

'Shall we risk it?' he asked May. 'The sun's come out. I bet they're copping it out in Essex.' He cleared a small patch of his desk. 'Everything gets so dusty.' He held up a brochure. 'Now this,' he pointed to the title page, 'is your bible. Davenport wrote it, so of course it's gibberish, but I can give you the gen. The unit was originally planned years ago as part of something called the Central London Specialist Crimes Squad, but they received unhealthy publicity after they failed to solve the Paddington trunk murder of nineteen thirty-five. The squad never really flourished, and was finally disbanded three years later.

'The following year our superintendent persuaded West End Central and the City of London police that their more troublesome cases should be siphoned off to a renegade group. Davenport's no diplomat, and he upset them right from the outset. Whenever we're criticized I send a letter to the HO reminding them that we handle only the files no one else knows how to tackle. I've been granted powers to develop my own specialist team, the brief being to deal with fringe problems, but in reality this means becoming a clearing house for everyone else's rubbish. The unit was defined by the Home Secretary as London's last resort for sensitive cases, but it's becoming a home for dubious and abnormal crimes. It's also acting as a resource for officers seeking to close long-term unsolved murders. London's regular forces have their hands full with looting, not to mention the assaults and robberies they're getting in the blackout, although of course we're not allowed to talk about those.'

Bryant sucked hard at his pipe, made a face and relit it. 'We've been given autonomy, but the problem lies in the types of witnesses and materials I attempt to have included in our cases. The lawyers kick up a fuss about admission of evidence. They're not open to new ideas.' He decided to spare his new partner the details of how the testimony of a spiritualist proved the last straw for a Holborn judge, who refused to hear any more from the unit's witnesses until Bryant could assure him that they were all technically alive and in human form.

The PCU worked on unaided, unappreciated and unloved in rooms above Montague Carlucci, the bespoke tailor's next to Bow Street station, holding the front line against all that was malevolent and profane, until war broke out and their casebooks suddenly filled, at which point Davenport saw a chance to please the Home Office. The unit had started to draw crazy people like moths to a flame. It was the war, everyone said; the war was to blame for everything that could not be explained.

For the time being at least, it suited the purposes of those in power to use the unit as a clearing house for unclassifiable misdemeanours. London faced an accelerated crime rate. It was to be expected in a place where everyone thought that each day was to be their last. Nobody wanted the city to get a reputation as a centre for spies, crime syndicates or murderers. It was important now, more than ever, to show the world that Britain could cope. Privately, though, Bryant wondered how long the line would hold.

'We had a lot of fuss about a man who was frightening the wife of the Greek ambassador. She said he appeared in their garden walking strangely, and that it looked as though his head was on back to front. Naturally it turned out to be an Italian, putting some kind of curse on the poor woman by wearing his coat the wrong way around. Silly, you'd think, but dangerous too. Given the current situation between Greece and Italy, we had to be very careful. The Eyetie eventually led us to a man who supplied Mussolini with cheese, and the War Office immediately started developing plans to poison him. They're working on something similar with Hitler and watermelons. Or was it bananas?'

As the afternoon waned, Bryant described his favourite case histories, even acting some of them out, and revealed the nonconformist methods he was keen to introduce into standard investigative procedures. He left the barmier-sounding ones for May to discover in his own time. For Bryant, the important thing was to make sure that he had an ally against the cuckoo, Biddle, whom he suspected of making mental notes against him.

By the time John May left the alleyway in Bow Street it was night and the traffic had virtually ceased, leaving him alone once more in the disconcerting darkness of a city under siege. As he groped his way home, the case file of a murdered dancer was making its circuitous way towards the unit.

10

COLD FEET AND ROASTED CHESTNUTS

'Can't you tell him I've already left, John?' It was early on Tuesday morning, and Arthur Bryant had just been informed that Farley Davenport was on the telephone for him.

'He knows you're here. He says he can hear you in the room even when you're not saying anything.'

'For someone who appears to be deaf most of the time, he has very acute hearing when he needs it.' Bryant searched his jacket pockets, looking for his pipe. He was forever losing it, especially when it was lit, and had a habit of setting fire to things. 'Is he still holding on?'

May gingerly returned the heavy Bakelite receiver to his ear, then covered the mouthpiece. 'I can hear him breathing.'

'Oh, for God's sake give it here.' He held out his hand so that May could pass him the telephone before busying himself on the far side of the office. 'What can I do for you, Davenport? I was just on my way out.'

'Alvar Lidell mentioned that business with the Leicester Square Vampire on the wireless this morning, Mr Bryant.'

'I know. I found his report fanciful in the extreme. He's in danger of developing a sense of humour. One can't help feeling it would be detrimental to the war effort.'

'Be that as it may, I believe I had expressly instructed you not to attract any publicity to the matter. We shall have to issue denials.'

'Someone from the *Daily Sketch* came creeping around asking questions. I told him the absolute bare minimum. I didn't think for a moment that he'd pass the information on to anyone else. I can't for the life of me imagine how the BBC got hold of it.'

May waved his hand at Bryant, requesting the receiver. 'Ah, our Mr May would like a quick word with you.' He threw it as though it was burning his fingers.

'Mr Davenport? That account was treated as a jocular endpiece to the news. It couldn't possibly be taken seriously, provided no further information is released. To refute the report now would only validate it.'

There was a pause on the line. 'I didn't realize you were an expert on the subject, Mr May.'

'I'm not, sir, but a fire can't burn without oxygen to feed it.'

Another pause. 'Perhaps you're right. Let me have another word with your colleague.' May hastily passed the telephone back.

'I'll let the matter lie there, Mr Bryant, provided there are no further security breaches of this sort,' warned Davenport. 'These are the kind of propaganda victories Goebbels is praying for.'

'Fair enough, point taken,' said Bryant. 'I'm in receipt of your new boy, by the way.'

'Ah, Mr Biddle,' said Davenport cagily. 'Thought you could use an extra hand.'

'I now have the perspicacious Mr May, for whom I thank you. Biddle is rather over-egging the pudding, don't you think?'

'Don't push your luck, Mr Bryant. He's there to keep an eye on things.'

'I'll make sure he spells our names correctly in the reports he prepares for you.'

There was a small, deathly silence on the other end of the line. 'As long as you're spending government money, you must be made accountable to the public.'

'I wonder that they don't have a right to know at least some of the things that go on.' Bryant winked at May across the cluttered desks.

'The news must be managed correctly if it is to have the right effect on the morale of the nation,' barked Davenport. 'You will not let this happen again.'

'Righty-ho, message received and understood.'

There was a pop and the line went dead.

'I say, thanks for getting me off the hook,' said Bryant, replacing the receiver.

'What's Davenport like?'

'He can be a bit of a stick. He's incredibly old, of course, and I've seen a happier face on a pilchard. I hope I never get to be like that when I'm past forty. He's utterly convinced that Goebbels is watching our every move.'

'They say Goebbels has a cloven hoof,' said May, 'did you know?'

'Oh, *that*, it's a club foot. He was exempted from fighting because of it.'

'It's a strange feeling, not being involved in the physical battle when so many others are.'

'I know what you mean. We saw an internal memo about the number of dead. Fourteen thousand civilians have been killed in the last two months, with another twenty thousand seriously wounded, and four-fifths of them are Londoners. They're keeping that quiet.'

'One looks at the sheer scale of the suffering and feels so useless. I would like to have taken part in Dunkirk.'

'You're here to use your brains, John. The government knows how to put its good minds to work. The boffins will win the war in other ways. You'll see.' He grinned mischievously. 'Something rather odd has just come in, as a matter of fact. Come and join me in about an hour, will you? I'll be—let's see,' he checked the address he had scribbled down, 'at the corner of Shaftesbury Avenue and Cambridge Circus, opposite Marks and Co. You'll have to go the other way round from here, cut over to Long Acre and work your way up. They've closed the top of Bow Street for bomb clearance.'

'Well, what do you make of this?' asked Bryant, glancing at the chestnut stall parked at the edge of the road. They were standing outside Marks and Co., the bookshop later recognized by its address, 84 Charing Cross Road. 'The gentleman here found something unusual on his chestnut stand last night, and called the police. They had a look and passed it on to us.'

May looked at the nervous young man of Mediterranean descent who stood beside his brazier. There was a sharp chill in the morning air, and very little traffic. Frost glittered on the rooftops of the houses in Shaftesbury Avenue, silvering the tiled turrets.

'This chap started heating up his brazier and noticed something that shouldn't be there among the chestnuts. Two somethings, to be precise. A pair of women's feet, very small. Heavily calloused, toes quite deformed.'

'Good Lord.'

'I always think anyone who eats pavement food deserves an upset stomach, but this is beyond the pale. There were a few raids reported after dark last night but they soon stopped, and no enemy aircraft managed to reach this far into the city, so I don't think we're looking at body parts from an explosive device. Besides, take a good squint at them.' He poked at the discoloured feet with the end of an HB pencil, carefully turning them over.

'Do I have to?' asked May squeamishly.

'Oh, you'll get used to sights like this. See here, the flesh at the edge of each ankle is neatly torn. Bombs leave limbs and appendages ragged. The skin's quite dry and hard to the touch. No blood. Look at that, clean bone. So we're looking at death earlier than discovery, perhaps twenty-four hours before. Do you want a boiled sweet?'

'No, thank you.'

Bryant rustled the bag. 'Warm you up,' he said, 'Bassett's Winter Mixture. I've mislaid my pipe.'

'I'm fine, thanks.' May blew on his hands and briskly stamped his feet.

'You must get yourself a decent winter overcoat. There's a lot of standing around in this job, and that suit isn't warm enough. If you're short of cash or coupons I can sort something out for you.'

'I'm sure I can find something,' May promised, eyeing his partner's eccentric choice of apparel. Today Bryant was dressed in a suit of large green checks, over which he had thrown a fawn cashmere coat clearly manufactured in the nineteen twenties for someone much larger. He had topped off the ensemble with another unravelling hand-knitted scarf of indeterminate length, shape and colour.

'Now that you've had a look at the feet in situ, I suppose we should pop them into a bag and offload them.' Bryant produced a pair of red rubber gloves and slipped them on. He lifted the feet from the pan of the chestnut stall. 'Mercifully not scorched. Our vendor here had the good sense to leave everything just as he found it. He should really be taken in for questioning, but he hardly speaks any English. I think he's an Ottoman, and rather frightened of losing his work permit, if indeed he has one. I should make a friend of him. I've always wanted to sail up the Bosphorus.'

Bryant produced a cloth bag from his pocket with all the flair of a magician, opened the zip that ran along one side and dropped the feet in. He offered May another chance to study its contents.

'So what's this chap's routine?' asked May. 'I imagine the vendors store their braziers in a lock-up overnight.'

'Just off Soho Square near the Henry Heath hat factory. They don't bother to clean them out very often, although they're supposed to, they just lock the lids. He hasn't let the brazier out of his sight since he wheeled it from the lock-up this morning. The holding bay was shut by the last man to leave, and remained sealed until this morning.'

'So the feet must have already been in the brazier last night. How could he not have noticed?'

'He was in a very nervous state when he closed up. The air raid, remember?'

'Did he leave the stand unattended at any time?'

'He went for a wee in Moor Street earlier, but didn't want me to know. I spoke to a couple of the other sellers before you got here. It's a sackable offence, leaving your stall unattended. They're meant to get another stall runner to cover for them but obviously they can't during the raids. He'd just got back when the sirens started up, so he had to leave the cart and head for a shelter. That time, he was gone for about an hour.'

'Do you need someone to translate for him?'

'He's proved to be a pretty good mime so far. I think he's told us all he knows. Besides, we can't get any decent translators. They're all working for the War Office.'

'I wonder if the rest of the body will turn up. Let's see if anything's been reported overnight, and check with the river police.'

'God, it's cold,' complained Bryant, who had hands like ice even in midsummer. 'Good idea. There's a box in Charing Cross Road, save us going back to the unit. Take this chap's name and address.'

'Aren't you worried he might do a bunk?'

'I'm not going to drag him back to Bow Street for questioning. The bully Carfax will simply frighten the life out of him, and then he'll tell them nothing.'

The pair made their way along Charing Cross Road, past bookshops that stacked salvaged paperbacks on tables outside their shops, and chemists advertising a peculiarly furtive mixture of products for gentlemen: trusses, contraceptives and nudist health magazines. They passed the old match-seller who stood on the corner of Newport Street, his blindness and missing leg testifying to an earlier conflict. Finally they reached the blue police box, and Bryant used his key to unlock it. He talked to a woman on the switchboard, and after a few minutes she called him back.

'Seems they've already got the rest of her,' he told May cheerfully. 'At least, they've found a body without feet. They're waiting for formal confirmation, but she's already been identified informally. A dancer named—hang on, I've got to write this down somewhere—Tanya Capistrania. Rather exotic. Being taken out of the Palace Theatre right now, *sans pieds*. The cleaners found her with her legs wedged into the trellis of the goods lift. Suggestive, isn't it, when you consider that the chestnut man left his stall in Moor Street, which runs alongside the theatre? Come on, let's go over and take a look. There's a woman who works in the box office who's waiting to show us around. Smile nicely and she might give us the kind of tidbits she wouldn't divulge to some ox in a police uniform.'

'Shouldn't we see where that chap left his chestnut stand first?'

'Good idea.' Bryant was still dangling the cloth bag containing the pair of feet. 'I wouldn't mind getting rid of these as soon as possible. I don't want anyone thinking I've nobbled a couple of black market pig's trotters.'

They slipped back through the early morning traffic, crossing Cambridge Circus, and passed under the side canopy of the Palace Theatre. May bent down and checked the gutter. He touched his index finger to the cobbles. 'Look at this. Someone has tipped coals out. I'm surprised they haven't been nicked. There's quite a bit of dust around. No footprints, which is odd.'

'The coals could have come from any one of the houses over there.'

'You're right.' He rose, brushing his hand on his coat. 'But this is where the Turk must have parked while he went for a Jimmy. It's a very short street.'

Bryant cricked his knees to take a closer look at the coal dust in the gutter. 'It's like hunting in reverse, isn't it?'

'How do you mean?'

'Finding the spoor from an act of cruelty, and trying to perceive the fading traces that lead away from it, following the dispersal of the participants rather than their convergence.' He thought for a moment, then leaned on May's shoulder to raise himself up. 'There's something out of joint here. What's that German word? *Unheimlich?*' He pulled his scarf protectively about his protuberant red ears. 'A cold wind. And a rather forbidding building. Definitely sinister.'

They stepped back into the road and looked up at the theatre. The exterior of the Palace was one of the most impressive examples of late Victorian architecture left in London. Standing alone on the west side of Cambridge Circus, finished in soft orange brick with peach-coloured stone trims, it sported four domed pinnacles, matching sets of stone cherubs, complex frescoes and decorative panels, with a peaked central pediment topped by the delicately carved figure of a god (miraculously intact, given the bombing that had taken place in Shaftesbury Avenue), and below it, nearly fifty arched front windows, currently boarded up to protect its patrons against flying glass.

'A suitably Gothic building in which to begin a murder investigation,' said Bryant, relishing the thought. 'But our duty is to the innocent. For that reason we must enter the realm of darkness.'

11

FORGOTTEN PEOPLE

... *A duty to the innocent,* thought John May, as he paid the miserable landlord of the Seventh Engineer and made his way back to rainswept London, the London of the new millennium, a place that bore only a superficial resemblance to the dark city of the Blitz. He felt old and tired, because Bryant was no longer alive to keep him young. Throughout his career he had been treated like the junior member of the team, even though there was only a three-year age gap between them. Now he was finally alone, and so bitterly miserable that there seemed little point in going on. But he had to, he decided, at least until he knew how his partner had died.

He stared through the train window at the cumuliform dullness blurring the horizon of the city, and tried to imagine what had been going through his partner's mind. Second-guessing Arthur Bryant had never been easy. A few days before his death, Bryant had returned to the site of their first case. The memoir's addendum suggested that he had been hoping to shed further light on the events of the past. Could he have upset someone so badly that he had placed his life in danger? Surely there was no one left to upset. The case had been solved and sealed. The characters it involved were as deeply buried as London's bomb rubble, and just as forgotten.

In 1940 the pair of them had been little more than precocious children. They had stumbled through their first investigation, and had somehow discovered a murderer. It had been a very different world then, more private, more certain. Nearly everyone they knew from that time was dead. Who was there left to question? Who would even remember? He knew he could expect no help from the unit; they were too busy confiscating Chinese-made assault rifles from the hands of drug-addled teenagers.

May's taxi pulled up outside his flat in a spray of effervescent drizzle. He had recently sold his house and moved to St John's Wood, to a small apartment with bare cream walls and a marble balcony that very nearly overlooked Regent's Park, if you stood on a chair. The old house had become hard for him to manage. Now he had a lift and a porter, and invisible neighbours who arrived and left without so much as a shoe squeak or latch click. Here he could sit and dream, and wait for death. Without Bryant, there seemed to be no alternative. It was as if the future had suddenly been walled off. He had always known that his partner would die first. Dreams of loss had disturbed his sleep for more than a decade. Bryant had laughed when he had described his nightly fears. Arthur had always been the stronger one. There was something callous in his nature that protected him from pain. Now the nightmare had sprung to life, and with it a new enemy. He wondered how he would cope alone.

May paused in the hall and sifted through the pizza deals on the mat. Beneath them he found a folded sheet of plain paper posted from the flat next door.

Dear Mr May,
I thought you ought to know that someone has been looking
for you.
—Mrs R. Mamoulian

May rang the doorbell of number 7, and it was answered by a tiny old lady with unruly grey hair knotted in a bun as big as her head. She beckoned him inside with a wave of her noodle ladle. Around her slippered feet scampered a kickable dog with bug eyes. May inched his way through a blue corridor lined with fragile china animals, into an obstacle course of a sitting room. Every available inch of space was taken up with occasional tables covered in doilies, glass ducks, ceramic fish, glazed birds, antelopes, tiny gilt cups and, above the fireplace, a large porcelain bear in the coils of a snake. He wondered how the dog managed not to smash anything.

'I wouldn't have put a note through—we keep ourselves to ourselves,' explained Mrs Mamoulian, 'but he was loitering in the corridor with the lights out, and frightened the life out of Beaumont'—the dog yipped at the sound of his name—'so I called my husband. Maurice spoke to him, but the man refused to give a name or explain what he was doing outside your door.'

'What did he look like?' asked May, carefully unsnagging himself from a china okapi.

'Creepy, with these awful glaring eyes and huge fangs, like a werewolf.'

'Oh, really?' May's assessment of his neighbour expanded to include the option that she might be insane.

'My eyesight's not that good but I'm sure he was trying to force open the latch. I wanted to call the police but, well,' she eyed the neat arrangements of china ornaments as if they contained secret mysteries, 'you don't want everyone to know your business, do you?'

May opened up his flat, leaving his wet bags in the hall, and seated himself in the lounge to make some calls. Ringing the Wetherby clinic, he managed to locate the doctor Bryant had seen the day before he had been blown up, and explained the situation.

'Of course I remember him, he walked straight through into the private ward without stopping to get permission from our duty officer.' Dr Leigh sounded distracted. He was trying to talk to someone else in his office while fielding the police call. 'At first I thought he was one of the patients.'

That sounds like Arthur, thought May. 'Did he tell you what he was looking for?'

'Yes, eventually. He seemed to be in a great hurry. He wanted to check our files for long-term residents, but he wanted records going back sixty years. I told him we didn't keep them for such a length of time, and anyway, they were incomplete because we'd had a fire here a few years ago, so he left.'

'Did he give you the name of the person he was looking for?'

'You'll have to hold on.' The receiver was dropped, to be picked up half a minute later. 'That was the odd thing. He told me the patient was male, probably suffering from deep trauma, and would have been admitted without a name. I tried to help him but didn't know where to begin looking. What could I say? Those who enter the clinic as residents usually have a history of treatment. Their cases are heavily documented. Mr Bryant seemed to think that we might have taken in war victims who'd lost their memories, or at least their identification documents. I told him if we had, they'd be deceased by now. I'm afraid he became rather abusive.'

'Yes, he does that,' May sympathized. 'But were you able to help him?'

'Look, I'm really not sure. We're very busy here.' Dr Leigh was not prepared to admit that one of their patients had set fire to the ladies' toilets and was now locked in a cubicle, threatening to swallow his tongue if his demands weren't met, and as these demands included the reinstatement of the Great Hedge of India and a meeting with the late singer Freddie Mercury to discuss the hidden meanings in his lyrics, they were all in for a long day.

'He was going around questioning the nurses,' said the doctor impatiently. 'Wanted to know when various patients had arrived, how long they were staying, that sort of thing. But I don't think we were able to help him.'

'Why not?' asked May.

'Well, when my staff tried to answer his questions, he ignored them and went off to talk to someone in the day room.'

'Do you know who?'

'I have no idea. But he was making notes on some kind of a list.'

Alma Sorrowbridge put down her squeegee and gave him an odd look. She was the only woman in the Battersea street who still washed her front step, and was proud of the fact. 'What sort of a list?' she asked.

'Names of people—patients. Something from the Wetherby clinic. In his room, perhaps.'

'I've disinfected his floor but I left everything where it was,' she said dolefully. 'I couldn't bring myself to throw nothing away. There's a lot of boxes.'

'Fine, then that's where I'll look,' said May.

Alma folded her arms across her chest. 'There is seventy-two of them.'

'Good God, where have you put them all?'

'I'm an old woman, Mr May, I got no strength left to start moving stuff about. They're where he kept them, in the basement. Besides, I been Mr Bryant's landlady on and off since the war. I'm not going to start touching his things now, just 'cos he's with God.'

'Would it be all right if I had a quick look through?' asked May.

'I suppose so,' Alma sniffed, 'but remember,' she raised a fat finger at the ceiling, 'he can still see you.'

'He always did like watching me work. Take me to the boxes.'

May spent several fruitless hours wading through the files and papers in the cartons, but they were arranged according to the workings of Bryant's disordered mind. The human male possesses a powerful urge to collect things; Bryant had collected books, papers and magazines that revealed a lifetime of idiosyncratic behaviour. As May rummaged through the photographs of forgotten faces, the absurd news clippings, the abstruse monographs of disbarred lawyers, maverick scientists and mentally unstable professors, he knew he would find little of use. Sixty years of tangled memories; there was simply too much to decipher.

A papery cloud of moths fluttered out of a carton containing nothing but old razor blades. One box contained several hundred keys, another held only seed packets and raffle tickets.

May raised himself from his knees and dusted down his trousers. Perhaps Bryant had thrown the list away. His partner had, to his certain knowledge, visited one other place in his final days. The archive room of the Palace Theatre.

He dug out his mobile and rang ahead for an appointment. It felt good to be doing something, however uncertain. Positive action was the only way to keep his mind from sinking back.

12

INTO THE PALACE

Dr Runcorn had already instructed the Palace not to open its doors to the public that morning. The last thing he wanted was for customers to tramp any remaining evidence through the magenta pile of the foyer carpets.

Theatrical rehearsals were under way for *Orpheus in the Underworld*. The production was due to open without previews on the coming Saturday night. The unusual step of premiering on a day when the critics had normally gone to the country was deliberate. Nearly all of the first week's performances were sold out, thanks to shocked stage whispers along Shaftesbury Avenue that the production would not survive for more than a few performances before the Lord Chamberlain closed it down. Nobody knew exactly what had been altered in this radical reworking of Offenbach's operetta, but the scenery going in depicted all the damnations of Hell, including several freshly invented for the occasion. The carpenters were telling their mates in the public bars that they had never heard such dirty language recited on the London stage, and there were tales of skimpy costumes on the girls that put the Windmill in the shade and left nothing to the imagination.

Bryant knocked at the theatre's main entrance. PC Crowhurst nodded to him through a gap in the boarded-over glass, and hastily unlocked the door. The interior of the Palace was mock-Gothic, with a central marble staircase that offered views back on itself like a recurring image from an Escher etching. Its steps and walls were worn pale, scoured by their nightly brush with more than a thousand bodies. Dusty electroliers hung down through the stairwell, their crystals gleaming dully like ropes of low-grade pearls.

'Hm. Nobody home.' Bryant peered into the frosted-glass lozenge of the box-office booth. 'Let's try the floor above.' He enthusiastically took the stairs in pairs and triples, forcing May to trot beside him. 'We're not going to give the press anything on this one. Davenport wants us to screw the lid down tight because of the victim's background.'

'Which is what?'

'Apparently her parents are Austrian. She trained in Vienna, mother's dead, father's Albert Friedrich, the international concert organizer. He's a pretty well-known chap, worked with C. B. Cochran here in the twenties, but Friedrich has lost a lot of good faith lately over his attitude towards the Jews. He has enough right-wing connections in neutral territories for the FO to keep files on him. He's also a professional litigant. I imagine he'd be prepared to make trouble for everyone if anything unsavoury leaks out about his daughter. Do you have a girl?'

'I'm sorry?'

'I was wondering if you had a girl. You know, a sweetheart. I don't, more's the pity.' Bryant sighed and shook his head with incredulity. 'It's not through lack of trying. I don't understand it. There's supposed to be a shortage of decent men. You just don't seem to meet the right ladies in this job.'

'I don't have a girl at the moment,' May admitted. 'I was seeing someone, but she's been posted to Farnham and isn't keen on writing letters.'

'Oh well, we anchor in hope, as the sailors say. Our contact here is a woman called Elspeth Wynter, supposed to be a mine of information.' He held up the cloth bag and checked that it was still dry. 'I must walk these feet back soon so that Oswald can get started on them.'

'Which one is Oswald?' asked May.

'Finch, our pathologist over at West End Central. Keen as mustard but such a stick you can't help winding him up. At least, I can't.' He stopped and studied the framed posters arranged along the corridor ahead. 'Thank God *No, No, Nanette* came off. All those performances of "Tea for Two" would turn anyone into a murderer. I don't understand it; America gets Ginger Rogers and we get stuck with Jessie Matthews. Nobody up here. Let's try again.'

Bryant turned on his heel and dodged past the confused May, rattling back down the stairs to pass into the theatre's centre foyer. 'I used to be quite a fan of the theatre,' he called over his shoulder, 'but I haven't been since the war began. They're all variety halls now, of course. People have lost the taste for anything serious. Who can blame them?' He looked about and sniffed the air. 'Theatres have a particular smell, don't you find? Mothballs and Jeyes fluid. It's so gloomy in here with the windows boarded up and all this cold marble, like a morgue. I wonder what D'Oyly Carte would make of the place now.'

'Wasn't this where Carte set up his national opera house?' asked May.

'Oh, it was to be his crowning glory. Nearly one and a half thousand seats spread across four floors, five bars, unrivalled backstage facilities, a modern mechanical marvel with room for more scenery than any other house in London. Poor chap opened it with Sullivan's *Ivanhoe* in 1891. The thing ran for a while, but it was a real plodder by all accounts, po-faced, arse-numbing, no good tunes, riddled with self-importance. Audiences wanted the bouncy songs and jokes of *The Mikado,* not wailing British epics about duty and fortitude. They tried a few more serious operas, then gave up the ghost and turned the place into a variety hall.'

He rapped on the box-office window with the handle of a furled umbrella he had spotted leaning against the wall. 'I say, are you in there?'

The frosted glass slid back to reveal a small tired-looking woman in a shapeless brown jumper and skirt. Knitted into the jumper was the title of Offenbach's operetta, the capitals picked out in blue wool. An overpowering smell of 4-7-11 cologne assaulted the detectives. The woman had an old-fashioned marcel wave, her hair held in place with kirby grips, and wore a pince-nez. May guessed that she was nowhere near as old as she appeared to be. She had nice eyes, large and rather sad.

'Ah. You must be Mr Bryant. I was wondering when you'd get here.'

'Miss Wynter? I see you're already advertising the show.'

'Oh, this.' She pulled at her jumper, embarrassed. 'Isn't it awful? Insistence of the new management.'

'John, this is the front-of-house manager, Elspeth Wynter. My partner, John May.'

'I'm pleased to make your acquaintance, Mr May.'

'A pleasure to meet a lady of the theatre,' said May, in the charming tone he unconsciously reserved for women.

'We looked in once but couldn't see anyone.'

'No, you wouldn't. I was on the floor with Nijinsky.' Elspeth opened the door of her office and emerged carrying a tortoise in a straw-filled cardboard box. 'I keep him under my stool because of the electric heater,' she explained, 'but I can't leave him alone because he chews through the wiring. Nijinsky's supposed to be hibernating but he's an insomniac. It's the bombs, they're enough to wake the dead. Do you want to go down and meet the company? They're about to start today's rehearsals.'

Bryant looked surprised. 'Have they been told what happened?'

'Only that Miss Capistrania went missing yesterday and will be replaced.' She walked ahead of them with the tortoise box under her arm, leading the way to the stalls. 'The artistic director is a lady, Helena Parole. This is a bit of a comeback for her. She's been away for a while, if you know what I mean.' She made a drinking gesture with her cupped right hand. 'Problems mixing grape and grain. The insurers aren't allowing her to touch a drop for the entire run.' She pointed down to the group standing in front of the bare stage. 'Not all of the sets have arrived, and everyone's getting nervous because they can't finish blocking.'

'Forgive me—blocking?'

'Fixing their physical movements, Mr May. Talk to me if you want to know anything. I'm always here, and I keep tabs on them all. The one in the yellow bandanna is Helena. The coloured gentleman with the artistic haircut is Benjamin Woolf, Miss Capistrania's agent. The confused-looking fellow is Geoffrey Whittaker. He's the stage manager. The girl beside him is Madeline Penn, the ASM, she's on loan from RADA because our other girl got bombed out and had a nervous breakdown. The man sitting down on the box steps in the snappy cardigan is Harry, he keeps the peace around here. They'll introduce you to the company.'

'Is it necessary to meet them all?' asked May, who was not at home in theatrical surroundings.

'It might throw some light on Miss Capistrania.' Bryant shrugged. 'We need to know if she was close to anyone, that sort of thing.'

Helena Parole had a handshake like a pair of mole grips and a smile so false she could have stood for Parliament. 'Thank you so much for taking the time to come down and see us,' she told May, as though she had requested his attendance for an audition. Her vocal cords had been gymnastically regraded to dramatize her speech, so that her every remark emerged as a declaration. May felt the hairs on the back of his neck bristle with resentment. 'I haven't told them a thing,' she stage-whispered at him. 'The spot where we found the corpse has been made off-limits, but they think it's because of repair work on the lift. Everybody!' She clapped her hands together and waited for the members of the company to quieten down and face her. 'This is Mr May, and this is Mr...' She leaned over to Bryant. 'I'm sorry, I didn't catch your name.'

'Mr Bryant.'

'Oh, like the matches, how amusing. Is that a *nom de plume*?'

'No it's not,' snapped Bryant.

Helena turned back to her cast. 'Mr Bryant,' she enunciated, thrusting her tongue between her teeth in an effort to extend the name beyond two syllables. 'They're going to be asking you a few questions about Miss Capistrania. It shouldn't cut into our time too much, should it, Mr May? We do have rather a lot to get through. Perhaps you can conduct your interviews out of the sightlines of my principals. It throws them off. I'll have a folding chair put out for you over there, and do try to keep the noise down, thank you so much.'

Having put May publicly on the spot, she accepted his silence as agreement, thrust her hands into her baggy khaki trousers and went back to directing her cast. Bryant felt as though he had been dismissed from the auditorium. Helena's eye rested easiest on men she found attractive, and clearly John May was in her sights. With a grimace of annoyance, Bryant stumped off to the side of the stage.

He found the goods lift separated off by wooden horses with warning boards tied to them by bits of string. The lift couldn't have drawn more attention if Helena had given it a part in the production. The electrics had been switched off at the mains, but Bryant dug a torch from his pocket and shone it into the shaft, quickly spotting the vertical brown streaks that marred the concrete barrier between the floors. On the other side of the stairwell, another slim beam of light illuminated a crouching figure. It turned and stared at him.

'God, Bryant, you frightened the life out of me,' said Runcorn. 'Must you creep about like that? I could have dropped this.' He held up something in a pair of tweezers.

'What is it?' asked Bryant.

'Muscle tissue by the look of it, probably torn from the victim's ankle as it shattered. Don't these lifts have fail-safe devices to halt them if a foreign body gets caught in the mechanism?'

'It's half a century old. Safety wasn't a priority then. The Victorians lost a few workers in everything they built, rather like a votive offering.'

Dr Runcorn, the unit's forensic scientist, was one of the top men in his field, but his air of superiority, coupled with the punctilious manner of a civil servant, made him disliked by nearly everyone who came into contact with him. That was the trouble with a unit like the PCU: it was destined to be staffed with the kind of employee who had been rejected from other institutions in spite of their qualifications. Dr Runcorn was especially irked by Bryant, whose intuitive attitude to scientific investigation seemed at best inappropriate and at worst unprofessional.

'I haven't finished here yet,' he warned, 'so don't start walking all over the area touching things.'

'I wasn't going to,' said Bryant, affronted. 'You surely don't think it was an accident, do you?'

'A damned odd one, I agree, but stranger things have happened.'

'Hard to see how her feet ended up on a chestnut brazier, with that hypothesis,' Bryant pointed out.

'Oswald Finch took receipt of the cadaver from West End Central and has already run a few tests on it, reckons she might show positive for some kind of drug, possibly self-administered.

These artistic types are noted for it.' Runcorn sniffed, rising from his crouched position and cracking his back. 'I don't know why he can't test for more obvious causes of death first like any normal person: heart failure, stuff like that. I just know that her feet were cut off and she didn't struggle. There are a couple of scuff marks here on the landing, the heel of a shoe, nothing particularly out of the ordinary. Suggestive, though.'

'Why?'

'Oh, I don't know.' Runcorn tugged at his ear, thinking. He was awkwardly tall and so thin that he looked lost inside his clothes. 'It's a backward scuff, but it faces forward to the lift. Like this.' He adopted an angular pose, something that came easily to a man who was six feet three and pigeon-chested. 'As though you were bracing yourself against the trellis. You might make it if you were pulling something through the bars of the lift. As if you were trying to drag out a heavy box. Or pull something through the cage. Legs, perhaps.'

That was the good thing about Runcorn, thought Arthur. Like Finch, he operated on a secondary set of signals, pulses that passed invisibly beneath his rational senses.

'There's another mark on the linoleum several feet away. It looks like it could be a match. If we can place someone outside the lift with the victim inside it, then you might have a murder case. But why cut off her feet?' Runcorn stared gloomily down into the lift shaft.

'She was a dancer,' Bryant replied.

'Meaning what, exactly?'

'Suppose she had somehow survived,' said Bryant. 'Can you think of a better way to guarantee that she'd never perform again?'

13

LIVES IN THE THEATRE

Elspeth Wynter had spent her whole life, or rather the thirty-two years she had so far experienced, in the theatre. She came from a long line of theatre folk. Her grandfather had been a Shakespearean, once spoken of in the same breath as Burbage, Garrick or Keane. His wife had been cast in his shows as a perennial parlourmaid, and in true theatrical tradition had borne him a son in the rear of the stalls. Eight years into the new century, that son fathered his only child, Elspeth. Although his wife survived a pelvic fracture when she fell from the stage of Wyndham's Theatre, she ignored her doctor's warnings about the perils of motherhood in order to bear a daughter. The birth killed her.

Elspeth's father took the King's shilling for the Great War, but grisly memories of Ypres wrought changes in his life from which he never fully recovered. Prevented from returning to the front by the state of his nerves, he resumed the family profession. In the twenties he delivered a shaky baritone in countless threadbare Gilbert and Sullivan revivals, but the shows closed as unemployment began to bite and the cinema became affordable to the lower classes who had filled the music halls.

Elspeth's father could not look after himself, let alone a teenage girl. He had no family beyond his colleagues in the theatre, and drink coarsened his acting. Elspeth was raised by sympathetic ushers and nursed from fretfulness while her papa performed in the twice-nightlies. As they trooped from one cold auditorium to the next, shivering in damp dressing rooms, shaking the fleas from lodging-house beds, playing in faded costumes to dwindling audiences, this daughter of the stage looked about her moth-eaten, mildewed world and began to wonder if the possession of theatrical blood was really the gift that her father's boozy friends claimed it to be.

Elspeth knew from an early age that although she was not destined for the boards, she would always be a part of the theatre; watching her father declaim each night from the box kept empty and permanently reserved for royalty—there seemed to be one in every playhouse—she watched the painful changes time wrought on his performances. The twenties were uncertain years, but not as lean as the thirties. Her father drank more as the audiences dried up. He too dried on stage, nightly forgetting his lines, relying on prompts, booed by an unforgiving audience weaned on cinema newsreels. The new medium had no truck with forgetfulness. Celluloid eradicated variable performances. To no one's surprise, he finally died in make-up and costume, during a trouser-dropping farce in which he had already been dying nightly.

Elspeth did not attend his funeral; there was a matinee. She had graduated from programme seller to bar cashier to ASM, through the various stressful stages of management until she suffered a nervous collapse and returned to front-of-house work. She was a West End girl, one of theatre's dedicated personnel, invisible to audiences but essential to everyone who worked there. As one show closed, another began rehearsals, and each run marked the periods of her life more completely than any calendar notation.

She had experienced a moment of passion just once, at the age of fifteen: pushed into a dressing room at the Palace and thrust into by a man she had only ever seen from the aisle of the stalls. He was playing the villain in a revival of *Maria Marten, or The Murders in the Red Barn,* and had barely paused to peck her on the cheek and pull up his trousers before returning to catch his entrance cue. While her seducer ranted across the boards, twitching his moustaches, his shirt-sleeves flecked with Kensington Gore, she too bled and suffered, and burrowed away in the crimson darkness to forget the world outside.

The theatre held no terrors for her. It was home, and filled with secrets, just like any family. It encompassed every happy moment in her life. As Elspeth paced the indistinct aisles of the Palace, its pervasive calm seeped into her. She could tell when the half-hour call was coming without looking at her watch. She sensed the rising tension of backstage activity, even though she was stationed in the front of the building.

Geoffrey Whittaker was also dedicated to the theatre, as invisible and essential as a spark plug to a car. He too was the latest—and the last, it turned out—in a long theatrical line. As stage manager to the incumbent company, he was in charge of the administration, the set, the lighting, the props, the health and safety of his audience, the scene changes, the laundry mistresses, the wardrobe people and the carpenters. He knew how to get scorch marks out of a starched collar, how to fix a cellulose filter over a follow-spot, how to unjam the springs on a star trap and how to keep bills unpaid until the receipts were in.

Like Elspeth, he was unmarried and probably unmarriageable, because his career constituted a betrothal of sorts. Unlike Elspeth, he had a sex life, rather too much of one. In addition to dating girls in the shows, he made visits to a private house in the East End, where for a reasonable fee his needs were taken care of. This abundance of sexual activity allowed him to concentrate on his job without becoming distracted by the dancers' bodies during rehearsals. He had grown up in the Empires and Alhambras, helping his parents prepare for the night's performance, and could imagine no other world. Colours were duller outside, and the skies were not painted but real, which made them untrustworthy. In the theatre, you always followed the script. Beyond this world there were only unrehearsed moves, mistimed entrances, lines spoken out of turn.

The start of the second great war brought unwelcome transitions to Geoffrey's hermetic world. Venues were changing hands, falling empty, getting bombed. Philanthropy had been replaced by the desire for quick profit. Boxing matches and coarse variety acts moved in to entertain a new type of audience: commoner, louder, one that

lived from moment to moment. Now there was something less comforting in the atmosphere before a show, something contaminated
by the urgent, hysterical laughter that nightly rang from the stalls.
Theatres were more frenetic, and companies diminished as the most
able-bodied men went off to war. The Shaftesbury was bombed, the
Strand and Sadler's Wells went dark. It was like a game of musical
chairs, and nobody knew when the music might suddenly stop.

But Elspeth and Geoffrey still heard the audiences of their child-
hoods above the sound of hot water gurgling in the pipes, still listened
to the ticking of the warm-air conduits, the backstage footfalls of
departing painters. They were still the sounds of home.

And something had irreversibly changed. Elspeth had sensed it
first at the outbreak of the war, a creeping disquiet that felt wholly out
of place between the gaudy vermilion aisles of the Palace Theatre.
She was alive to the smallest changes around her, and could detect
any eddy of emotion in the silent building.

Late one night, closing up after a performance, she had suffered
a terrible premonition, and her life had passed before her eyes. She
told no one about the dark, scarred thing that stalked behind her in
the rufescent rows of the dress circle, creeping down the vertiginous
steps of the balcony. She experienced a sense of panic more with each
passing performance, never knowing at what hour it might strike, for
there is no day and night in a theatre. She only knew that it was there,
watching and waiting, that it meant harm, and that something
wicked had to happen.

Anxious to escape, she slipped out of the building and into the
blackout, following the white stripes that had been painted on
the paraffin lamps hanging from the protection boards around the
front wall of the theatre. The Palace was her habitat, but she was
lately being driven from it. She stopped and looked up at the entresol windows, and glimpsed the terrible visage, a pale oval peering out of the smoking salon at her, its features so distorted that it
could barely be considered human.

Geoffrey had seen the faceless creature too, scurrying between
the rows of the balcony, loping across a distant corridor, but he
had not believed his senses. It was the war, he told himself, shaking
his head. The constant fear played tricks on you. Last month a

bomb had fallen through the roof of St Paul's Cathedral, destroying the high altar. For many it had seemed like a blow struck against God himself. If Hitler was the devil kept at bay, perhaps his acolytes were already here, moving among them, and wouldn't they choose such a godless place as a theatre from which to corrupt the innocent?

Geoffrey Whittaker sat in his office on Sunday evening and smoked, but his hands shook. Nothing could drive him from the only world he understood. He told himself that, at forty-six, he was too old for an attack of nerves. There were men out there less than half his age fighting to preserve his freedom, even though he did not want to be free. He was a willing prisoner of the theatre, its plans and strictures. His life was patterned on the stage directions of a dog-eared script. But something had crept inside his world that had no place in the production. His trembling fingers pulled another cigarette from the pack and inserted it between his lips.

Outside the Palace, Elspeth Wynter ran on into the blackout, through the empty city streets, her breath ragged behind her ribs, daring herself to go forward into darkness, frightened to return. But the home that had nurtured her for so many years could not be left so easily. It too was her domain, and beyond it, beyond the black-outs, there was no structure, no control, only the terrible light of freedom.

For Elspeth and Geoffrey, and hundreds like them, theatres were the last repose of stasis and sanity in a world hurtling beyond sense. But even they would be touched by the bloody hand of madness.

14

DOUBLE ACT

'What the hell are you talking about, keep it out of the press?' asked Benjamin Woolf. 'I've already had a call asking why she didn't keep an appointment with a photographer this morning. What am I supposed to do?'

'This is a tragedy for all of us, Ben,' said Helena Parole, whose earnest attempts to empathize with others were undermined by the fact that she didn't care about anyone else. 'I understand your feelings entirely.' She compounded the hypocrisy by rolling her eyes at May coquettishly.

That Tuesday morning, the mood at the Palace Theatre was fractious. Thanks to a night of bright moonlight there had been bombing raids until dawn, and no one had slept well. Sloane Square tube station had been hit, killing many. In the morning's papers, questions were being raised about the efficacy of public shelters. Not enough people were using them, and there were rumours among those who did that infection was rampant. Sanitation remained haphazard, and there was a general feeling that the unchanged air spread all manner of germs. Most Londoners preferred to stay at home, tucked inside cupboards, under the stairs, sleeping in ground-floor rooms or outside in an Anderson shelter: fourteen arched sheets of corrugated iron bolted together and half buried under earth that flooded in wet weather but could survive everything except a direct hit.

The stage was still empty. Few of the cast had yet arrived, but members of the orchestra were seated in the pit, patiently waiting to resume rehearsals. They usually practised in airy rooms behind Waterloo Station, but those had been requisitioned by the War Office, and now the musicians were crammed before the stage in a dimly lit theatre instead of playing in a sunlit space overlooking the river. The most able-bodied among them had been taken by conscription, and they had been forced to fill up their ranks with fiddle-scratchers from the twice-nightlies and even a couple of Leicester Square buskers.

Luckily their conductor, Anton Varisich, like many great conductors, was as adept at diplomacy as he was at extracting mellifluous harmonies from his motley crew. He had topped up the percussion and woodwind sections with exiled Spanish and French players, lending the arrangements a jaunty cosmopolitan air in keeping with Offenbach's play, but previously unheard in London. The nation's music still owed more to the palm court than the boulevard, and consequently the players were having a whale of a time because they were doing something new. Quite how they'd manage to rehearse when the cast turned up and wanted to practise their lines would remain to be seen.

'Will you understand when I tell the next person who calls that your star dancer might be a little late for rehearsals on account of not having any *feet*?'

'You can't be serious.'

'That's what they're saying.' Woolf threw his long body back down onto seat C15 and smoothed a hand across his brilliantined hair. There was an ever-present aura of sarcasm about him that no one responded to positively. 'The police are crawling all over the building, you won't tell any of us what's going on and I'm supposed to act like everything's tickety-boo.'

Helena glared up into the darkness beneath the roof. 'Benjamin, please, you're an agent, lying is a professional qualification for you, like a merit badge or something. You can tell the press she's joined the WAAFs and flown to Timbuktu on a mercy mission if you want, and they'd have no choice but to believe you. She's frightfully upper class, and her reputation will need protecting.'

Their conversation was punctuated by the noise of the wind section practising scales. Woolf had to raise his voice to be heard, but Helena did not wish to shout back. She knew how easily panic could infect a cast facing a deadline under already difficult conditions, but she was going to make sure that the Windmill wasn't the only theatre to stay open throughout the war.

'It's difficult for all of us,' she explained with feigned sufferance. 'You'll just have to do the best you can. I'm out of gaspers, darling, would you light me?' Benjamin touched a match to a Viceroy and passed it to her. 'These gentlemen are detectives, and hope to have the whole thing quickly sorted out. You know how easily these girls fall in with the wrong types.'

'Perhaps we should continue this discussion in Miss Parole's office,' May suggested. 'I think we're in the way here.' He looked back at Bryant and followed his partner's gaze to the stage. Bryant's attention had been drawn away by the arriving dancers, half a dozen long-legged girls who stood whispering and giggling in the shadows of the wings.

Bryant was captivated by what he saw. The theatre held a special fascination for him. When John looked at posturing actresses angling their best sides to the audience, he saw nothing but mannequins and painted flats. Arthur saw something fleeting and indefinable. He saw the promises of youth made flesh, something beautiful and distant, a spontaneous gaiety forever denied to a man who couldn't open his mouth without thinking.

In Helena's office May raised the window behind the battered oak desk and looked down into Moor Street, where men in black heavy rescue and white light rescue helmets were clearing sections of charred wood from a blackened shop front.

'Am I right in thinking that, as the company's artistic director, the production's success lies in your hands?' Bryant asked.

'Absolutely.' Helena looked tense and angry. She brushed at the cigarette ash smudged in the cleavage of her tight white blouse. 'I have a board of directors to answer to if *Orphée aux enfers* fails. I tried to keep Offenbach's French title. They felt it would put people off. I said, "It shows solidarity with the people of France, and it's the cancan, how much more accessible can you get?" Eighty years ago this was considered a trifle, an after-dinner joke. Now the English think it's high art because three words are French. They're such peasants. They'll queue to see a mayoress open a fête but only fall asleep in opera houses. It's not like this on the continent, you know. The French have more respect for their artists.'

The thin November sunshine threw slats of light across her make-up as she unfurled a plume of cigarette smoke into the coils of her coppery hair. The exhalation softened her harshly painted eyes. Bryant realized that she was probably his new partner's type, firm-jawed, full-busted, full of life. She had presence, like an expensively upholstered piece of furniture, a reminder of more luxurious times.

Helena knew that it was important to care about the members of her cast. They weren't actors, Benjamin had once told her, they were her children. But she had no children. What she had was a failed three-year marriage to her agent which had foundered over the argument of raising mixed-race infants in a land where black skin was still seen as a peculiarity. Now, because of the war and the lack of jobs in the theatre, she and her former husband had been forced into each other's company again.

'We have to find a way of keeping it out of the press.' Helena joined May at the window. 'Although the story would do wonders for the box office.' She closed the window. Smoke still loitered in her hair, momentarily recalling an image of the Medusa. 'This show represents a massive commitment of time, energy and money. It's going to brighten up London and raise the morale of thousands of people every week.' She turned to the detectives. 'The board has been planning it for years, setting *Orpheus* up as a public company, raising finance on an international scale, waiting for cast availability. The war has made us redouble our efforts. None of us can afford a flop. We're putting our futures on the line. If *Orpheus* fails to recoup its costs, the insurers will step in, and one of our greatest theatres will fall dark for the remainder of the hostilities, perhaps for ever. So, does anybody have to know what happened? They're more concerned with their own safety than hearing about some dancer's misfortune. We open in four days.' Helena felt safer when others considered her incapable of kindness. 'As far as we knew, she was working late on Sunday night and went home. Couldn't she have decided the role wasn't for her and left the country?'

'Don't you think you owe her something, Helena?' asked Benjamin. 'Suppose somebody has a grudge against the performers? What about the safety of the rest of the cast? The safety of the audience?'

'You know as well as I do that the audience is always separated from the stage.'

'Is that really true?' asked May.

'Backstage and front of house are two entirely different worlds. You can get from one to the other only by going through the ground-level pass doors. There are just two of those, and one has been locked for so many years I don't think anyone knows where the keys are.' She ground out her cigarette. 'It was probably someone from the cast of *No, No, Nanette,* driven insane by Jessie Matthews.'

'I can make a case for press restriction if you really think the play is in the interests of the city's morale,' Bryant offered.

'It'll be tough keeping things quiet this end. So long as an actor's near a telephone, word always gets out. Death poisons the atmosphere in a place like this.' Helena knew that performers were sensitive to the slightest undercurrents rippling the still air of an auditorium.

'How are we going to explain that our dancer has disappeared?'

'She had no friends.' Helena stole another cigarette. 'Nobody who pushes that hard ever does. She told me she was getting weird letters, Mr May. Sex-crazed men wanting her to walk on them with stilettos, that sort of thing. People were drawn to her aggression. It could be any one of them. They follow the movements of performers in the papers and turn up in the front row every night applauding in the wrong places, and there's nothing you can do about it.'

'There is something,' said May. 'The telephone bookings for which you mail out tickets, we can cross-check the addresses of all the reservations so far.'

'And what are we supposed to do in the meantime?' asked Benjamin.

'Resume rehearsals,' said Bryant, taking his partner's cue. 'Behave as if nothing untoward has happened.'

'You could make an announcement to the effect that Capistrania has been taken ill and has been placed in quarantine,' added May. 'Scarlet fever perhaps.'

'Thank heaven someone around here is ready to take charge.' Helena gave May a reassuring smile. 'I already feel safer in your capable hands.'

Bryant made a face behind Helena's back, and was caught in the act when she turned round. He transformed his grimace into a cough as, somewhere far below, an oboe hit a warning note.

'I thought you were jolly impressive with La Parole back there,' said Bryant, bouncing along the corridor to the box office as they left. 'We make a bloody good double act. Perhaps we should take to the stage: Bryant and May, detective duo, some juggling, a patter song and a sand dance, what do you think?'

'I think you're completely loopy,' answered May truthfully. 'It's a murder investigation. I don't have the training for this.'

'You're young enough still to have an open mind,' said Bryant, laughing. 'That's all the training you need.'

15

SOMETHING POISONOUS

'Hello, Oswald, something's different in here, have you had the place decorated? I'm rather partial to the smell of new paint.'

'Very funny, Mr Bryant.'

Oswald Finch, the pathologist, sat back from his desk notes and cracked the bones in his wrists. His team had been forced to disinfect the department at West End Central after Arthur had presented him with a cadaver so slippery with infesting bacteria that it had reacted with their usual chemical neutralizers, causing the entire floor to reek of ammonia and rotting fish. This was no problem for Finch, who had the occupational advantage of being born without a sense of smell, but Westminster's health officer had threatened to shut them down unless they did something about it.

Apart from the nuisance factor of dealing with council officials, Finch couldn't see what all the fuss was about. He found the process of bodily decay fascinating. Bryant had suggested that, as a longtime supporter of Tottenham Hotspur, he was used to seeing things slowly fall apart.

'At least we got you a nice fresh one this time,' May pointed out cheerfully. There was something so depressing about being in Finch's presence that people adopted an air of forced jollity around him. He had the suicidal expression of a Norwegian painter and the posture of a unstuffed rag doll. No one in the unit had been surprised when Oswald's glamorous wife had left him for a dashing

RAF officer. Rather, they were amazed that he had managed to marry anyone at all.

'She's been dead since Monday evening. Come and take a look.' He rose and led the detectives through to a windowless green-tiled chamber behind his office. Scrubbed wooden workbenches and ceramic sinks alternated along opposite walls. One table was in use, its occupant covered with a white sheet more to reduce temperature change than to spare feelings.

Unlike most autopsy rooms, this one had variable light settings instead of bright overhead panels. The reason became apparent when May studied the laboratory's centrepiece, a mass of counterbalanced mechanics so advanced for the time that, as yet, the results it yielded could not be considered as admissible evidence. Having developed the system exclusively for the unusual demands of the PCU, Finch was now testing the prototype in the hope that it would become the new industry standard. The unit was so close to the discovery of computer technology that, years later, John May wondered how they had not managed to stumble upon the invention of binary code. But on that day, he had been so fascinated and horrified by the sight of a dead body that he saw little else.

'I assume you've definitely ruled out some kind of bizarre accident?' asked Bryant.

'I'm not so sure. According to your man Runcorn, she didn't fall down in the lift, she passed out. No fibre snags on the lift wall or something; you'll have to speak to him about it. And I don't think loss of consciousness was caused by anything natural like a narcoleptic fit. Her medical files indicate that she was in perfect health.'

'You've already raised her records?' asked Bryant. 'I'm impressed. We don't even have a typist.'

'We don't hang about here, Arthur,' said Finch pointedly, 'not when you can lose half an afternoon from an air raid.'

'Do we now have a formal identification of the body?'

'The theatre's registered doctor knew her. She has no family living here. We think her father's in Vienna. We're trying to notify him now. Look at this.' Finch drew back the sheet to expose the body's right shoulder, then pressed the end of a nail file against the inside of Capistrania's upper arm. 'Ignore the lividity. The flesh clearly retains any indentation marks you make on it. In my book that's a sign of infected tissue. The introduction of something poisonous. My first reaction was to check for evidence of a narcotic, stuff a dancer might possibly use to improve her performance.'

'Is that what they do?'

'I don't know,' Finch admitted. 'I don't know any dancers.'

'You go to that hoochie-coochie place in Clerkenwell. Forthright used to see you queuing up outside as she was going home. Anything come up in the blood samples?'

'This equipment's faster than most, but there's an awful lot to test for. I started by looking at cardiac glycosides, oldendrin, nerioside, toxic carbohydrate groups, but there's no evidence of vascular distress, no common signs of poisoning.'

'How can you be sure?'

'I can't, but convulsions in such a confined space would cause bruising on the limbs and some kind of organic material deposit at the site, which Runcorn has yet to find. There's no indication of haemorrhage, diarrhoea or vomiting. I checked the stomach contents. She'd eaten a sandwich about three-quarters of an hour before death, some kind of poultry in the filling, nothing unusual, and a type of chocolate bar, something with nuts in—don't Barker and Dobson do one? I don't think it's an allergic reaction of any kind. Still, the gastric juices are disturbed, and if we assume that assimilation was rapid, causing her to fall down shortly after she'd entered the lift, I'd say we were looking at something that paralysed her muscles. There's a lot of clenched tissue in her limbs.'

'So you know what she didn't die of. What's your initial reaction?' Bryant had come to trust Finch's instincts, even though they were unlikely to find their way into official reports until the appearance of corroborative evidence.

'There's some slight inflammation and discoloration on her right knee. Dancers bruise all the time, of course, but this one's very fresh, consistent with falling in the lift. I think she just dropped suddenly in her tracks, which suggests a fast fall in the supply of blood to the brain or some kind of synaptic disruption, but I'd still expect more electrical activity.'

'What do you mean?'

'Limbic convulsion. Aberrant behaviour from the nerve endings. Cuts on the hands, something to indicate a bit of thrashing about.'

'You realize what you're saying—it's possible that she collapsed and got her feet caught.'

'I have to say that because of the trace evidence.' Finch moved down to the base of the table and rolled back the sheet. 'You can see the avulsive trauma here in tissue dragged right from bone, separated from all of its connective materials. That's how we know the skin and musculature around the ankles have been torn, not cut. These parallel scrape marks are actually scored deep into the cartilage, and the bones are severely compacted to a depth of an eighth of an inch. That's consistent with the concrete ledge hitting the feet and breaking them off. You can get Runcorn to look along the ledge for vertical striations that include bone particles. Obviously the pain must have been appalling, and for a young lady to remain still while something like this happened, I just think it's unlikely that she would have been conscious. There's another thing. She's very short, slender, very small-boned, virtually no body fat.'

'A lot of dancers are tiny,' May pointed out.

'Small people are easier to poison, although there are exceptions to the rule. Women get drunk more quickly than men because they carry more fat. Dancers are a different kettle of fish, though. A fast-acting muscular poison, possibly something naturally occurring, would have taken care of her. I just ran tests for a substance called coniine, which paralyses the body in pretty much the same way as curare.'

'Curare? I thought that caused heart failure. One has images of blowpipes being aimed in the jungle.'

'That's because it was used by Orinoco Indians. A plant resin. But I believe there's a prescribed clinical version available in America. It's not unheard of for doctors to inject it into pre-op patients in order to reduce the amount of anaesthesia needed. The point is, we've got a positive match for coniine, but not for curare. Something was definitely introduced into her body, but I'm at a loss to understand how. There are no visible puncture marks of any kind.'

'What about in the feet?'

'Obviously I've yet to examine those.'

'But you don't think it likely that she was injected.'

'I didn't say that. I said there are no *visible* signs so far.

Hypodermic injection sites can heal very quickly and disappear completely within two days.' He tapped a pencil against his long yellow teeth. 'There is something here, though. Take a look at this.' He pointed to the small radiophonic monitor angled above the cadaver. 'One of our new gadgets. I'm not sure how reliable it is yet. It's taking subcutaneous readings from different levels in her body tissue. This is the balance of acids that occurs at cellular level. They should all be about the same height.' The screen showed a number of bright green lines, but some were much taller than others.

'And what does that mean?' asked May, looking up at the chartreuse-tinged face of the pathologist.

'That's rather the problem.' Finch narrowed his eyes as he studied the drifting pulsations. 'I haven't the faintest idea.'

16

OFF THE RADAR

Janice Longbright was seated on a stack of Tampax boxes trying to type with two fingers. Outside, on the steps of Kentish Town police station, a gang of teenagers were screaming at each other. The former detective sergeant forced herself to block out the noise and concentrate. With the Mornington Crescent offices blown to smithereens, the unit's surviving personnel had been evacuated to the nearest annexe, but with the force on full alert, no chairs or desks were available for them to work from. The Tampax boxes had been found in the boot of a boy's car, cushioning a number of rifles and stolen army pistols, and made a passably comfortable seat.

The sounds in the street were becoming more confrontational. Longbright looked around the overcrowded office at men and women barking into phones, and was unsurprised that no one had the energy to go outside and stop the fight before someone got hurt. The gang members would be at each other again the second the police departed. Trying to help them was like sticking a plaster on a cut throat.

With John May still off on leave, Longbright had reluctantly agreed to return to the unit for a few weeks. Balancing the telephone on her knee, she tried Sam Biddle's number. This time she got through to him. The Home Office's new police liaison officer was supposed to be providing them with relocation plans and news of emergency funding, but was proving evasive.

'I can't give you anything concrete at the moment,' he insisted. 'There are too many other priorities.'

'So I keep being told,' replied Longbright impatiently. 'Presumably we all have to be firebombed before we get your attention.'

'We have to make sure the police can protect civilians first. Yesterday we had tourists getting caught in crossfire at Stockwell tube station. Once this situation is under control we can take a look at the unit's future.'

'What's happening in this city isn't a "situation", it's an epidemic, things are out of control. And who said the unit's future was in question?'

'Your building is gone, Longbright.'

'We still have our staff.'

'No, you have one of your two directors left alive, and he's beyond retirement age.'

'We have DuCaine and the other new recruits.' Longbright was stung by Biddle's reversal of attitude. Only days ago he had been talking about recruiting amateurs, in accordance with the Scarman Centre's findings.

'The minister's position on this is that Mr Bryant was caught up in some kind of internecine feud that resulted in his demise. We don't have the manpower or the money to investigate all of the surrounding circumstances. Obviously what happened is unfortunate, but it's our position that Bryant was acting alone and knew the hazards of doing so. We're concerned about the dangers to the public posed by the collapse of the building, but as mishaps go these days, it's pretty much off our radar.'

'Your grandfather was a great friend of Arthur Bryant's. He would be ashamed of you now, Mr Biddle.' Longbright slammed down the receiver just as the stack of boxes slid away beneath her.

To calm herself she went to her car for a cigarette. A young girl with a sharp face and scraped-back blond hair challenged her.

'This your motor? You gonna give me a tenner for saving your stereo?' Her hands were thrust defiantly into the cheap cotton of her jacket. Longbright presumed she was carrying a knife.

'I'm a police officer. Fuck off before I arrest you.'

'You can't arrest me, bitch.' The girl stuck out her chin. She was all of fifteen. Longbright knew without looking that she had track marks on the backs of her legs.

'I'll think of a reason if I have to.' Longbright moved her aside and climbed into the car, quickly locking the door. She watched the girl walk back to her mates, feeling almost sorry for her.

A cigarette soothed her nerves. She exhaled smoke and sat back in the seat as sirens started up in the police station car park. Poor John, she thought. Wherever he is, he'll have to figure this one out by himself.

17

IMPRESSIONS

'There is no precedent for what we're trying to create here, Mr Biddle,' explained Bryant. 'There are no superior officers correcting our mistakes. The last thing I need is you going to Davenport and informing him of our progress.'

Bryant had received another scalding telephone call from the unit director about the amount of time the detectives had spent at the theatre, and he could have found out only through his newly appointed agent.

'I'm just doing my job,' said Biddle hotly. 'Mr Davenport wants the matter cleared up quickly, and for the law to be observed. How else can he report back to the victim's father? Your absence from the office contradicts—'

'You don't decide how I choose to work.' Bryant ran his hands through his floppy fringe and thumped down behind the desk, then dug about in a drawer for a packet of 'Nervo' fortified iron pills. Bryant did not enjoy the best of health, and was forever testing new cold remedies. In this case his cold symptoms were more to do with the resentment he felt at losing DS Forthright to something as pointlessly career-damaging as the state of matrimony. He studied Biddle resentfully. He had seen the type before. Thin-skinned, competitive, angry with the world. School had been filled with boys who saw everyone else as a threat. Half of them became so confrontational that they lost their friends by the time they left and ended up in the Territorials, where the war would take them.

'We can investigate this case in any way we see fit,' explained Bryant. 'We have none of the prejudices of the regular police force.'

'You have none of the resources. No equipment. No manpower. They've given you nothing at all,' muttered Biddle. 'That's why they leave you alone, you don't cost anything.'

'We have our minds, Sidney, the most powerful weapons we possess.' As far as Bryant was concerned, his office was a monk's cell, a sanctified if incredibly untidy billet where acolytes concentrated on their devotions to the cause. It was not simply a cheap place to dump dead cases.

'You'll see I'm using a blackboard,' Bryant pointed out. 'I gave Mr May a chance to explain his audiophonic filing system and it failed to impress me, so I'm falling back on a tried and trusted method.'

'You didn't give it a chance, Arthur,' May pointed out. 'It'll work if you just learn how to use the deck.' He had borrowed the cumbersome tape machine thinking it might help, but Bryant had managed to wipe the tape clean and irreparably damage the recording heads, although quite how he had managed to do it remained a mystery. It didn't help that he kept magnets in his overcoat pockets.

For Arthur this was the start of a lifelong stand against technology that would one day result in his crashing the entire central London HOLMES database and part of the air traffic control system at Heathrow. The young detective possessed that peculiar ability more common to elderly men, which produces negative energy around electrical equipment, turning even the most basic appliances into weapons of destruction. The more Bryant tried to understand and operate technical systems, the deadlier they became in his hands, until, at some point in the nineteen sixties, just after he had set fire to his hair by jiggling a fork in a toaster, man and machine had been forced to call a truce.

'So,' Bryant brandished a chunk of chalk, 'Runcorn's mysterious footprints suggest a second person at the death site, but not much else.'

'We can't be sure who was in the theatre at the time,' said May, pulling on the overcoat he had borrowed from his uncle. The office was freezing. The radiators had packed up again.

'Everyone is required to sign in with—what's his name?' asked May.

Bryant consulted his notes. 'Stan Lowe checks members of the company through the rear stage door. Elspeth Wynter keeps an eye on the front of house. Geoffrey Whittaker sees everyone in the auditorium. Between the three of them they usually know who's in the building. We'll have a roll call by the end of the day.'

'She was a beautiful girl,' May pointed out. 'Too beautiful for others to get close to.' The cast at the theatre had proven reticent on the subject of their friendships with the dancer.

'But somebody did, though, didn't they?' said Biddle fiercely. 'Maybe she led her boyfriend on, drove him to attack her. It happens all the time.'

'No, Sidney, ordinary murders do not happen like this. Most occur at home, within the family unit, where the perpetrator is a spouse, sibling or friend. War changes that. Crimes start to happen without reason, because people are upset, or angry, or just frustrated. Acts of violence are squalid, casual, mundane. Contrition, misery, fingerprints everywhere, children in tears. This death was absurdly theatrical, to mutilate someone in the home of Grand Guignol. That's what makes it unique, that's why the case has come here.'

'You think someone in the cast is trying to stop the production?'

'It's unlikely to be anyone involved with the show, because they're the ones with the most to lose. If you were working with Capistrania and had a violent grudge against her, why not wait until she left the theatre for the night? Why draw attention to your own workplace?' Bryant's eyes were bright with enthusiasm. 'There's enough danger out there on the streets right now, what's one more casualty? Go on, whack her over the head with a brick and dump her on a bombsite, who would know? Anything can happen in the blackout if you've a mind for it—a calculating, egotistical, opportunistic mind. One thinks of the Rosicrucian Robert Fludd and his theories of anti-magnetism, brilliant and deranged. The greatest dangers come from the man without a conscience. Look at the photographs of Hitler at Nuremberg two years ago, the deadness behind the eyes that denies humanity, just as it betrays the true darkness of the soul.'

May felt exhilarated around Bryant. He had always imagined that somewhere out there, away from suburban dullness, ardent young people were allowed to give freer rein to their thoughts. He felt as though he had arrived at a place he had always wanted to be.

'How can you concern yourself with the mind of the murderer when it's the victim who's been done wrong?' asked Biddle hotly.

'Because we can do nothing for the victim. John, surely you must agree?'

'I suppose so, but it's difficult to set aside sorrow for the death of someone young.'

Over the years, the detectives argued so much that eventually their polarized altercations mellowed into the kind of bickering that passed for daily conversation in married households. Bryant was more receptive to unusual paths of thought. May's attitude was flexible, but he seemed in a permanent state of surprise. He was warmer, more approachable. He empathized with victims. Bryant was the opposite. He hailed from a sphere of arcane textbooks and borderline beliefs. There was something mad about him, as if he had lived in the city for centuries. Biddle couldn't imagine how his mind worked, or what had made him place his trust in John May so quickly. Bryant appeared untouched by the horrors of war, except on a level of academic interest, and showed no capacity for kindness. May's mental processes were easier to follow. Bryant just frightened people. He smelled of some weirdly pungent aftershave and looked like a distracted, misanthropic student. He trusted books more than other human beings.

Biddle was an observer. He stayed silent and noticed the things others missed. He could already feel the undertow of loyalties that might pull the two detectives in different directions. It was worth making a note of. In terms of career advancement, it could prove useful.

'Sidney, we seem to have lost you.' May pointed at the blackboard. 'Points of correspondence in these footprints.'

Biddle studied the photographs pinned at the top of the board and tried to concentrate. 'The design is similar in shape and dimensions, and there's what looks like a faint worn area on the instep common to both,' he pointed out. 'The moulded sole probably means plimsolls, which is good, given the distinctive patterns produced by different companies.'

'I noticed that many of the cast members wore a specifically styled stage shoe with a rubber sole like that,' added May.

'What would you suggest we do with these prints, then?'

'They were made on lino and concrete respectively, so I'd try to raise a more detailed image with an electrostatic mat.' May knew that you could pass an electric charge through a sheet of foil layered between two sheets of acetate, photograph it at an angle that contrasted the surface, and it would reveal details of the shoe that might otherwise be lost.

'No need. I was informed that such shoes come from a specialist shop in St Martin's Lane. That's your job sorted out for the rest of the day, Sidney. Till receipts.' Biddle looked uncomfortable. 'What's the matter?'

'We should be looking for her enemies.'

Bryant's face clouded. 'What does forty-eight mean to you, Mr Biddle?'

'The first forty-eight hours are the most important in any murder investigation,' he mumbled.

'And would you mind telling us why that is?'

'The evidence starts to deteriorate.'

'Exactly. The physical surroundings of violent death become muddied. The people who knew this unfortunate young lady will still be around after those barely visible heel marks have gone.'

'I think what Mr Bryant is trying to point out,' said May, 'is that no matter how hard we try to preserve the site, someone or something will stir the air, touch the floor, imperceptibly change the scene. The city we live in now is not the city we lived in five minutes ago.'

'Oh, but it is, John,' stated Bryant, annoyingly. 'The growth circle sees to that.'

'I'm not sure I follow. Growth circle?'

'Natural forces create order out of chaos in specific sites, and there's nothing you can do about it.'

'I hardly think this is the time for an argument in semantics,' said May.

'It's not semantics, it's psychogeography. Ask yourself to name the most soulless and depressing central thoroughfare in London. New Oxford Street would be high on your list. Why? Because it's a forced nineteenth-century creation; it was noted to be atmospherically dead when it was built, and it always will be. Natural growth fails in a spot that was artificial to begin with.'

'I must agree with that,' said Biddle, then quickly shut his mouth.

'Fine,' said May, surrendering. 'Would you like me to check out the number of murders in nineteenth-century Cambridge Circus, or shall we go back further, to the age of the Black Death, say?'

'Where we need to go is back to the theatre,' said Bryant. 'You and I will take Miss Wynter's tour of the building. We shall sense the impressions left behind on the air. The auditorium of the theatre, that's where the drama is playing itself out.' He waved a warning digit at Biddle. 'And not a word to Davenport, you, or I'll put pinholes in your gas mask.'

18

GRAND TOUR

Elspeth Wynter replaced the receiver and made a note in her theatre order book. Many of the *Orpheus* opening-night guests were unable to attend because of war commitments. Even so, word of mouth had provoked enough intrigue to sell out most of December. Audiences scented a success in the making. They recalled snippets in newspapers, heard wireless reports, remembered names, gradually assembled facts. The director was suitably infamous, the cast was on loan from the finest companies in the world, including Offenbach specialists from Lyon, and a strong whiff of scandal hung over the show. The play's ribald new script had incurred the suspicion of the Lord Chamberlain; there was a rumour that he might have it banned.

Elspeth suspected that Helena Parole wanted to court controversy. She knew what would happen once word reached the censor's office that this production featured virtual nudity, simulated sex and a salacious translation. There would be demands for its immediate closure. But the owner of the theatre company had apparently made contingency plans, though nobody knew what they were.

Elspeth climbed down off her stool and studied the figures. The production was to be the most spectacular depiction of Pluto's Underworld ever attempted. The designs for Hades and Olympus were sure to provoke outrage—and generate welcome column-inches.

But part of the original cast had been lost to ENSA commitments, most of the chorus girls were inexperienced and under eighteen, and good actors were scarce.

Across from the booking office, downstairs in the auditorium, she could hear the orchestra limbering up as rehearsals got under way. It was a special sound, unique to the theatre. Those tentative first chords told her that a new production had started, and that the public would soon be on its way.

It was cold in the foyer. In the last few days the close dampness of autumn had dissipated, to be replaced by diamond skies and too many freezing clear mornings. It meant that daylight raids could be carried out, and bombers had been sighted brazenly venturing deeper into the city. Messerschmitt 109s, fighters equipped to dart in and drop small-calibre incendiary bombs, were being seen more frequently. Everyone now recognized different aircraft by their outlines and the sounds they made. The Heinkels were German bombers, rearguarded by Junkers during night raids. Hurricanes and Spitfires were ours, and provoked cheers. Sometimes pieces of plane fell right into the road. Oxford Street had been knocked flat, as had the whole of Stepney.

On the first night of the Blitz, the East End fires had burned so fiercely that you could read a newspaper by their light in Shaftesbury Avenue. 'Get-You-Home' booths had been set up around town, staffed by officials who could explain alternative routes. Commuter trains were being bombed and strafed with machine-gun fire. A direct hit had killed twenty in a Marble Arch subway. A group of teenage girls had been buried alive in a busmen's canteen. Parachute bombs drifted through the dust-filled skies like deadly jellyfish, frightening the life out of passers-by. A bomb had destroyed a London perfumery, filling the air with the scent of tropical flowers. A sixteen-year-old boy had appeared in court charged with lighting fires to guide German aircraft inland, Nazi paraphernalia having been discovered in his bedroom. These were disturbing times.

Elspeth felt a draught across her legs and looked up, thinking that someone had opened one of the doors, but the entrance hall was empty. She was waiting for the detectives to return for their tour of the theatre. She instinctively knew when someone was in there with her—the foyer of the Palace was more familiar than her own bedroom—but now it felt different, tainted by death.

At the stage door, Stan Lowe set aside his newspaper and listened. The pastry girl in Maison Bertaux swore she had seen a body being carried out to an ambulance parked in Greek Street. Now Stan had been informed that Tanya had gone—you didn't need a sixth sense to figure out that something wicked had happened to her. Dancers suffered falls that could wreck their careers in a single mistimed step, but to take someone out in silence suggested that she was dead.

Although he had barely met her, it was the idea of bad luck befalling someone in the theatre that disturbed him. Acts of betrayal and revenge unfolded nightly beneath the proscenium arch, but something like this, with police and doctors spiriting away a covered body, felt like an ill omen.

As the sound of the orchestra died away, the balding velvet curtains tied back above the entrance to the stairs shifted slightly, as though a theatrical ghost had just brushed by them. Could somebody have come in and slipped past the window? The buzz of the stage intercom made him start, but he was thankful for something to occupy his mind.

'The theatre first opened as the Royal English Opera House on the thirty-first of January eighteen ninety-one, five years before the first films arrived in London.' Elspeth Wynter pushed open the rear door to the stalls and led the detectives down the centre aisle. 'It was the fulfilment of a lifelong dream for Sir Richard D'Oyly Carte, but the dream lasted only a year. Sullivan's grand opera *Ivanhoe* was not the great success everyone had hoped it would be, and as no one else stepped forward to write an English opera, this magnificent building became the Royal English Variety Theatre, then the Palace of Varieties, and finally just the Palace.'

Elspeth had clearly conducted the tour before. Dressed in shapeless brown cardigan and skirt, she marched between the rows, pointing out details as she passed, keeping her voice in a practised low register. 'We've lost the key to the left-hand pass door, and it's been painted over so many times I doubt anyone could get it open without a chisel, so we have to use the right one. Stan Lowe keeps the key to that and won't lend it out to anyone he doesn't know. Follow me.'

Bryant watched Elspeth's wool-clad bottom as she walked ahead and wondered what it was that attracted him to older women. He speculated on the idea of asking her out. 'Is there any way of turning more lights on?' he asked.

'This is as bright as it gets, I'm afraid. Parts of the theatre are always in darkness. It gets worse beneath the stage and up near the roof.'

May peered up into the gloom, but could discern little more than the vague outlines of four boarded upper windows. The interior had once been green and gold, with red draped curtains, but had subsequently been painted a depressing chocolate brown because a job lot of railway paint had become available at low cost. The sepia walls were rubbed through to the original gilt where members of the audience had paused to touch the plaster cherubs in the friezes, as though they had the talismanic power of saints.

'Theatres are much more artificial than most people realize,' said Elspeth, leading them down a passage beside the stalls. 'Much of the auditorium decoration is built from painted papier mâché. The marble panels you see around the proscenium arch are false. There are no pillars blocking views because the whole structure is made from steel cantilevers, like Tower Bridge. The bricks are mere cladding. Along this side used to be the entrances to the cheaper seats. There were several kiosks selling drinks and cigars, and here is the royal entrance, nine steps up to the royal box, which is partitioned and has its own retiring room, the idea being to keep the classes quite separate. There are other boxes, ten in all. The sightlines are poor, but of course they're for being seen in, not for seeing from. The company office is to the right of the stage door, as is dressing room two. All the dressing rooms are on this side, along with the front-of-house changing room and a number of quick-change areas, but it would take a week to discover all the hidden spaces.'

'You'd have to find a way of gaining access to the building before you could hide yourself,' Bryant pointed out.

'Quite,' agreed Elspeth, opening the door that led to the lift where Capistrania had died. 'We'll take the stairs if it's all the same to you. The entresol floor has three dressing rooms, a smoking lounge and salon, and the booth for the projectors.'

'Projectors?'

'The music hall would show a short silent film as part of the variety bill,' Elspeth explained. 'In nineteen twenty-two they premiered *The Four Horsemen of the Apocalypse* with a live orchestra and a staff of thirty making the sound effects.' She led them higher. 'Next is the dress circle, more dressing rooms, then the upper circle, also the wig room, and finally the balcony, formerly the amphitheatre. The casting offices are right at the top, along with the conference room, the archive rooms, storerooms, the fly gallery and the loading gallery, and a ladder leading up to the grid that I've never seen anyone use.'

'I had no idea the place was so enormous,' said May.

'Five floors no member of the public ever sees.' Elspeth pulled back a curtain leading through to the balcony. 'Be careful here, it's so steep that some people become sick. Please use the handrails.'

Bryant took one look down and put his hand over his eyes. 'I can't,' he admitted. 'How could anybody sit up here?' Some fourteen rows of seats were arranged in plunging descent to a low parapet over the auditorium. 'I don't think we need to see this, do you, John?'

'You've seen the public and business side of the theatre. Now I'll show you the mechanical areas. We'll have to go single file.' She led the way into a musty narrow corridor filled with boxes and wiring, and pointed through an archway. 'I can't get you across without returning to the pass door, but you can see from here. There are three gantry levels, a carpenter's bridge, five stage bridges, two hanging bridges. The slopes and bridges raise scenery, and there's a flying counterweight system that's hardly ever used. At the top is a drum and shaft mechanism capable of lifting half a dozen backcloths at a time. There are a further three floors under the ground,' explained Elspeth. 'I hope neither of you has a problem with confined spaces.'

If Bryant had discovered that he suffered from vertigo, May found the backstage areas claustrophobic. It was impossible to imagine what these areas were like when they were filled with staff and actors. They were now inside an *Alice in Wonderland* arrangement of wooden columns and twisting corridors, their tracks crossing over each other like ghost-train tunnels. There was nowhere to move except slowly forward. The lights, hanging from bare wires and wedged into corners, only disorientated May even more. He felt beads of sweat breaking out on his forehead.

'As you can see, the lower levels are crowded with chariot cuts and sloat cuts. Sloats are cut-out pieces of scenery. There's a chariot and pole system for the wing flats, but it's all too elaborate even for grand opera, and no one has ever really used it to the full extent for which it was designed. There's the grave trap and the revolve, the star traps, and lots of other little doors. It's terribly over-elaborate.'

'What powers it all?' asked May, peering uncomfortably into the darkness.

'In nineteen hundred and seven they started producing their own electricity from three coal-fired boilers which drove the steam turbine engines.'

May tried to imagine the hellish scene below, with stagehands stoking glowing furnaces, and felt sicker than ever.

'I wonder how they managed to top up the engines with water,' Bryant mused, fascinated by the chaotic machinery of beams, cogs, wires, pulleys and rods.

'Oh, there's an artesian well down here too,' Elspeth explained, pointing out the eerie green shimmer of water reflected on the distant bricks opposite. 'The pump is under the orchestra pit. They're supposed to keep the hatch cover on the well because it's very deep and hard to see in the dark.'

'Can we go back up?' asked May, wiping his forehead.

'I say, are you all right?' Bryant shot him a look of concern. 'Feeling shut in?'

'I hope it's helped you get the lie of the land,' said Elspeth, returning to her box office.

'Absolutely,' Bryant told her enthusiastically, but all she had shown him was how easy it would be for a murderer to hide in such a building and never be found.

19

THE WEIGHT OF THE WORLD

'Ten minutes, everyone,' warned Helena Parole. 'We've still got a lot of work ahead of us tonight.' She rose and gathered her notes from the seat next to her. 'Harry, where are you?'

'Over here, Helena,' called her assistant. 'I wonder if I could talk to you for a moment.' He was standing at the back of the stalls with Olivia Thwaite, the show's costume designer. Olivia's wardrobe designs had graced enough Noel Coward productions to inspire new fashions at the Café Royal, but the Blitz had forced her family back to their country home in Wiltshire, and she was now thinking of retiring. She intended to make *Orpheus* her swan song, and would not settle for anything less than perfection. Consequently, the costume manufacture was running late, which at least kept this aspect of the production in step with everything else, even though it was giving Harry heart failure.

'It's about Eurydice's first-act costume,' he explained as Helena strode up to him. 'Olivia would like to double the amount of flowers sewn on her dress.'

'I know the material's in short supply,' said Olivia. 'I promise you it's entirely necessary. The bodice is transparent, and since you specified no undergarments, her breasts and buttocks will clearly be seen beneath the lights. I'm sure I don't need to remind you that the Lord Chamberlain's rules forbid nudity except in motionless tableaux under special lighting arrangements and a special licence, a licence I understand we do not have.'

'I assure you there will be no vulgarity,' promised Helena. 'The semblance of nudity is entirely as I intended.'

'But not as Miss Noriac intends.' Harry spoke for Olivia. It was something he was in the habit of doing whenever possible. It allowed him to defuse tension between stage personnel by rephrasing overheated arguments into the semblance of reasonable conversations. 'She is concerned that as a woman with a voluptuous figure, she will not look her best if the audience can see her entire body.'

Eve Noriac had joined the production on loan from the Lyon Opera House, and represented a heavy investment as their Eurydice. It was important to keep her happy in order to maintain courteous relations with the prestigious French company.

'She's somewhat on the portly side, but she has a marvellous *poitrine* and should be proud of it. Olivia, can't you make her see that?'

'I don't see that it's my job to tell your female lead that she has to appear in the buff before one and a half thousand people every night,' reasoned Olivia.

'I think Olivia would like to add flowers in the top half of her costume for the sake of decorum,' said Harry gently.

'I don't want her to go on looking like a walking advertisement for the Kensington Roof Gardens, thank you, Harry. Go and talk to her, would you? Tell her I'm not having daffodils sewn over her nipples just because she can't leave spuds alone.'

'I'll suggest she speaks directly to you about your perception of her appearance, bearing in mind her reservations about the décolletage.' Harry didn't mind liaising between the director and her cast, but it had reached the point where he was acting as an interpreter.

He left Helena and Olivia arguing about the wardrobe and made his way backstage. The scenery for the opening tableau had arrived, and he squeezed between freshly painted scrims depicting sheaves embroidered with hand-sewn cornflowers, courtesy of the ladies of the Bank, Holborn and Aldwych underground stations, who had wanted something to do in the evenings.

Above his head hung a great globe painted a rich cyanic blue and topped with a set of opened steel compasses, a symbol of cartography and freemasonry denoting the mapping of the earthly world. The globe had been manufactured for a Glyndebourne production of *The Magic Flute,* then junked after the production was cancelled on account of the site's proximity to the exposed Sussex coastline.

The shepherds and shepherdesses of the chorus had returned to the flies. The principal players were familiarizing themselves with the finer details of their roles, having taken musical direction at rehearsal rooms in Covent Garden. At this stage of the production, when the librettist was belatedly putting the finishing touches to his new translation of Offenbach's work, it seemed that nothing would ever come together, but this was how it always was. The production would not coalesce into a performance until the dress rehearsal on Friday.

'Corinne, I don't have you in my diary until late this evening,' said Harry. 'You're not due on for another two hours.'

'I'm recording a talking book for the blind over in Greek Street,' explained the diminutive comedienne who had been cast in the role of Mercury, a tenor role usually played by a male. 'The producer's called a break while they sort out their wiring or something, so I thought I'd come and see how everyone was coping with La Capistrania's mysterious disappearance. I'm dying for a snout, love. You haven't got one on you, I suppose?'

'You know you're not supposed to smoke back here,' said Harry.

'Don't give me that. I've seen you creeping out the back for an oily rag. Go on, chuck us a Du Maurier. Has anyone dared to mention Tanya today?'

'God, no. You can cut the atmosphere with a knife. I've only got a Woodbine, but you can have it. Helena's still waiting to see if her replacement is up for tonight's run-through.'

'There'll probably be an air raid and we'll all spend the evening under the stage trying to play whist by the light of a forty-watt bulb again. I suppose you know they're saying she's been murdered?' Corinne airily brandished Harry's proffered cigarette. 'Working as a spy for her father and assassinated by fifth columnists, apparently.'

'I've heard rumours,' admitted Madeline Penn, the skinny, nervous ASM. 'Stan's been putting the fear of God up everyone as they sign in, but there's been no real news. She's walked out of jobs before, hasn't she?'

'He reckons she was carried out of this one in the dead of night,' offered Charles Senechal, a chubby Anglo-French baritone who, like their Eurydice, was on loan from Lyon. 'Slaughtered by a lover. Body parts missing.'

'Well, if that's the case, somebody made a jolly good job of cleaning up the blood,' said Corinne.

'If I had a franc for every story I heard circulating around a theatre I'd be rich by now.' Charles had been assigned the role of Jupiter. It was a part he had performed so many times before that his performance was in danger of becoming petrified, but audiences loved him.

'Apparently she was having a torrid affair with someone right here in the theatre,' whispered Madeline.

'I haven't heard about that.' Harry looked shocked. 'I'm sure I would have seen her with someone.'

'The trouble with you, Harry, is you never notice flirting between the sexes,' snapped Corinne. 'She was being rogered by someone in our esteemed cast. I should know, because I caught them at it. Walked into her dressing room thinking she'd gone for the night and there she was with her heels in the sink and her bloomers hanging from the light. She didn't even make the effort of trying to look embarrassed.'

'Who was it?'

'That would be tittle-tattle, Harry, and I know you don't approve. Besides, I was fascinated by the sight of his hairy bottom poking out of his shirt-tails.'

'You should tell the detectives.'

'What, and have them hanging around all week ogling the chorus girls? You know how I feel about outsiders. Elspeth, put that thing down, love. It weed all over the stage yesterday.'

Elspeth Wynter had been watching from the wings, where she had gone to retrieve Nijinsky. The tortoise refused to stay in its box, and regularly headed for the dim warmth of the backstage areas. 'Sorry,' she called, picking up the animal and putting it inside her cardigan. 'Is that another air-raid warning?' She cocked her head and listened to the distant rise and fall of the siren.

'Bugger, does that mean we all have to go down to the understage again?' Corinne complained. '*Quelle* bore. I'll have to get another coffin nail from somewhere, I can't do Woodies, they slaughter my throat. Doesn't anyone smoke Park Drives or Kensitas these days? Charles, have you got *un clope*, love?' Nearly all of the French contingent smoked.

'I only have roll-ups,' said Charles. 'Three Nuns or Dark Empire Shag, take your pick.'

'God, no thanks, I want some voice left.'

'Then try the sparks.'

Corinne pushed past Jupiter and the young assistant, crossing to the far side of the stage, where Elspeth stood. Harry looked over and saw her searching for an electrician. As he idly watched, he noticed something was wrong. The stage had been cleared but the spotlights were still on, and the house lights had been dropped. The spots should have been off and the stalls lights raised. He could barely see beyond the edge of the stage.

'Charles,' called Corinne, her gravelly voice absorbed by the sound-deadening backcloths of the Hades set, 'there's nobody over here—ask someone on that side, would you?'

Harry turned in the direction of the shepherdesses, but they had gone down to the section of the basement that had been designated a shelter. He looked back over at Corinne, who was waiting in the flies, but could barely make her out. He felt Charles brush past him, and saw an unlit cigarette in his hand. Either he had asked someone for Corinne, or had decided to palm her off with one of his home-made specials.

Harry noticed that Charles was halfway across the stage when he heard something rip—later, he recalled the sound as being like someone tearing a sheet, which was also the noise a bomb made as it fell—and glanced up just in time to see the great blue planet break loose of its moorings.

He wanted to call out, but the words were stuck in his throat.

Charles had not noticed. The globe was swinging towards him in a graceful arc. Harry heard the impact that lifted the Frenchman off his feet. The sound was followed by a dull crack as Senechal's head was slammed into the brick wall at the rear of the set. When Harry looked again he saw that the sphere had come to rest on the floor. It took him a few moments to realize what had happened.

As he lurched towards the giant prop he heard other shouts in the auditorium. Blood the colour of crushed blackberries pumped across the floorboards. A thick dark puddle was soaking into the backcloth. One end of the compasses had speared the baritone through his ribcage, just below his heart. Charles coughed loudly in the sudden silence, and sprayed the stage with blood. His left foot beat a reflexive tattoo on the floorboards before falling still.

He was dead before Harry, or anyone else, could reach his side.

20

SOMETHING IN THE ARCHIVE

'Two deaths in the same theatre,' said Bryant, rubbing the chill from his hands as they descended the stalls staircase of the Palace. 'I'd call that a bit more than coincidence.'

'You sound sorry you didn't see it,' May remarked.

'Well, I am. Of course I am. From a professional point of view it would have been instructive.'

'Two talented people just had their lives cut short,' said May hotly. 'You might be able to put their relatives at peace as to how and why they died.' He was growing tired and irritable. The air-raid siren had proven to be a false alarm, and had caused them to miss the real drama. Bryant's heartlessness bothered him. 'People are suffering all around us, and there's nothing one can do except try to keep the lives of their survivors in some kind of order. One must heal wounds by providing answers to questions.'

'Quite, old chap. Still, two extreme acts of violence in a public auditorium.' Bryant lightly tapped his partner's arm. 'They feel like symbolic rites, don't you think? Signs that the mad illogic of the war is entering places of sanctuary. After all, British theatre is a bastion of common sense, civilized, safe, middle class, old-fashioned. Theatrical performances are structured on the principles of cause and effect. The auditorium exists outside of time or place, and only comes alive with the rising of the curtain.'

'I really don't see your point,' said May.

'My *point,* dear fellow, is that these murderous acts went unwitnessed by any audience, in a place where people come expressly to revel in sensation. Come on, let's see what we've got.'

Charles Senechal's body had been removed to an ambulance parked in Romilly Street. The stage had been cleared of all flats and cloths except the cotton duck and hessian frames that stood in the up-centre area against the gaudy crimson cyclorama of Hades. The great blue globe lay where it had fallen, sparkling beneath a profile spot and a pair of par lights.

'What's it made of?' Bryant asked Mr Mack, the head carpenter, whose first name nobody seemed to know. Bryant walked round the globe, his fingers trailing lightly across its surface as if trying to divine some inner purpose from its topography.

'Plaster, built around a central wood core. It weighs a bloody ton. Took three of us to get it up there. I hope it ain't cracked.'

May followed the arc of the planet back up to the raised iron platform on the right side of the flies, the area above the stage where much of the scenery and lighting equipment was suspended. 'How was it held in place?'

'Two steel cables attached at forty-five-degree angles, locked in by bolts. One of the wires must have broken at the top end. The rest of the cable is still attached.'

'So the right-hand wire snapped, leaving the globe to swing down on the left wire like a wrecking ball. Ever seen an accident like this before?'

'Never, and this is my forty-third production,' Mr Mack replied. 'Those cables can take a lot of weight. Go up there and take a look.'

Bryant wasn't thrilled by the idea of climbing along the gantry. He ascended the narrow steps leading to the first of the stage bridges like a man condemned. From where he stood he could see a large steel hook screwed into the wall. About two feet of wire hung limply down from it. 'In order to be sure of catching someone, you'd have to keep them on their mark from when the wire was cut until the globe hit,' he said absently.

'What do you mean, their mark?' asked May.

'The prearranged spot you reach onstage, where you stand in any scene. All stages are divided into nine squares: up right, centre right, down left and so on. Sometimes there's a front extension, an apron that makes a tenth area. Performances are spatially three-dimensional, and have to be learned accordingly, like chess moves.' Taking a deep breath, Bryant reached over the catwalk railing and pulled up the wire, examining the end. 'Tell me about the compasses, Mr Mack.'

'They're just pieces of pressed tin,' the carpenter explained, 'but each arm is four feet long, and we had to put a sharp point on the end of one because it didn't look like a real set of compasses without a needle.'

'Who told you to do that, the set designer?'

'No, I answer to Geoffrey Whittaker, the stage manager. He takes care of my practical needs. Raymond leaves the materials up to me. He's only concerned about the look of the stage once it's lit, although he'll tell you the difference between hardwood and composition board by the way light bounces off it.'

'Raymond Carrington is the lighting chief,' May pointed out.

'The only access to the wire is from this gantry,' said Bryant. 'And you saw no one.'

'No. This stage is narrow as working areas go, but it's deep and we're capable of producing a lot of mechanical effects. That's why it gets the big song and dance shows; there are more scene changes in musicals, and more scenery has to be flown in. You can bring someone up from any part of the floor, lift whole sections of the stage, do revolves, put in a lot of filler flats and wing divisions, drop dozens of backdrops, scrims and props from above. The lighting is handled from a master board in one of the dress boxes, so there's more room backstage for physical effects. Even I get confused up there sometimes, trying to figure out where each part of the scenery is.'

'It's not your job to fly them in and out?'

'No, the stagehands do that, but I have to check and repair them all the time. Scenery gets damaged after virtually every performance.'

'Had you repaired the globe recently?'

'We've had no dress rehearsals yet, so there's been no need to.'

'You don't think a stranger could have come in from the street after the siren sounded, climbed up the right-side gantry and waited for Mr Senechal to walk across the stage?'

'I don't see how,' said Mr Mack, scratching the top of his head. 'The only time the side bay doors are open is when we're bringing scenery into the dock, and there's always someone manning the stage door whenever the theatre's being used. Besides, the gantries are in virtual darkness. There's no way of easily climbing along them unless you know exactly where the footholds are.'

'So, Miss Betts was in the wing looking for a carpenter with a cigarette. Miss Wynter was there with her retrieved tortoise. Miss Penn, Mrs Thwaite and Miss Parole were all in the process of heading to the basement, as were Harry, Mr Woolf and Mr Varisich. Up until the siren sounded, Mr Woolf had been watching the front entrance from the box office, and the stage door keeper—'

'Stan Lowe. He has an assistant called Mouse. I s'pose he has a real name but I don't know what it is—'

'—was still in his booth at the base of the stairs, and neither of them saw anyone enter or leave. You were by the bay doors, which were locked. And there's no other way in or out.'

'I wouldn't quite say that,' said Mr Mack. 'There is a pair of exits on to the roof, and they're unlocked from the inside because of the current ARP regulations.'

'You can get out of the building via the roof?'

'Yes, but you can't get in from them, and you can't go very far once you're out. Sometimes we have firewatchers stationed out there, but not today. They have to prop open the door with fire buckets when they go up because we've not enough keys.'

The Palace Theatre was one of the few London theatres standing in grand isolation. Its facia overlooked Cambridge Circus, but its sides were separated by Shaftesbury Avenue and Romilly Street. Only the rear section touched any other buildings, a short row of houses in the lower part of Greek Street, and the Palace roof stood considerably higher than those.

'So no one entered or left during the rehearsal. See here, John.' Bryant held the end of the wire aloft. 'Even with my hopeless eyesight I can tell this was cut. A clean shear. There is no way that you could arrange it in advance.'

He carefully made his way down onto the stage to examine the wires that had been drilled into the globe. Corinne Betts, the comedienne playing Mercury, had been sedated by her doctor. Chorus girls were talking in shocked whispers in the wings.

'Where would I find a copy of the design for the globe?' asked Bryant.

'The prop designs and stage plans are all in use,' said Helena Parole, walking into the light thrown by one of the Fresnel spots. 'They're changed and updated all the time, so they'll be scattered about in different offices. We mimeograph copies of everything and work from those.'

'What do you do with the originals?'

'They go up into the archive room. They'll be clearly labelled.' The lack of concern in her voice bothered May. 'Do you want me to send someone for them?'

'John, I wonder if you would oblige?'

'Of course.' May left the stage and went to the company office for the keys. He took the lift to the fifth floor, pulled open the trellis doors and stepped out into a dingy hall. The boarded-up end windows prevented light from entering, but the pairs of defunct gas mantles at either end of the hallway would have done little to dispel the creeping gloom, which was deepened by chestnut walls and threadbare brown carpets.

May flicked a brass switch at the head of the corridor, but nothing happened. According to Helena, there was barely a time when the electrics functioned correctly. The faint glow from the electroliers in the main stairway allowed him to make out the doors to his left, but none of them was labelled. He checked the first door but found that it had been fitted with a Yale. The key he had taken from the company office was a long-handled Victorian affair, scabbed with rust.

He located the theatre archive in a room at the darkest turn in the corridor. Within the cramped suite were dozens of overstuffed boxes and damp cardboard files cataloguing productions and stars. Dim light was provided by the bare bulb overhead. He glanced across the titles on the lids of the boxes and pulled out some of the Palace's monochrome publicity photographs. Buster Keaton performing with his father, the pair of them bowing to the audience in matching outfits. The jagged profile of Edith Sitwell, posturing her way through some kind of spoken-word concert. A playbill for W. C. Fields starring in a production of *David Copperfield*. Another presenting him in his first appearance at the Palace as an 'eccentric juggler'. The four Marx Brothers, gurning for the camera. Fred Astaire starring in *The Gay Divorcée,* his last show before heading to Hollywood.

The dust on the lower boxes betrayed an even earlier age. The infamous Sarah Bernhardt season of 1892; Oscar Wilde's *Salome* was due to have been performed at the theatre, but had fallen foul of the Lord Chamberlain's ruling about the depiction of religious figures. The legendary Nijinsky, seen onstage just after his split with Diaghilev. According to the notes, he had left the Palace after discovering that he was to appear at the top of a common variety bill. Cicely Courtneidge in a creaky musical comedy, her dinner-jacketed suitors arranged about her like Selfridge's mannequins. The first royal command performance, in 1912. Anna Pavlova dancing to Debussy. Max Miller in his ludicrous floral suit, pointing cheekily into the audience—'You know what I mean, don't you, missus?' Forgotten performers, the laughter of ghosts.

An accordion folder labelled *Orphée aux enfers* lay on the nearby desk. May pulled it out and began sifting through the floor plans and set blueprints. He found the design for the second tableau, Mount Olympus crowned by clouds, its great azure sphere pinned in the heavens, and carefully folded it into his jacket pocket.

The anguished cry that tore its way along the corridor made his scalp tingle. It was the call of a human in terrible pain. May jumped to his feet and ran outside, but there was nothing to be seen. He heard it again, softer and more in sorrow this time, but the acoustics were so dead that it was impossible to pinpoint the location of the sound. The other doors along the corridor were all sealed. Some looked as if they had not been opened for many years. Panic crawled over his skin, sending him back to the lift and the light.

He had just pulled the trellis door shut when he heard the cry again, a miserable low bellow that reverberated in the lift shaft. May jammed his thumb on the descent button and the cage dropped down through the building, recalling him to life and safety. He was nineteen and impressionable. The city was blacked out every night, and the dark held hidden terrors. In years to come, his dreams would vividly recall his haunted week at the Palace.

'You imagined it,' said Bryant, poking about in the pockets of his battered gaberdine raincoat for a Swan Vesta. 'Nothing to be ashamed of, old chap. We're all a bit jumpy. This building hasn't seen daylight since the start of the war.' He lit his pipe while May unfolded the sheet of paper he had removed from the archive. 'So this is the original design for the globe and compasses?' Bryant asked Mr Mack as May smoothed the stage plan flat on a workbench.

'It looks the same as the finished model,' commented May distractedly. He was still thinking about the deep cry echoing in the corridors.

'Does it? Would you say that the compasses occupy the same position as they do in the drawing, Mr Mack? Do you have a first name?'

'Mr Gielgud always calls me Mr Mack because of his memory,' explained the carpenter. 'We used to talk about table tennis.' He spat a mouthful of chewing tobacco into his handkerchief and examined the plan. 'Blimey, you're right. The point of the needle is higher on the full-scale version by about a foot.'

'Who told you to raise it?'

Mr Mack studied the drawing in discomfort. 'It's not like me to make a mistake. There should be a master diagram. This is one of the earlier sketches. Someone must have moved the globe.'

'I don't know how much more evidence you need to prove a case of premeditation,' Bryant told his partner.

'The carpenters reckon accidents happen all the time in the theatre,' said May.

'That's right,' agreed Mr Mack. 'You've got a lot of people jumping about in a very small space, surrounded by moving mechanical objects, some of them weighing tons. Feet get crushed, arms broken, ankles shattered. Arthur Lucan fell through this very stage.'

'But they don't normally die, do they?'

'That's true, sir, they don't.'

'And the problem with these two deaths is that we lack any kind of a link between them,' whispered Bryant.

May consulted his notebook. He felt that someone should keep a record in case Davenport decided to question their tactics. 'Well,' he pointed out, 'they were both represented by the same agent, weren't they?'

21

FREEDOM FROM MEMORY

He was searching for something in the files. John May sat in the archive room of the Palace Theatre and rested his aching, aged bones.

He was perched on a canvas stool with a mildewed cardboard box on his lap. Many of the photographs, plans and notes beneath his fingers were stuck together with time. They bore marks of damp, tea, candle grease. He wished he knew what he was looking for. He knew only that Bryant had been here before him, just days before he died.

In the years following the investigation, more photographs had been added to the files of the Palace: Jimmy Cagney, tap-dancing in a USO camp show; Betty Grable singing; Laurence Olivier grinning gap-toothed in Osborne's *The Entertainer;* John Tiller's Girls, high-kicking their way through the 1958 season; a thousand forgotten variety acts armed only with funny walks and silly catchphrases; the cast of *Les Misérables,* changing yet changeless across the years. And a grey police file on the Palace Phantom, dated November 1940, left to be rediscovered over sixty years later.

Here were the typed interviews they had conducted with the cast and production crew of *Orpheus* at the onset of that terrible season. The last pages of the file were missing. Only the interviews remained. But there had clearly been other pages here. The freshly torn staples at the top of the file attested to that. He looked through the interview list again. Corinne Betts, Miles Stone, Eve Noriac, Geoffrey Whittaker...he could barely put faces to the names. Elspeth Wynter, Arthur had fallen for her, but had it been out of love or pity? Who knew now, and what did it matter? He imagined the faces of Londoners, photographs pinned to an immense police board stretching hundreds of miles back into the past, across two thousand years of continued inhabitancy. So many dead, so many yet to come...

The ring of his mobile phone startled him. He pulled the Nokia from his pocket and answered it.

'John? It's me, Alma. I hope I'm not disturbing you.'

'Me? No, how are you?'

'My legs are wicked, no change there, just getting old. Janice said you were back, and I was worried because someone's been in Mr Bryant's flat.' She called him John; she always referred to Arthur as Mr Bryant.

'How do you know someone's been in there?'

'There was some stuff left out and now it's gone. I know because I did the dusting. I told you I didn't like to throw anything away. I don't want to let the rooms out no more.'

'Was the door forced?' asked May. 'Did they break in?'

'No, nothing's damaged, the front lock's in one piece. They must have got them skeleton keys.'

'I don't think that's very likely, Alma. But it's a standard lock, it isn't too hard to open. I've done it before now. What did they take?'

'Just some pieces of paper from the table.'

'You don't happen to remember what they were, do you?'

'I know because I typed them out for him myself,' explained Alma. 'They were Mr Bryant's dental records.'

May walked down Charing Cross Road and cut through to the back of the National Portrait Gallery, carefully avoiding the junk-food swill of Leicester Square. He detested the swirling scrum of the pedestrianized zone, the latent danger, the shoving, dislocated crowds that filled a once-beautiful space. It was hard to imagine, but the area had been pleasanter to stroll through when traffic had traversed it. Now, the tourist hot spots of the city were the very parts that made it like everywhere else. Was it possible to imagine those buildings without inhaling the animal-fat stink of McDonald's or KFC? He never thought London would cease to appeal to him, but the little faded glory it still possessed was being scuffed away by the dead hand of globalization. On his down days he saw London as a crumbling ancient house, slowly collapsing under the weight of its own past.

As he pushed his way through a herd of name-tagged visitors in matching baseball caps, he wondered if he had left it too late to retire to the continent. France seemed a good bet, more at ease with its history. Crucially, he had never visited the place with his old partner. Perhaps he could be freed from memories there. He thought of his embittered son, recovering from years of addiction in a French commune, of his wife and daughter, and how he had survived them both, but even then he remembered Nathalie, how Bryant had loved her and lost her...

Damn you, Arthur, he thought, let me go.

He knew there was only one way he could stop himself from subsiding into the silent past: he needed to settle the murder of his alter ego. Without the truth, there would be no rest. Not now, not ever.

22

BLOCKING

'I'm offended that you should even ask,' Benjamin Woolf bristled. He never looked more suspicious than when he was trying to appear injured. 'I represent a great many artists.'

'I'm not saying you had anything to do with their deaths, even though no one actually saw you at the time of Senechal's impalement,' Bryant snapped. 'You're very touchy for an agent.'

'We don't all have hides like rhinos, Mr Bryant.'

'How many other performers in the company do you represent?'

'Oh, quite a few.'

'*Exactly* how many?'

Woolf made an effort to look innocent and failed. 'I'd have to work that out and get back to you.' The detectives had set up a base in the company office, and were seeing everyone who had been present in the auditorium when Charles Senechal had met his death.

'Do you have some kind of special deal going on with the cast members you represent?' asked Bryant.

'Something like that.' Woolf ran a finger along his thin moustache.

'Are you on friendly terms with them all? How close were you to Miss Capistrania and Mr Senechal, for instance?'

'I keep a respectable distance from all my clients. I'm there when they need me. I give them advice and support, I listen to their problems, nothing more.'

'But it's a twenty-four-hour job, isn't it? You take their calls when they come off stage at night, cope with their insecurities, as-suage their doubts?'

'Of course. All theatrical agents worth their salt do.'

'Do you know much about their personal lives? Who they were closest to, who they were amorously involved with?'

'Some are forthcoming, others aren't. I don't pry, if that's what you mean. They have to tell you some things, obviously.'

'What did Tanya Capistrania have to tell you?'

'You must understand she had very few friends in this country. She told me she was seeing someone in the company. I don't know much about Charles except that he's married and has a flat in Paris. His wife and son are on their way here right now.'

'So Miss Capistrania was having an affair and Charles wasn't.' Bryant sucked hard on his pipe, trying to keep it lit.

'For all I know he could have been. Performers become very tight-knit during the course of a run. They form liaisons that last only while they're working together.'

'Would you care to divulge the identity of the man Miss Capistrania was seeing?'

'I suppose it won't do any harm to the young lady now,' sighed Benjamin. 'But you musn't say I told you. It was Geoffrey Whittaker.'

'The stage manager?' Bryant was surprised. He didn't look the type to conduct a torrid affair.

'It's not the first time he's got up to this sort of thing. He's pretty well known by the Piccadilly commandos.' He was referring to the squad of prostitutes who brazenly worked around the Circus, step-ping out of doorways to accost servicemen on leave.

'He's a bit old to be a Lothario. What about Miss Capistrania?'

'Tanya was famous for upstaging her fellow players. She was very driven to succeed. The usual story, pushed by her family from an early age. Nobody's got much good to say about her.'

'And Charles Senechal?'

'The opposite. Everyone thinks—thought—he was wonderful. He's played all three of the baritone roles in *Orpheus* before, a con-summate professional and a wonderful singer.'

'I see. What about some of the others who were there when it happened, Harry—what's his surname, Cowper? And Corinne Betts?'

'Corinne's seeing one of the shepherds. A boy in the chorus. I don't think it's anything more than mutual convenience. Harry, well, he's a bachelor. Let's leave it at that.'

'So there are a few *amours* in the background. Any risk of blackmail with Harry?'

'I suppose there's always a risk, but the theatre's safer than most places. Outside the Palace, people keep asking if I'm a visiting calypso player. In here, nobody cares about the colour of my skin. Why are you interested?'

'The globe could have been intended to hit anyone, couldn't it?'

'Oh, I see. Harry's well liked. There's often someone like him in a theatre company, born to be a den mother to the rest. Runs around after people making them feel better. Nurses the bruised egos. Corinne's got a bit of a mouth on her, but I don't know that she's made any real enemies. Some of the cast went to Café de Paris to see her perform her comedy routine a couple of weeks ago, and she bought them all drinks afterwards. It won her a lot of friends.'

'So there are no real connections that you can see, apart from the fact that Miss Capistrania and Mr Senechal were both performers represented by you.'

'May I remind you that I'm the one losing out here.' Woolf made a further effort to look pained, but appeared to be suffering from heartburn. 'They were more than my clients. They were investments.'

'I'd say everyone's investments are in danger of disappearing now, wouldn't you?'

'No,' replied Woolf, 'no, I wouldn't. Don't you know the show always goes on?'

'If I find reason to suppose that anyone else's life is in danger, I won't hesitate to close down the production.'

'Aren't you a bit young to have that authority?' asked Woolf, alarmed.

'I'm not sure,' Bryant admitted, giving up on his pipe, 'but it would be interesting to find out. Let me get this clear in my head. While the globe was being cut loose, there were four people actually on the stage: Mr Senechal, Miss Betts, Miss Wynter and Mr Cowper. Mr Mack was further back in the wings, Miss Parole was in the stalls with Mr Whittaker, Miss Penn, Mrs Thwaite and

Mr Varisich, heading in the direction of the pass door. Stan Lowe was manning the stage door, and you were out in the front box office. What were you doing before the siren sounded?'

Benjamin thought for a moment. 'I was talking to Elspeth. I left the auditorium, but then I heard the commotion and ran back in.'

'To your knowledge, was there anyone else near the stage or in the stalls?'

'I don't think so—wait, Anton was still in the orchestra pit. Eve and Olivia were arguing about something as they came out, a problem with a dress, so they must have been nearby.'

'Do you think it likely that any of them could have climbed the gantry to the globe and cut it loose?'

'I don't see how,' interrupted May. 'The gantry is clearly visible from the stage.'

'Then there's someone we haven't accounted for,' said Bryant, prodding his partner in the shoulder. 'Someone else in the theatre. Someone up there, in the dark.'

23

OFF TO THE REALM OF DARKNESS

'Have you heard? They're killing all the poisonous snakes and rep-
tiles at London Zoo, in case the cages get bombed,' Betty Trammel,
one of the *Orpheus* chorus girls, told John May that afternoon.
Like most of the other female dancers, she had long legs, a tiny
midriff and shapely breasts that the detective found himself covertly
watching. 'And they've had to put sandbags around the pink flamin-
gos because they're suffering nervous breakdowns.' She smiled at
the detective and rolled her enormous eyes. They were set in a
heart-shaped face, framed with blond curls. 'I used to cut home
through Regent's Park to my place in Camden, but they've closed
the public path past the zoo. It's getting so a girl doesn't know
what's safe any more.' Betty spoke with more refinement than the
other chorines. She had a smile that could put a froth on a cup of
coffee, and she knew it.

'I'm in Camden. I can walk you home if you like,' May offered
gallantly.

'I might just take you up on your proposal.' She placed her hands
on spangled hips and grinned. 'Give me two minutes to get changed.'

Bryant watched in disgust as Betty bounced off into the wings.
'What is it,' he asked, 'that makes girls go so damnably gooey-eyed
over you? I don't understand it. You only have to stand next to
them and they start rolling bits of themselves about like Betty
Boop.'

'I think they just feel, you know, comfortable around me,' said May, surprised by his own powers.

'Well, they don't do that with me,' Bryant complained, scratching the back of his ear in puzzlement. 'I can't see why not. I'm a bloody good catch. I have prospects. I have an enquiring mind. You'd think that would be appealing.'

May stared at the aisle carpet, embarrassed. He could not tell his new friend that there was something about his fierce energy that disturbed people. The more Bryant tried to be sympathetic, the less believable he was. It was an unfortunate effect that was to bedevil him throughout his life.

'And the types that go for you,' Bryant continued, 'well!'

'What's wrong with their "type"?' asked May, offended.

Bryant searched the air, almost at a loss for words. 'You can't see it? My dear fellow, they're so—obvious.'

'Look, if it bothers you that much, I don't see why you don't find a date of your own. Go down to the box office and ask Elspeth out, she's keen as mustard. I've seen the way she looks at you.'

'Oh, I don't know about that.' Bryant poked his pipe-stem down into his top pocket, considering the idea. 'Do you really think so?'

'I'm sure of it. Go on, ask her. She'll be glad to get out of here.' The blackout made houses stuffy and airless at night. Even in a building as large as the Palace, the still atmosphere weighed heavily in the lungs.

'All right,' vowed Bryant, grinning bravely, 'I will. I'll go and ask her right now.' And he did.

She turned him down. It didn't take her long either. He was gone for only two minutes.

'She has to look after a sick relative,' said Bryant on his return. 'I wasn't convinced.' He grumpily kicked at the ground. 'Here's your bit of fluff.'

Betty had rouged her cheeks and changed into a fox-fur coat. Divested of her blond wig, she was revealed as a mousy brunette. She waltzed into the company office and seized May's arm as though it was a lifebelt. 'Are we going for a drink, then?' she asked cheerfully, pinching May's cheek.

May was almost pulled through the doorway. 'I'll see you in the morning, Arthur,' he volunteered. 'Stay out of the light.'

'Yes, you go and have fun. I still have a police investigation to run.' Bryant shoved his trilby onto his head. 'I think I'll go back to Bow Street and ruin Biddle's evening.'

By the next morning, the mood of the company had become morose and belligerent. To have a member of the cast killed by a stage prop was not unheard of, but after a long night of bombing raids that frayed the nerves and lasted until dawn the idea of it panicked everyone. Performers were at the mercy of stagehands when there were a large number of scene changes to incorporate in the action. Three years earlier, two members of a Belgian dance troupe had been fatally injured at the Albert Hall when a vast steel wheel had collapsed on them. The scenery at the Covent Garden Opera House, with its newly overhauled hydraulic system, had nearly decapitated one of its principal players in front of a horrified first-night audience. Recently, a trapdoor in the Palladium stage had opened without warning, dropping a chorus girl down a dozen steps, breaking both her ankles. Players were superstitious and productions easily made bad reputations for themselves.

Helena Parole was aware of the cast's sensibilities, but hoped they would be cheered by today's arrival. Their Orpheus was landing, fresh from a triumphant American tour of *The Tales of Hoffmann*, the opera wrongly regarded as Offenbach's only serious work. Miles Stone had hit the big time, but his *Orpheus* contract pre-dated his rise in stock, and he had not managed to wriggle out of the agreement in time to seize his Hollywood break. MGM was offering him a role in a screwball comedy that would help to cement his image as the smart girl's sex symbol, but unless something went wrong with *Orpheus* and the production was cancelled, Miles knew that he would be forced to remain in bomb-strewn London throughout the winter. The film would be recast with someone else, and his window of opportunity would slam firmly shut.

Consequently, the company's leading player found himself in an ambivalent mood when he arrived to find that Jupiter was dead. It was a tragic loss, of course, but if the cast were so demoralized that the production could not continue, he would be freed.

'Everybody back to their positions and we'll take it from

Eurydice's invocation to death.' Helena Parole rubbed her eyes. The cast was nervy and out of sorts. Anton Varisich, the conductor, was particularly bad-tempered, and seemed unable to control his orchestra, who were coming in late on their cues. On stage, Eurydice lay in the cornfield as Aristaeus stood over her, feeling her pulse.

'*La mort m'apparaît souriante, qui vient me frapper près de toi,*' sang Eve Noriac.

Helena threw her script over the seat in front of her. 'For Christ's sake!' she shouted. 'What the hell do you think you're doing?'

'I'm sorry,' called Eve, rising on one elbow and squinting down at her. 'I'm used to singing in French. It's easier for me to remember my lines this way.'

'The management has decreed we're to use our sovereign nation's native tongue,' snapped Helena. 'They want a popular hit. The only people who can speak another language in England are foreigners. Let's go again from the top.'

'*Death appears to me smiling, coming to strike me while I'm near you...*'

Helena sat back and listened. Eurydice had a remarkable soprano range. The plot was of no consequence to a modern audience, a once-saucy parody of classicism that held little meaning for anyone now, and yet Eve invested her words with such conviction that you would listen if she sang addresses from a telephone directory.

Helena was suddenly aware that the music had stopped. 'What now?' she cried, sitting up.

'Someone's taken my fork,' complained Aristaeus. 'It was here a minute ago.'

'Will somebody find his bloody fork?' called Helena. 'Harry, go and look for it, would you?'

'Can he just mime it for now, Helena?'

'Helena?' Aristaeus had walked to the front of the stage and was shielding his eyes from the key lights. 'Is this a practical?'

'You know it's not. I told you that earlier.'

'So the trapdoor's not going to open when I reach "Off to the realm of darkness"?'

'No,' she replied wearily. 'We won't start using the drops and lifts until the end of the week. No sense in wishing more accidents on us, is there?'

'I can see you're busy,' said John May quietly. 'I'll wait here until you're ready for me.'

Helena checked her watch in alarm. 'I'm sorry, I didn't realize it was time for our meeting, Mr May. We're running behind this morning.'

'That's quite all right,' said May. 'I'm enjoying the rehearsal.' He felt like sitting in the dark for a while. Betty had kept him out later than he had intended, and the AA guns stationed in Regent's Park had been booming for most of the night. On top of this, he had now spent his entire first week's wages on a girl, and he hadn't been paid yet.

'We're still interviewing everyone who was with Miss Capistrania and Mr Senechal on the days of their deaths,' May reminded her as they seated themselves in Helena's arched office above the balcony. 'I need to talk to your assistant.'

'Harry, yes, he was there when Charles was killed.'

'And Corinne Betts, who I'm told actually saw the globe fall.'

'She's not on today's call sheet but Harry has her landlady's telephone number.'

'Mr Bryant reckons that casts grow into extended families during the run of a production,' said May. 'Is that true?'

'For better or worse, yes.' Helena opened the window behind her chair and lit a cigarette, waving the smoke out. The management had asked the company to reduce their daytime smoking because the new auditorium upholstery absorbed the smell. Nobody had bothered to point out to them that the whole of the city stank of burning varnish and brick dust. 'We've got a cast of real troupers. Normally a deranged German sniper could burst in and machine-gun the audience, and they wouldn't miss a line. I know many of the boys and girls from previous productions. They've been doing scenes in groups for a while. They've received musical direction and attended rehearsals with the same choreographer. Now it's just a matter of keeping them calm.'

'So it's still going smoothly?' May felt as though he should be taking notes, but wasn't sure what to write.

'I wouldn't say that. The thing never fits perfectly from the outset. Steps get in the way of recitative, cues come in the wrong places and have to be rearranged. You get a lot of masking and scissoring, but nothing that can't be worked out.'

'Scissoring?'

'Actors crossing each other's paths onstage. We're over the worst. I shout at them, but it doesn't mean anything. By opening night we'll be a big happy family.'

'Then why do Mr Bryant and I feel shut out?' asked May.

'Because you're outsiders, darling,' laughed Helena. 'You expect backstage to be a hotbed of gossip and intrigue, but this one's not. There's too much riding on the production for anyone to behave in an unprofessional manner.'

'Perhaps you're right,' May admitted. 'I suppose I was expecting histrionics. Highly strung actors, the usual clichés.'

'So long as you realize that they are only clichés,' said Helena reproachfully.

Just then the door to the artistic director's office burst open and a tall, angular woman of about forty flew in.

'I'm not going to work with that dreadful bitch for one more minute!' she cried before chucking herself lengthwise onto Helena's sofa. 'He's ruining my entrance. I said to him, "Darling, I wouldn't let any man step across my entrance, let alone an old cow like you," and he said, "I can't see how you would know, dear, you've never been with a man in your life," waving his whip at me in front of the shepherdesses. I said, "I've played bigger houses than this," and he said, "Only when you were working the back passage of the Alhambra, love." He said, "I've played the Duke of York's, Her Majesty's, the Queen's," and I said, "The Queen's is an ice rink, dear, no wonder you're so frigid." Oh, you're not alone, I'll come back later.' She threw herself back onto her feet. 'So I'll leave you to sort that out then, if you would.' And she was gone in a cloud of Arpège, slamming the door behind her.

'You were saying?' said May gently.

'Well, there are a few exceptions to the rule,' Helena admitted, blanching.

'Who was she, by the way?'

'Valerie Marchmont. She's playing the role of Public Opinion, God help us,' said Helena.

Down in the foyer, Arthur Bryant knocked on the window of the box-office booth. Elspeth Wynter looked up from her booking forms and smiled vaguely. 'Hello, Mr Bryant. A pleasure to see you again.'

'I'm glad you feel that way,' said Bryant, tugging his scarf straight. 'We're conducting interviews—'

'Of course, I understand,' she said hastily. 'Can we do mine here?'

'We're supposed to record them at the unit.'

She looked hesitant. 'We're absolutely frantic, what with the schedule running behind.'

'Perhaps I could arrange something.' Bryant attempted a smile, liked the effect and widened it. 'On the condition that you have a bite to eat with me.'

'I don't know, it's our busiest day so far for bookings. I can't be away from the telephone.'

'Half an hour,' said Bryant. 'A bowl of soup somewhere nearby. I won't take no for an answer.'

Elspeth was flustered. 'All right, but it will have to be just over the road. The little Italian place in Moor Street?'

'It's a deal.' He pulled on his hat and flicked the brim of it non-chalantly. May was right. Persistence paid off after all. While his partner had been out with Betty Boop, Bryant had passed a miserable evening filing reports and being covertly studied by Sidney Biddle, who appeared to have nothing better to do than watch him and surreptitiously scribble notes in a diary. Biddle's visit to the St Martin's Lane shoe shop had proved disappointing. Although shoes matching the prints were sold only to theatres, they went to nearly every theatre and variety hall in the country.

Bryant stepped outside the theatre foyer and back into the natural light of the morning. Across the road, workmen had barricaded the pavements and were digging holes, searching for cracked gas mains. The Pioneer Corps were salvaging furniture from a bombed office in Shaftesbury Avenue. In schools across the city, children were swapping souvenir incendiary bomb fins from the night's raids.

At this point in the war, over two hundred tons of high explosives were being dropped on London every night.

He took a deep breath. The burning smell lingered in the air even on the freshest days. He wondered whether they were mad, trying to discover how just two people had died, when all around them men, women and children were being killed violently and unexpectedly. The AFS men had been putting out oil bombs in the next street all night long.

Some theory, he knew, would have to reveal itself soon or he'd be in for it. With a sigh of resignation, he stepped back into the chill shadows of the theatre.

24

READING SIGNS

Sidney Biddle was getting angrier.

From what he had seen so far, the Peculiar Crimes Unit was aptly named. The place was a total shambles. There was no excuse for it, war or no war. Everything was just as Farley Davenport had predicted. Procedural policy appeared to be non-existent. There was no chain of command, and members of staff were allowed to do exactly as they pleased. True, Arthur Bryant was the last to leave each night, after diligently entering the day's activities into the unit's logbook, but he kept it locked up in his office, so it was impossible to guess whether his entries were accurate or fanciful.

More bothersome was the fact that he, Biddle, appeared to have been excluded from Bryant's circle. He had been identified as the enemy in the camp and was shut out of all conversations, notes, briefings and interviews concerning the events at the Palace.

And the black-marketeering that was going on! All around him, all day, everyone was on the fiddle. Runcorn and Finch bartering tea, sugar and armfuls of rhubarb with the boys in the tailor's shop, PC Atherton, Crowhurst and the Bow Street constables coming in with buckets, kettles, clocks, tin openers, gardening tools, boots, pencils and tins of furniture polish. Everyone seemed to know that a potato peeler in good nick was worth two spanners.

Once again, he was an outsider. Sidney sat in the window of the office behind Bow Street station and morosely sipped his tea, watching the clearance boys at work. The empty offices beyond the Royal Opera House appeared to have been commandeered as fire-alarm stations and first-aid posts. Perhaps he should have taken a job with the Press and Censorship Bureau. At least they were performing an essential duty. Last month, the corner of Leicester Square had been bombed flat, and holes had been blown in the District Line railway tunnel at Blackfriars; right now the bureau would be busy suppressing the truth, retouching photographs, stemming negative information, tucking away all morale-damaging reports until after the war.

With a twinge of annoyance he realized that he would rather have been accepted by the others in the unit than marked out as someone to avoid. Even Runcorn, the miserable forensic scientist, ducked back into his office whenever he saw him approaching.

Everyone associated with the unit appeared to hold Arthur Bryant in high regard, although what Bryant had done to earn their esteem was far from obvious. And the other new chap, May, was creeping around in his partner's footsteps, clearly filled with awe.

Biddle checked the spelling in his report and recapped his fountain pen. By the end of his first week he hoped to have a dossier on Bryant that would draw a constricting ring of common sense around the unit. Davenport had made it clear that he wanted them closed down before the month was out. He'd clearly had enough of boffins being allowed a free hand while everyone else had to buckle down.

Biddle knew something else the others didn't know, because he had taken the call himself. DS Gladys Forthright would soon be on her way home, because her fiancé had backed out of the wedding. All they needed now was an unstable woman moping about the place. He smiled to himself as he blew on the page and closed it. She might just prove to be the straw that broke this peculiar camel's back.

'I'm so glad you could spare the time to have lunch with me,' said Bryant awkwardly. He never knew what to say to women. Consequently his behaviour around them was formal and slightly unnatural.

'I've always had a soft spot for the police. My brother's a crown court duty officer, not that I ever see him. I have to be getting back in a minute.' Elspeth pushed away her soup plate. The café was steamy and crowded with customers queuing for tables. 'There's a dress rehearsal this afternoon. Helena feels that several of the scenes aren't working so she's changing them. There are no out-of-town try-outs, and unless you tour first, the team only has rehearsals and previews to get it right.'

'Do shows change much before opening night?' asked Bryant, scooting a fork around the remains of the suspiciously unmeaty gravy on his plate.

'Oh, some of them become unrecognizable, especially the musicals. Of course, I'm strictly FOH so I'm not privy to everything that goes on, but you hear it all from the front of house because stages are designed to project sound forward. Do you think Helena will be able to keep the show running?'

'I don't know,' Bryant admitted. 'Westminster Council will have to be given our crime reports because of the Palace's status as a public building, but they've already got their hands full, so it's pretty easy for me to stall them. Their final decision will be swayed by the Lord Chamberlain's attitude. If he decides that it's a threat to public morality, there's nothing I or anyone else can do to keep it open. An appeal to Churchill might work, I suppose. I understand that when he was young he used to champion the ladies of the music hall.'

'All this talk of the chorus girls appearing nude is sending the box office through the roof,' said Elspeth. 'We'll soon have the Christmas season fully booked. If the Lord Chamberlain does shut us there'll be nothing else to put in after it. We'll go dark for the first time in thirty years. It doesn't bear thinking about.'

'If the Lord Chamberlain objects, couldn't a compromise be reached?'

'Yes, if Miss Parole would just agree to cover up the girls' ... you know...'

'What?'

'Nipples,' she mouthed at him, looking down at her chest. She dabbed a napkin at her forehead, embarrassed. 'It's so hot in here, Arthur. That scarf must be strangling you. We never overheat in the foyer, even in the middle of summer. So much marble.'

'You're all very loyal to the theatre,' Bryant conceded. Just being outside the building made Elspeth uncomfortable. He wondered how she would cope if the directors closed the show down and fired the permanent staff. Theatre management seemed a separate breed from the acting companies, one of the oldest and least recognized London tribes, working long hours for low salaries, never in the limelight themselves, unable to imagine any other life apart from the stage. 'Mr Whittaker's like you. I'm surprised you aren't...'

'What?'

'Well, together.'

'Me and Geoffrey?' It was good to see her smile. 'God, no. The theatre would always be in the way. We'd never talk of anything else. Besides, he's a terrible womanizer.'

'Are there really no problems between Helena and members of the cast?'

'None that I know of. The only row is with the stagehands, because of these accidents. I mean, we're all assuming the rumours are true about Miss Capistrania suffering something similar. Everyone's wondering who'll be next, but they all get on with their work. It's incredible how the press has managed to twist the whole thing around. Have you seen the article by Gilbert Riley in this morning's edition of the *Evening Standard*? He's suggesting we're the victims of some ancient theatrical curse. And then there are those photographs.' Elspeth was referring to the fact that someone had managed to take several shots of semi-naked chorus girls through the door of a rehearsal room several days earlier. 'Where's Mr May today? He seems ever so nice.'

She fancies him, thought Bryant immediately. Well, why not? He had the same effect on every woman he met. Presumably it was some kind of chemical reaction, scientifically quantifiable and easily explained. Some men had it, he decided, and others didn't.

'He's finishing the interviews,' said Bryant, pushing his plate back and picking up the bill. 'I have to submit a report to my superior by tomorrow. The process would normally take longer, but the war is speeding everything up.'

'The last fourteen months have passed so quickly,' agreed Elspeth. 'So many horrors, so many changes. I just celebrated my thirty-second birthday. Not a good age for a single woman.' Her hand absently brushed her cheek. In the dusty light from the restaurant window she suddenly looked much younger, as if she had been kept all her life within the walls of the theatre, untouched by the ravages of the outside world. Bryant felt a sudden pang of desire for her. 'It's rather ironic still to be working in a shrine constructed for a man who made merciless fun of spinsters.'

'Oh, Gilbert, you mean. Yes, he was a bit hard on the ladies. But Sullivan balanced him. He loved women too much. It must have been an interesting alliance.'

'I daresay you see the parallels with your own partnership,' said Elspeth carelessly.

Bryant pretended to bridle at the thought. 'Crusty curmudgeon and laconic ladies' man, whatever can you mean?' he said.

Elspeth's eyes sparkled with mischief. 'Oh, I don't think you're such a curmudgeon. You have the heart of someone who's been in love. Trust me, I know the signs.'

'Well, once was enough.'

'You're young. You have plenty of time yet, provided you can manage to stay out of harm's way.' She checked a tiny gold watch. 'I need to get back. Perhaps we can see each other when I get out.'

'And perhaps we can eat somewhere other than here,' said Bryant, paying the bill. 'Their meat sauce tasted as though it had been boiled up from the innards of a horse.'

'If they keep reducing our rations, I imagine that's what we'll end up eating.' Elspeth rose and straightened her hat as a woman shoved past her to claim her seat.

The young detective laid a gentle hand on Elspeth's shoulder. 'I've overlooked something. You know the theatre better than anyone...'

'I know it well, but so does Geoffrey. And Stan Lowe, and Mr Mack.'

'Am I making mistakes? What have I missed?'

'I think perhaps...' She hesitated for a moment, studying his wide blue eyes. A connection tingled as she opened herself to him, then quickly cooled as she remembered her place. 'I think you should talk to the owner of the theatre company. You might learn more than you imagine. Everyone has secrets.' She pushed open the restaurant door and glanced guiltily at the theatre. 'I've said enough. I really must go.'

For the briefest of moments Bryant had read something in her eyes that he could not interpret: fear, mistrust, the pain of hidden knowledge. He was young, and still had much to learn about people, especially women.

25

THE NATURE OF ILLUSION

Every time May passed near the footlights of the Palace stage, chorus girls would peer round the wings at him and start giggling. He wondered what Betty had told them. The evening had been a lot of fun, though bloody expensive, and the pretty chorine had made it obvious that she would welcome entertainment again at the weekend. Knowing that Bryant had returned to the unit the previous night, May felt an odd sort of disloyalty to his partner. It was only the end of his third day, and he was fraternizing with potential suspects instead of working late.

'I thought I'd find you down here,' he said, spotting the unruly fringe of chestnut hair that stuck above the back of a row of stalls, six rows from the orchestra pit. Bryant was sprawled with his legs hooked over the seat in front. The stage was partially lit with Fresnel spots to reveal a hellish scene. Crimson caverns of oil and fire glittered with droplets of lava, and the petrified purple bodies of demons jutted from priapic stalagmites. The effect was, if not quite obscene, very near the edge of public toleration in 1940.

May pushed down the seat next to his partner and leaned over. 'Did you know that while the theatre company is occupying the Palace, it owns the stage, the backstage area and all rights of access, but not the front of house or its offices? Those are in the control of the theatre's owners. Each of the companies is placing the responsibility on the other, so now we're not allowed to talk to staff on the premises. I'm trying to make arrangements to continue off site.'

'We should have done that from the start,' said Bryant grumpily. 'It'll shake them up to be questioned in official surroundings. I wish I hadn't tried the mystery meat pie at luncheon, I feel most uncomfortable.'

May pointed at the semi-naked women cavorting with each other onstage. 'I suppose all of this offends your purist sensibilities.'

'Not a bit of it,' said Bryant. 'Offenbach was far from pure. In fact, he outraged the purists of his age, so he'd probably approve of the nudity, although he might think some of the sex scenes are going a bit far, even in our supposedly enlightened times.'

'Perhaps you could tell me what's supposed to be going on'— May waved a hand at the stage—'all this operatic hellfire and brimstone.'

Bryant unbuttoned his waistcoat and massaged his podgy stomach. 'For a start it's not an opera, it's an *opéra bouffe*.'

'What's the difference?'

'It has mythological, supernatural elements. It's fanciful. It's intended as a comic diversion.'

'So there's no fat lady singing at the end?'

Bryant swivelled his head and studied his partner coolly. 'You're not much of a music lover, are you?'

'Oh, I don't know, I like a bit of a dance to Glenn Miller. I'm always willing to learn.'

'I know a numbers-and-fractions merchant when I meet one. You're a science bod. I saw you listening to Oswald Finch when he was going on about body fluid ratios. Your ears pricked up.'

'I just thought I should know a bit about all this.' He bounced his fingers in time with the music.

'I must say, it's suspiciously appropriate.' Bryant unknotted a few feet of his scarf and sat up. 'Jacques Offenbach was a forerunner of Gilbert and Sullivan. He's the reason they started writing together. He had huge successes with these romps in Paris, even though the critics were sniffy. *Orpheus in the Underworld* is over eighty years old. Back when it was first performed, everyone who could afford to visit the theatre had a decent working knowledge of the classics, so Offenbach could make fun of Greek legends and everyone would get the joke. Here, he's taken the most famous part of the Orpheus myth and reworked it. Orpheus was the son of a muse who saved the Argonauts from the Sirens. He ventured into the Underworld to get back his beloved nymph, Eurydice, who had been bitten by a snake.'

'Oh, I remember that bit. Pluto let him have Eurydice back on the condition that he didn't look behind him at her until she reached daylight, but he did.'

'Well done. Offenbach's version breaks with traditional mythology. He cynically parodies the characters and makes the story a social satire. He turns Orpheus into a salacious violin teacher, makes Eurydice a tart and has her old man moaning about having to go off and save her.'

'Who's that, then?' May pointed out a statuesque woman in vast grey crinolines. He had last seen her throwing a histrionic fit in Helena Parole's office.

'That's the figure of Public Opinion. In Offenbach's version of the myth Orpheus is pleased to see the back of his wife, and goes down to Hades only because Public Opinion threatens him with exposure about his own dalliances. Eurydice lusts after a shepherd called Aristaeus, who is really Pluto in disguise. She gets bitten, and is taken down to Hell, but finds it more boring than she expected. Meanwhile, on Mount Olympus, the gods are grumbling to Jupiter about their rights, he gets hot for Eurydice and they all go down to Hell.'

'I think I get the idea,' interrupted May. 'Presumably it all ends in tears.'

'No, it ends with the cancan. A real trouser rouser, sends you home with a song on your lips and a lump in your drawers. In those days, the stage used to be lit with floats, oil wicks that were floated on water to reduce the risk of fire. It was an effect designed to show up the dancers' thighs, so you can imagine the excitement it caused with a lot of saucy high-kicking. The ladies of the Paris chorus rarely bothered to wear knickers, and performed all kinds of athletic motions to reveal themselves to the wealthy patrons in the front rows.

'As well as stuffing his recitative with knowing jokes, like Morpheus being the only god awake when all the others are sleeping,

Offenbach filled his entertainments with references to other nineteenth-century operas, so the trio of the last act of *La Belle Hélène* is lifted from the *William Tell* Overture, and in this opera there's a direct pinch from Gluck's version of *Orpheus* that got screams of laughter from the audience. The ending's topsy-turvy too, because Eurydice doesn't want to go back with boring old Orpheus, and he doesn't want her, so Pluto's condition of not looking back at her on the way out of Hades is really an escape clause for both of them. Eurydice ends up as a bacchante, one of Hell's call girls, merrily high-kicking in the inferno.'

'Sounds rather immoral.'

'That was the whole point. What interests me,' Bryant continued, warming to his subject, 'is Offenbach's capacity for deceit. Here was a man who used tricks and jokes, paradox, caricature and parody, who lied about when and where he was born, a man who was not French at all but probably a German rabbi, who conned his way into the Paris Conservatoire despite the fact that foreigners were banned from attending, who was a published composer at nineteen, a virtuoso on the cello and, bizarrely, the toy flute, who had five children and became a Roman Catholic, whose success was so great that *le tout Paris* had to be nightly turned away from his theatre. He was a conundrum, a shamelessly charming scoundrel. He had what our Jewish friends call "chutzpah".' Bryant folded his arms across the back of the seat in front of him, lost in admiration. 'Offenbach's been out of favour for the last few years. But he was capable of scandalizing in his time.'

'People really take offence at this sort of stuff?'

'Not any more. Classical Greek scholars find the whole thing particularly amusing.'

'So we're not dealing with a deranged Greek?'

'Oh, I wouldn't rule out anything at this point.' Bryant turned his attention back to the stage. 'But I wonder if someone wants to stop the production for another reason.'

'You have one in mind?'

'Actually, yes. Elspeth told me I should talk to the owner of the theatre company.'

'I don't see what the owner could have to do with this.'

'Somebody's spending an awful lot of cash, several thousands of pounds, to get the show to opening night.'

'When the country needs money for manufacturing weapons? That's almost treasonous.'

'Not if you strengthen the spirit of the people. And sell the production to other countries, of course. These days plays are like motion pictures. A production can be simultaneously staged around the world.'

'You can't strike prints like you can a film.'

'No, but you can licence other companies. *No, No, Nanette* is probably still going strong in Addis Ababa.'

'I don't see what someone would gain by stopping the show from opening.'

'That's where it gets murky. Rival businesses could be searching for a way to lower the value of their enemies' stock. Or the backers themselves could sabotage their own production because it has to be insured to the hilt. If they found they'd misjudged the market, or sensed that the show was shaping up badly, they could halt it and claim the insurance. It depends on the equity structure, how the deal is underwritten.'

'They'd have a tough time convincing the insurance company in this climate,' said May. 'War damage must be bankrupting them. Can we check out the backers?'

'I've already briefed the pen-pusher Biddle on that.'

'I take it you're not intending to do any more work today, then.'

'Look here, I had four hours' sleep last night. There was a frost this morning, and my bedroom ceiling has a hole in it that's open to the sky. I actually felt like kipping down in the tube, just for warmth.'

'I don't know how people can do that. The smell of unwashed bodies on the platform of Covent Garden this morning was terrible.'

'John, people can get used to anything. Our job is to make sure they don't get used to murder. I'm going up to place some telephone calls.' Bryant hauled himself from his seat. 'Enjoy the rehearsal.'

'Wait,' said May. 'Tanya Capistrania's role in the show. The method of death. A dancer loses her feet. And the performer assigned to play Jupiter—'

'Is hit by a planet,' said Bryant. 'Yes, the idea had occurred to me that perhaps there's some grander plan. It's just so odd that it should happen on a stage.'

'Why?'

'Oh, the illusory nature of the theatre, I suppose. The whole thing about the stage is that it's a huge trick, a visual paradox. If you could see the set from overhead, you'd realize that the scenes you see from the stalls only exist as a series of angled flats, with actors slipping between them. The perspectives are far more false than you realize. Designs have an almost Japanese sense of construction, layer upon layer.'

'I'm not sure what you're getting at,' said May.

'I'm not sure I'm getting at anything,' Bryant conceded. 'I need to sleep on the problem. If indeed any of us are allowed to get some sleep. We'll have to see what the moonlight brings.'

26

REPAIRING THE PAST

What did the moonlight bring? John May walked to the centre of Waterloo Bridge and stopped. Behind him, the suspended wheel of the London Eye stared out along the line of the Thames. May adjusted the nylon Nike backpack strapped between his broad shoulders. He liked modern clothes; they had freed an older generation from constricting suits and ties and tight-fitting toe-capped shoes. He wore trainers and jeans without embarrassment. He was too old to be concerned with the strictures of fashion.

The river had the flat grey dullness of a plastic groundsheet. There were hardly any boats to be seen in either direction. If he closed his eyes he could see the wartime fire barges. The sound of traffic faded from his ears, and the city fell silent. Those Blitz mornings were so quiet and still that one could slip further back in time, to an age of cart-tracks and wooden slums. Now, the past and the silence were gone for ever. The city survived in fragments, as though it had been painted on glass and the glass had shattered.

He was on his way to meet Janice Longbright. He had found a yellowed picture of her mother in the archive at the Palace Theatre. It had been taken by PC Atherton in 1940, clowning around in the cell at Bow Street, just before she had supposedly gone off to marry Harris. Their wedding had finally taken place at the end of the war, in disastrous circumstances—but that was another story.

He wanted to be with Longbright, even if there was nothing to say. She was his only remaining connection to the past.

He had to find out who was stalking them, and why Bryant's dental records had been stolen. Could someone have wanted a souvenir of the dead detective? It was the first thing he asked her when they met.

Longbright was sitting in the corner of a black-and-white-tiled fish restaurant in Covent Garden, tearing the claws from the sockets of a crab shell. She had a cigarette sticking from the corner of her mouth, and was squinting through the smoke at the eviscerated crustacean. 'I'm sorry, John, I was starving and started without you,' she apologized. 'You've lost a bit of weight.'

'They say bereavement does that to you.'

'Well, don't lose any more. You're half an hour late.'

'Am I? I didn't mean to be.' May slid onto the bench seat opposite and poured himself a glass of wine from her carafe.

'I suppose you were standing in the middle of Waterloo Bridge, staring into the filthy water and thinking bad thoughts.'

'You know me too well.'

'You can't bring him back that way.' She wielded a vicious-looking pair of pliers, cracked open a claw and dug out its flesh.

'I realize that. I was wondering if someone else is trying to bring him back.'

'By nicking his dental records? I hardly think so. I called the dentist, by the way, but it's a new bloke. Bryant's regular man has gone on holiday, nobody seems to know where. They're going to call me back. Did it cross your mind that the bomber might have been trying to get the both of you?'

'I don't think so. If he'd figured out how to get into the unit, and knew about Arthur's habit of working on a Sunday night, he must also have known that I rarely stay late at the weekends.'

'I've got people checking the station CCTVs, but there's a lot of coming and going around that place because of the club next door, and they're nearly all wearing hooded jackets. You can't see a bloody thing.'

May watched Longbright disembowel the crab. 'My neighbour told me someone tried to break into my apartment. She said something about teeth. The man had huge fangs.'

He studied the former detective sergeant. Her make-up looked thick in the pale morning light. She reminded him of her mother, not least because she styled herself on the forgotten film star Ava Gardner.

Janice dropped the crab claw and stabbed her cigarette into a tin ashtray. 'God, I miss him, don't you? Stupid question. I've been trying to find out too, you know. One hundred and forty-two major cases between nineteen forty and two thousand and three, not counting the thousands of small unsolved dramas the pair of you waded through. It could have been anyone.'

'But it wasn't,' said May. 'I'm sure it's connected with the Palace.'

'You can't know that. There's no one left. Stone, Whittaker, Wynter, Noriac, Parole, that poor creature who committed the murders, even Mouse, the stage door boy, they're all dead. I've checked all the records and made all the calls.'

'Then we've overlooked someone,' said May simply. 'Just as Arthur did all those years ago. Here, this is for you.' He took out the photograph and handed it to her.

'My God.' Janice touched the edges of the faded monochrome picture. 'I could be her.'

'You are.' May touched her hand. It was hard to believe that Gladys Forthright's daughter was in her fifties. Looking at her he felt the present shift into the past. He was forced to shut his eyes and wipe them clear. 'Tell me, do you think we wasted our lives?'

Janice looked shocked. 'What do you mean? Of course not. All the people you helped, all the—'

'I'm not talking about work, I know what we did. I mean us, Arthur and me. He loved Nathalie and lost her. He was infatuated with your mother, but she didn't want him. He waited years for Gladys. I married the wrong woman, lost her and my baby girl. My son has a daughter who can't even leave her house any more. What was it all for? Sometimes I think Arthur and I worked so hard because there was nothing else for us to do.'

Longbright picked up the photograph and dropped it into her shoulder bag with an air of finality. 'Well, there's something for you to do now,' she said, taking up the crab once more and splintering its legs into pieces. 'If you want to save the future, you have to repair the past.'

'And how am I supposed to do that?'

'I may have found a way. Alma remembered another sheet of paper lying on Bryant's dining-room table, beside the dental records. She thinks it was from a hospital. It also went missing. I'm assuming it was his list of patients released from the Wetherby. The nurse who compiled it for him says there were over fifty names on it. But he might have made a mark against one of them.'

'I don't see how we'll find that out now.'

'It took me years to get him to keep copies of everything.'

'You think it was a copy?'

'Yes. And I imagine he would have left the original at the office.'

'Then it's gone. The unit was obliterated.'

'Your partner was an untidy man. He never put anything back in its rightful place.'

'You don't think it would still be in the photocopier?'

'If it is, it's between a sheet of glass and a layer of heavy heat-proof plastic. I can't think of anything that would preserve it better.'

May dug for his mobile phone.

'Relax,' said Longbright, biting into the soft flesh of the claw. 'I've already called Finch. We're going through the remains after lunch. Bash in a crab first, I promise you'll feel a lot better for it.'

27

THE MASK OF TRAGEDY

'I've never seen anyone die before,' said Corinne Betts distantly, twisting a curl of hair at her ear, 'not actually go from living and talking to suddenly lying on the ground covered in blood, like a stage prop. You'd think you'd see something leave, a wisp of air.' The little performer was being interviewed by John May. They were seated in the tiny white-tiled dressing room that Mercury had been sharing with Jupiter.

'We have someone who can talk to you about the psychological aspects of witnessing death, if you'd like,' May offered. 'It's something they've set up for people who've been bombed out. It hasn't proven very popular so far, but it's supposed to help.'

Corinne dug out a bottle of Scotch and a pair of enamel mugs. 'I'm not bothered. Call me cynical, but I suspect institutional comforting is designed to give nosy people something to do. My sister was killed during the first week of the Blitz. She was working in a maternity hospital near the Guildhall. We weren't close; she didn't approve of the way I live. Even so... I feel all right now, a little strange, like I did when I heard about Maisie. As though something has shifted. At least they found her body, and I know why she died. Everyone is much more upset than they're letting on, you know. There's talk of spies, all sorts of rubbish. There's a theory that Tanya was just picked out at random and murdered. Was she?'

'It's certainly possible.'

'And Charlie? That wasn't an accident either?'

May shifted uncomfortably in his seat. 'Someone aimed at Mr Senechal and cut the wire attached to the globe.'

'Blimey. You think it's an inside job, someone trying to stop the production?'

'I don't see how anyone could have entered the theatre unseen.'

'I suppose you're waiting to be handed names. We're all meant to turn informer and blame the people we don't get along with.'

'Do you want to nominate someone?'

'Me? I've no axe to grind with anyone here, except perhaps Little Miss Perfect, and that's only because she gets on my nerves for being so gifted.'

'Who do you mean?'

'Eve Noriac. You only have to look at her. Haven't you met her yet? She's young, she's beautiful, she's rich and she's French so of course all the men adore her. She has the starring role and she deserves it. It's just that it all seems to come so easily to her. She's been rehearsing in splendid isolation with her own tutor, away from us commoners. She turned up late for this afternoon's rehearsal, and hardly concentrated at all while the rest of us were floundering around. She's touched by the muses. And I've heard she's set her sights on Miles Stone, our Orpheus, so they'd rather be living out their roles in the play.'

'What about Tanya Capistrania? Did she have talent?'

'She worked hard, but was never more than proficient. The parts you take on have to sit comfortably with you, otherwise your awkwardness transmits itself to the house. The audience is always aware that it's watching "acting". Real stars make you believe in them because they believe in themselves. The audience is on their side from the moment they arrive on stage.' Corinne leaned forward conspiratorially. 'I'll let you in on a secret. Acting is a confidence trick. You don't attract good roles without exuding confidence, and you only have that if you already know you have talent. The two go hand in hand, and without one, the other spirals out of control.' She knocked back her Scotch and grimaced. 'Tanya wasn't seeing just Geoffrey Whittaker. She was also having an affair with John Styx.'

'Someone from outside the production?' asked May.

'No, that's his *Orpheus* role. His real name's David Cumberland—you know, like the sausages. He doesn't get going until act three, basically gets one decent number to himself and joins in with the others for some melodramatic dialogue. But perfect for Tanya.'

'Why?'

'Darling, you can't have an affair with someone if they're always on stage the same time as you.'

'You say an "affair".'

'Yes, he's got a civilian wife tucked away somewhere. It was probably a matter of mutual convenience. There's nothing like a good tension-releasing fuck after you've been singing at the top of your lungs all day, pardon my French.'

'Any link between her and Charles Senechal that you can think of? Did they spend much time together offstage?'

'I don't think they even knew each other. In the early stages of a production you can address the most intimate dialogue lines to a stranger and not get to have a real conversation with them at all. Particularly if there's a celebrity performer among you. They make the less experienced members of the cast nervous. The stars have to break the ice first. Protocol, my dear. I'm not from a stage background like the rest of them, so it doesn't wash with me.'

'How did you get the part, then?'

'Mercury is a pretty physical role.' Corinne topped up their mugs. 'Lots of charging about on winged feet. I saw someone do it on roller skates at the Blackpool Tower Ballroom. Helena came to one of my humorous monologues and asked me to attend a casting session. They were seeing lots of other short fat people. Comedy women, you know the sort of thing. If they're fat they must be funny.'

'Will you do me a favour, Miss Betts?'

'Corinne, please. Theatres are intimate places. We should be on first-name terms.'

'You seem to have a fairly objective outlook. Would you tell me if you hear anything unusual?' He looked up at the posters of demonic heads lining the walls, different productions of *Orpheus* around the world. 'I mean, unusual by theatrical standards.'

'You can't ask me to spy for you, Mr May. They're my friends.'

'I appreciate that. But Mr Bryant thinks something is happening here that goes beyond the scope of normal criminal investigation.'

'And what do you think?'

'I'm not sure. This is my first actual case.'

'They've sent a boy to do a man's job.' She gave a dark chuckle. 'Isn't that the war all over.'

'We don't have the facilities to protect everyone. We don't even have the means of finding out who else might be at risk.'

'I see your problem,' said Corinne. 'It's like acting. You don't get very far with a role until you've established your motivation. If you can't find anything to relate to, you never get a grip on the piece.'

'Then perhaps we understand each other,' said May, smiling gently.

'You're a nice man, John.' Corinne brushed his jaw with the back of her hand. 'Don't let anything happen to the rest of us.'

Corinne Betts waited twenty minutes for a 134 bus, but it was raining and the first two were completely full, so she decided to start walking. She liked John May a lot. She had always been drawn to younger men. They had a sense of innocence that she no longer had the strength to muster.

She wondered if there was a link between Tanya and Charles that she had missed. It was fun in a Conan Doyle–ish way: an old, dark theatre, a murderer on the loose. Except that Conan Doyle had been dead for a decade. His *Strand* magazine stories now belonged on the bookshelves of elderly aunts, and the war had stolen away the vicarious pleasures of murder.

It set her wondering about motives again. You'd have to be pretty angry with someone to plan their death, particularly at the moment when there was every chance that they might disappear under a bit of falling masonry. And to be annoyed with two people as different as Charles and Tanya made no sense at all. If someone was trying to stop the production, why not just set fire to the theatre? It wasn't as if there were any likely suspects. In fact, the more she thought about it, the stranger everything became—an air of Greek tragedy, the severing of limbs, the compass falling from the sky. Something began to prick at her skin. She resolved to take a long bath and have a smoke before going to bed.

She had reached the top of Tottenham Court Road before another 134 came along, and although she waved at it, the damned thing refused to stop. The rainswept corner of Euston Road had become one of the bleakest and most exposed points in central London, now that so many craters of brick and stone had transformed tarmac into the surface of the moon. They said an old woman had been blown out of her house in her iron bedstead, and had not woken up until the rescue squad reached her. 'They' said a lot of things. It was becoming impossible to know who to believe.

The few people she passed were carrying bags and suitcases, heading to stations, or to houses that had roofs. A hearse passed her with perhaps a dozen children in it, their faces pressed against the windows, evacuees being taken to their train. The distant plane trees of Euston Road were just visible in the downpour, the tops of their branches rustling and twisting in the rain-laden wind. Here the street was preternaturally empty, the boarded-over shop fronts as dull as the terraced houses set back from the road. She hated the blackout, the dead carapaces of buildings, their rooftops darker than the sky.

Corinne was about to cross the road beside the tiled wall of Warren Street tube station when she became aware of someone else moving on the street. Grey veils of rain fell ahead of her, blurring the view, but a figure appeared to be waiting on the opposite pavement. It was dressed in a black rubber raincoat, with the hood raised. There was something wrong with its face, she thought: too white, too still. The figure twisted back and forth, clasping itself, its head bouncing from side to side, as though it was laughing, or in terrible pain.

Corinne walked to the striped traffic island in the centre of the road. From the corner of her eye she saw the figure shift again, passing across the dimmed lights from the station ticket hall. She watched as it reached the edge of the pavement, and found herself staring into a distorted face as pale as porcelain, the crying tragedy mask of traditional theatre. A passing truck churned its way through a lake of rainwater. When she looked up once more, the figure had vanished.

It had seen her alarm, she was sure. Angered and frightened, she ran across the road, moving past the taped crosses of shop windows, until she realized that she was running in a hard panic, and forced her pace to a walk.

She could not understand where the fear had come from. She was only aware that she had felt it, a chill prickling between her shoulder blades, a primal warning that someone or something meant her harm or, worse still, wanted her.

28

VENOM

'Mr Bryant, wait, I'd like a word with you.'

It was late on Wednesday evening when Oswald Finch came running after the young detective, who was backing a black Wolseley out of the half-flooded car park behind Bow Street police station. He had requisitioned the car from the pool in order to visit his aunt in Finchley. She had trouble getting about, so he was taking her a joint of beef. Bryant affected to ignore the pathologist and almost ran over his foot. Exasperated by the obstruction that had placed itself between his vehicle and the exit, Bryant jemmied open the window with the end of a soup spoon set aside for the purpose, and eyed him brightly. 'Oh, Oswald, it's you. They still haven't fixed this window. What do you want?'

'Mr Bryant, there's an enormous plant in my office. Your constable told me you put it there.'

'Well, I didn't personally move it, it's far too heavy for me to touch, with my back.' Bryant searched about for the handbrake. 'I had Atherton bring it up. Do you like it?'

'Well, frankly no, I don't.' Finch bobbed down to look at him. 'It's six feet tall and blots out all the light, and it smells strange.'

'That's just a bit of root rot. It's been sitting in contaminated water, a broken sewage main, I imagine. A house in St Martin's Lane got bombed out and they were clearing the site. There are insects of some kind living in its soil, I thought you might know what they are. They've got a bite rather like a mosquito, brought me up in livid red lumps, some kind of tropical necrosis. I once found something similar in a flat belonging to an Ethiopian student in Tufnell Park. We still don't know what killed him. I thought you'd be interested.'

'Floral virology's really not my field, and it's in the way. I can barely get the door open.' He rocked hesitantly back and forth in front of the automobile as Bryant throttled impatiently.

'I'd keep it open for a few days if you can, Oswald, just until you're used to the smell. It's quite overpowering. The buds shed a sort of purple pollen, very sticky, gets everywhere. I knew you'd be fascinated. Don't get any on your shirt, it seems to burn.'

'Look, I really don't think—'

'Jolly good. How are you getting on with the tissue samples from Tanya Capistrania?'

'Er, well, that's just it. I've carried out some more detailed analysis, and I think poison was ingested. In fact I'm sure—'

'Ingested? That could be anything, couldn't it? I mean, you can die from having water injected into your spine, or air into your brain or anything. Can't you be more specific?'

'Well, er, something she ate.'

'You mean the chicken? The chicken sandwich?' Bryant released the handbrake and the car hopped forward.

'It wasn't chicken. It was quail.'

'I don't see a difference.'

'Ah, but there is. You remember I got a positive test for coniine. Well, there's a plant rather like parsley or London rocket in appearance, *Conium maculatum*, not at all uncommon, springs up on waste ground, especially around bomb sites. Causes the kind of muscular paralysis I described. There's no real antidote beyond gastric lavage, and only if it's performed moments after ingestion. It's a long-recognized poison, most commonly known as hemlock.'

'Hemlock? It supposedly killed Socrates, didn't it?'

'I really have no idea. The thing is, some birds are immune to the plant. Quail eat the seeds without suffering any damage, but their flesh becomes highly toxic. It's feasible that the victim just got a bad quail. The perils of a rich diet.'

'Wouldn't she have experienced symptoms?'

'Yes, any time from half an hour to three hours after consumption, but she might not have recognized them as such. Dancers suffer muscular pain all the time.'

'You're telling me she may not have been murdered at all, Oswald?'

'That's right. She may simply have become paralysed, fallen down and been unable to move when the lift started up.'

'Well, thank you, that makes my evening.' Bryant ground the gear lever forward, forcing Finch to jump out of his path. Blithely ignoring the horn blasts from behind, the Wolseley thumped up the kerb in front of the station as Bryant beckoned to his partner. John darted towards the vehicle with a late edition of the *Evening News* held over his head as Arthur threw open the passenger door.

'John, Runcorn is going to conduct some kind of tension test on that prop globe, isn't he?' said Bryant, trying to clear the condensation from the windscreen with his sleeve. 'Can you run the wire ends under a microscope and check the shear?'

'I'll do it, but the waiting time for equipment isn't good. The samples will probably have to go over to Lambeth.' John smiled. 'I saw you talking to Mr Finch. He's very upset about that plant.'

'He works faster when he's upset about something. I'm annoyed about his chemical theory.'

'You should be pleased to hear about Miss Capistrania,' said May, puzzled. 'It may mean we've just stumbled upon an unfortunate series of circumstances.'

'Very unfortunate when you consider that her feet managed to turn up in the possession of a chestnut vendor. Who is entirely innocent, by the way. His movements are fully vouched for. If we're not looking for a murderer, somebody out there must have a pretty black sense of humour.'

'There's a lot of it about. None of Tanya's colleagues liked her very much.'

'How much do you have to hate someone to hide their feet? I'll tell you, John, right now the unit could do with a renewed funding pledge, and we'll only get that if we find a culprit quickly.'

May peered through the windscreen. 'Don't pull out just yet, there's a lot of traffic.'

'Well, I don't believe it,' said Bryant, twisting the wheel hard and stamping on the accelerator to a chorus of screeching tyres, 'it's all too absurd, quails and hemlock and falling planets. The chances of two people undergoing such colourful ends in close proximity is positively Jacobean, and I don't swallow it for a moment.'

'Strange things happen all the time,' May felt compelled to point out. 'Do you have something against the laws of chance?'

'I do, as it happens. I think while we're under bombardment, all sorts of peculiarities might emerge, just not in this fashion.'

'I say, you're driving awfully fast without lights. Why are you in such a rush?'

'After I've visited my aunt I'm taking Alma out tonight, and I'm running late.'

'Your landlady? You're taking your landlady out to dinner?' A traffic policeman loomed out of the dark at them, and jumped from harm's way like a startled hare. Bryant was a terrible driver. His priorities corresponded to none of the ones mentioned in the Highway Code. Nor did his signals, for that matter.

'Nobody mentioned dinner. She happens to consider me companionable.'

'Still, it's a date. I thought you were working on Miss Wynter.'

'Miss Wynter is already spoken for. Her first love is the theatre. I suspect she enjoys her status as a spinster. Alma knows how to enjoy herself.'

'Don't tell me you're planning a night of love.'

'If you'd met her, you'd know you were being disgusting. Alma is religious and respectable. We have a couple of shilling seats for *Gone With the Wind*. She has an unfathomable obsession with Clark Gable, and can't find anyone else to go with her.'

'Well, at least you can watch with an easier mind.'

'Far from it,' said Bryant, 'I'm going back to the theatre afterwards. They'll be rehearsing late because the weather's too bad for bombing. I want to make sure nothing else happens.'

'You mean you want to be there if it does.'

Bryant swerved the vehicle over to the side of the road. Horns honked and tyres screeched in the darkness. 'How's this for you?'

May reluctantly opened the door. 'It's not at all where I'm going but never mind, I'll get a bus, it's safer.' He pushed his long legs out into the rain. 'Try to have a relaxing evening with Alma. You know where your nearest shelter is?'

'Alma will, she's very practical. I won't take anything in, you know, I shall be thinking about severed feet. I daresay you're off to enjoy yourself with your busty sexpot.'

'Actually, I'm taking a night off to recuperate,' said May. 'From what you've told me, your landlady sounds most keen. Perhaps you should consider the benefits of matrimony.'

'It seems an awful lot of effort just to get regular sex and someone to wash your socks. I mean, she already washes my socks.'

'Which still leaves the sex. I bet you can't remember your last time.'

'Oh yes I can,' called Bryant, pulling away from the kerb. 'Saturday night.' He indicated left and turned the wheel right. 'It could have been perfect, but for one thing.'

'What's that?' May hopped onto the pavement and squinted through the rain.

'I wasn't with anyone,' laughed Bryant as he plunged back into the unlit traffic.

29

THE REFLECTED INFERNO

Eve Noriac loved the smell of an old theatre.

It was something no amount of carpentry or repainting could remove, a richly human odour. She had grown up on the south coast of France, in a small town outside Nice called Beaulieu, so sun-caressed that the area around it was known as La Petite Afrique, and her arrival in England had coincided with the most prolonged period of rainfall the country had seen in a decade. Within a fortnight she had resolved to go home, but then in May her homeland had been invaded, and she had been forced to stay.

It was then that she discovered the theatres. The Lyric, the Apollo, the Fortune, the Criterion, the Cambridge, each had its own stamp and style, but they all exuded the same sense of shared life. The diurnal passage of each play brought platoons of awestruck schoolchildren and seasoned veterans, locals and tourists, suffering spouses and devoted worshippers. The challenge was to unite them all and win them over.

No two shows were ever the same, even though they appeared identical from the front of the stage. A nightly war was waged for the hearts and minds of those watching. Ground was gained and lost as each evening peppered itself with small victories and defeats. Much-rehearsed movements were swallowed up or skimmed past unnoticed. Flaws were observed or concealed. Each script was a recipe for pleasing the crowd; moments rose perfectly to the intention of the text or fell flat. The subtle ebb and surge of the performances made for different emphases that could alter the total effect of the entertainment within the batting of an eye.

Eve's role as Eurydice was the essence of the piece, but for a young soprano it was also a stepping stone for career-making roles to come. Some sopranos were technical virtuosos who honed their skills through ceaseless training. Others were born with a natural undisciplined talent that merely had to be shaped. The second type was rarer, but more thrilling to experience. Technical singers never bared their souls. Naturals were destructive, dangerous, even doomed. Their voices could create an extraordinary atmosphere of tension.

Actors can believe strange things; Eve Noriac knew she was a natural, and that her gift was granted by the gods of the theatre. They looked down kindly upon her, and protected her from harm. On the previous Saturday she had walked from St Paul's to Blackfriars during a daylight bombing raid, while the wardens shouted at her to get off the street. Who you had faith in wasn't important; it was that you had faith at all.

Eve's only failure was in her choice of lovers; she knew she would have to do something about Miles. He had barely set foot in the theatre before they had fallen upon one another in an urgent, sweaty embrace. Thinking about him now, Eve knew he wasn't her type. Miles would cling. She would have to wait until after opening night to tell him it had been a bad idea. She had no wish to damage his confidence before the critics had their chance.

Miles Stone was Eve's counterpart, Orpheus to her Eurydice, and right now he was trying to keep the voice on the other end of the line from fading, but the building's acoustics were playing tricks on him. It was as if the theatre frowned on the outside world, and interfered with the line connected to the ancient two-piece telephone in the hall outside the company office.

'I don't understand what you're doing in London,' he shouted, pressing his finger into his free ear. 'I thought you were staying in New York. What do you mean, I invited you? I said don't come. Yes, I did.'

Rachel's reply was damaged by a searing crackle of static. This was all Miles needed right now, his mother staying in town. While everyone else's mothers were heading for the comparative safety of the countryside, his was coming to the city.

'Why don't you let me check you into a hotel?' he asked. He knew Rachel would prefer to stay in his damp apartment building. She distrusted English hotels, with their erratic service and weird plumbing.

'No, not in the centre, it's not safe,' said Miles finally. 'I'll find you something further out, but you can't just waltz along to rehearsals.' He was through taking Rachel's advice. She always promoted Becky, his ex-wife, acting as if he was still married to her. Getting divorced was one of the few good ideas Miles had ever had. Changing his name from Saperstein to Stone had been a less successful move. He'd liked the mnemonic sound of Miles Stone; at least, until he overheard his agent referring to him as the Millstone. He knew he would have to ask Eve to stay away for a few weeks. Although the decree absolute had been settled a year ago, he was sure that Rachel still considered him married in the eyes of God, and he had not helped matters by occasionally sleeping with Becky when he was in New York. Rachel would only get into an argument with Eve if they met, and she would ensure that there was a meeting because she would turn up at the theatre whether he liked it or not, and report back to Becky. He had been caught in the velvet trap all his life, betrayed by his love of difficult women.

He settled the receiver back on its hook and walked down to the stage, a fiery riot of red, gold, purple and indigo flats and skycloths. There was so much set-dressing that he wondered whether the audience would be able to see anyone at all. On Saturday night they would have a full house plus the critics, the police, the St John's Ambulance brigade and the odd ARP warden to add to the confusion.

An extraordinarily high note reverberated through the auditorium: that note was meant for him. Eve Noriac was standing at the front of the stage, stretching her throat and impatiently swinging her arms. As Miles set off down the stairs once more, he wondered how Orpheus had managed to avoid visiting Hell to save her in the past, seeing that she was not a woman to be kept waiting.

It was half past nine, and the few remaining performers were tired. Helena was slumped in a seat six rows fom the orchestra pit, sipping her hundredth cup of tea. On stage, Eurydice was having trouble adjusting to her new Jupiter in their duet, the *'Duo de la mouche'*. The understudy baritone was now transformed into a bluebottle, and was finding it difficult to hit his mark while managing the celluloid wings of the costume.

'All right, everybody, we'll resume this at ten o'clock tomorrow morning,' Helena called, clapping her hands. 'If anybody needs to share a cab, please let Geoffrey or Harry know.' She rose and walked up the aisle, lighting a cigarette.

'Helena?' Harry came hobbling up beside her. He had twisted his ankle in a pothole at lunchtime, and had spent the day on his feet. 'We haven't heard sirens yet, but the searchlights and sound locators have gone back up in Charing Cross Road. I was wondering if you'd prefer to have the cast stay over in here. We could open up a couple of the old practice rooms. I think there's some bedding lying about.'

'You can discreetly ask the girls,' Helena suggested, sucking blessed smoke into her lungs, 'but the boys can go home. There's enough hanky-panky going on without putting the girls in temptation's way.' She loosened her bandanna and shook out her hair. 'If any member of the audience complains about having to sit for two hours on a narrow horsehair seat I shall ask them to try it for a fortnight.' She grabbed Harry's hand. 'Come on, you. Let's lose the others, I don't want to talk about work tonight. I'll buy you a Scotch in that nancy-boy bar you like so much. If we get in before the raids start, they might lock us in all night.'

Betty Trammel awoke with a dry mouth and a throbbing head. After the rehearsal, the ladies and gentlemen of the chorus had retired to the Spice of Life for drinks, and had stayed until closing time. The bombing raid had made travel impossible, and she had decided to sleep on a canvas camp bed in the upper circle practice room on the condition that her friend Sally-Ann slept in the room next to hers. She had no intention of staying alone in the theatre. Not that it frightened her, it took a lot to do that these days, but she wanted someone to talk to. She knew she had chosen the wrong time to return to England, but her course was set, and now she had to make the best of it. She decided to lie awake and listen to the night city while planning her next move. Instead she fell asleep almost instantly, and only woke because she found herself desperately thirsty.

The room's single window was blacked out, and the street far below was so silent that she thought for a moment it must have snowed. Rubbing warmth into her goosefleshed arms, she swung her legs from the bed and made her way slowly towards the door, where she had left a torch. She knew there was a bathroom at the end of the corridor, and presumed she would find some potable water. The torch threw a dim yellow circle onto the brown walls. She paused before the room in which Sally-Ann slept and listened to her light snoring, then made her way through the darkness.

'*Chante, belle bacchante,*' she sang under her breath as she walked, '*chante-nous ton hymne à Bacchus.*' Too much bloody Bacchus, she thought, twisting the torch beam onto the bathroom door. Her head was killing her, and she had nothing to take for it. Behind her, the faint light of the candle she had deposited at the top of the main staircase flickered and shifted.

Betty shone her torch around the bathroom, checking that it was empty, then shut the door and locked it. To do so was an act of habit; at home she had three brothers. She set the torch down on the edge of the sink, beneath the bathroom mirror, with its thin beam pointing up. They weren't allowed to turn on the lights when they used the lavatory up here because the windows weren't covered, and Helena had warned them that any more fines would come out of their own pockets.

She ran the cold tap, listening to the ghostly sound of clanking pipes, then filled an enamel mug with water and drank deep. The water had been standing too long in the cistern, and tasted brackish. She made a face, then noticed the chiaroscuro effect of the torchlight on her reflected flesh.

Detective May was rather a dish, she thought, but obviously penniless, which was a pity because she'd been saving herself for a wealthy man. There was something appealing about the fact that he was so young and unsullied. He clearly found her attractive. Betty stuck out her tongue and examined its pale coat. Then she drew in a deep breath, and held it.

But someone continued breathing behind her.

She still had her mouth open in surprise when the great white mask of a face unfurled itself over her right shoulder. Its mouth was a tortured red gash, like an angry cut from a sword, the teeth unnaturally large and distorted. The eyes were wild and cloudy, scarred with shiny stretches of skin. Above his hairline she saw a scraped knob of gleaming, cracked bone. His sore red hands clawed out for her in a mannered pose, captured in the torch beam like a frame from some forgotten Chaney film, or a scene from the *Inferno*—Dante's version, not Offenbach's. He had the shape of some poor limbless creature from the First War, more mutilated than any of the old soldiers she still saw on the streets selling pencils.

She screamed so loudly that the sound of the torch being knocked over into the sink was lost. Her last sensation before losing consciousness was one of anger, that she could be so foolish as to strain her vocal cords in this manner, just days before her big night.

Bryant heard the scream and ran towards it with his hurricane lamp raised, but was forced to stop and retrace his steps when he realized that he had come out near the left-hand pass door, the one that was glued shut by years of paint. It took him another minute to climb the stairs to the rooms of the upper circle. Betty's friend Sally-Ann was awake and shrieking and clutching her shoulders, and waving her hands at the bathroom.

Bryant opened it and helped Betty to her feet. As he turned on the tap and splashed some cold water on her face, Sally-Ann grabbed his shoulder.

'Something ran up the stairs,' she yelled, pointing.

Bryant realized that he was meant to dash off after the villain, but didn't much fancy it. He trotted to the bottom of the staircase and looked up into the pitch black. 'What, up there?' he asked.

'Yes, yes, hurry, get him!' Sally-Ann's panic had infected the revived chorine, and now they were both jumping up and down, flapping their arms about.

Bryant reluctantly mounted the stairs. The landing was so dark it gave him claustrophobia. With his lantern held high he walked cautiously forward, and found himself in the deserted brown corridor of the balcony offices. He raised the lamp in the opposite direction. Nothing that way either. But when he returned to his original position he was startled to see the broad back of a man disappearing round the bend in the corridor, no more than fifteen yards away.

Where the hell could he have come from? Bryant asked himself. The corridor was empty. How can he see in the dark? He set off in pursuit of the retreating form. He reached the turn, stopped and gingerly held the lamp out further, half hoping that whoever was up there would be scared away by the light. He wished May was here, lumbering along beside him, big and sensible and brave.

Having waved the tin lantern for long enough, he finally peered round the corner.

And found himself inches from a white staring face. He yelled, the face yelled, and he dropped the lamp in terror.

Luckily the lamp had a safety wick, so it didn't splash burning oil everywhere, but it went out all the same. It took Bryant a full minute of fumbling in the dark with trembling fingers to get it lit again, and then he found himself sitting on the floor next to a full-length mirror.

From somewhere up near the roof he heard boots scraping on iron rungs, then the slam of a steel door. Whoever he had been chasing was now locked outside on the roof with no way down. Thank God for that, he thought, smoothing his hair and straightening his clothes into a more ordered appearance. I can tell the girls I scared him off.

30

THE THREE HUNDRED

Thursday morning brought evidence of the previous night's bombing, but the streets of central London were mostly quiet and unscathed. John May was alarmed to discover that he had somehow used up his week's rations of everything except lard. He hadn't the faintest idea what to do with lard beyond trying to swap it for something edible. On the second to last page of his ration book was a list of mysterious serial numbers and a government message that read: DO NOTHING WITH THIS PAGE UNTIL TOLD WHAT TO DO. It summed up the official attitude to everything.

But nobody seemed to mind. In 1939 it had been estimated that at least a quarter of the population of Britain was undernourished. Now, families were thinking carefully about nutrition, discovering vegetables they had hardly ever seen or used before.

May prided himself on his youthful fitness but had begun to put on weight. His aunt had taken the war to the kitchen front with a vengeance. Overnight she started presenting her favourite nephew with unappetizing combinations of shredded cabbage, spinach, beetroot and turnips. She rustled up scabby-looking potato pancakes and fish-head soups seasoned with sorrel and grated nutmeg, baked purées of bile beans with celery and chestnuts, liberally lubricated with dripping or stiffened with suet. One night she boiled something experimental with slippery elm and condensed milk that took the finish off the dining-room table so completely she was using Karpol on it for weeks after to restore the shine.

'Why don't you go and buy us a couple of coffees while I finish up here?' instructed Bryant as his partner arrived for work. 'We're out of tea, and the Carlucci brothers have traded all theirs. Get a couple of Bath buns while you're at it.'

'It's a bit embarrassing,' May admitted, 'but I'm afraid I'm low on funds. I've already spent my first week's salary.'

'Too busy impressing the girls. I suppose I'll have to give you an advance.' Bryant dug into the pocket of his voluminous woollen trousers. 'Here's ten bob. Don't worry about getting into debt. I'm spending wages I'm not due to earn until about six years after my death.'

'Thanks awfully. Biddle says you saw the Phantom last night.'

'Indeed, but I do wish you wouldn't call him that. I trapped him on the roof, actually. When I got up there I found a surprised fire-watchman sitting on a ventilation flue. He told me he'd seen someone come flying out of the door, only to rush at the side of the building and vanish over it. When he ran to the ledge and looked down, there was no sign of anyone. It was as though he'd simply flown off into the night air. Poor bloke was beginning to think he'd imagined it when I turned up.'

'Where on earth could he have gone?'

'Buggered if I know. There aren't even any windows he could have dropped through. Nothing but a sheer brick wall and a long drop to the street. I've sent Crowhurst up there this morning to take a look around. What bothers me more is that your chorus girl locked the bathroom door from the inside when she entered, and yet this creature materialized right behind her.'

'You're telling me it has the ability to walk through walls and vanish over the edges of buildings like a vampire bat.'

'No, you're telling me. I can see your lips moving. Go and get the coffees.'

May went and got the coffees, but the image of someone sinister materializing in the bathroom next to the semi-naked girl stayed with him.

'I feel it's my duty to offer Betty police protection,' he said when he returned.

'Hm. I thought you might say that. I'm studying you for tips, you know. Your manner of dealing with the opposite sex could form the basis of an anthropological study. The most annoying part is, you don't even realize you're doing it.'

May was anxious to change the subject. He was staying with his aunt because his father's philandering had destroyed their family, and May lived in fear of taking after him. He set down the coffees and looked over Bryant's shoulder. 'What have you got there?'

'Zurich. They came back to us overnight. Damned efficient, the Swiss, although not to be trusted, of course.'

'What's in Zurich?'

'We've been tracking the money,' Bryant explained. 'The finance to stage the show. From Lloyd's of London, across to the continent and into neutral territory.'

'And you can find that out from here? I'm very impressed.'

Bryant studied the teleprinter paper for a moment and isolated a number of addresses. 'The production is being presented by a financial group registered in Victoria under the name of Three Hundred International.' He unravelled another foot of paper and carefully folded it. 'Listen to this. Three Hundred International Banks is registered in Zurich but is Greek-owned. Central European office, Athens. Other companies in the group include shipping, automotive accessories, property, blah blah, ah, here, a chain of theatres. Shipping and theatre, odd bedfellows, don't you think? I wanted a profile of the whole group but all I've managed to find so far is a general prospectus, and that tells me nothing. I spoke to some jobsworth in the Victoria office, but he wouldn't give me any information. What would make a shipping magnate diversify into the theatre?'

Shortly before he died, Arthur Bryant was interviewed about his earliest case. He told his interviewer, 'After the hostilities ended in nineteen forty-five, over a fifth of London's theatres had been destroyed or rendered unusable by bomb damage. The rest were bought up by a single consortium. The old theatrical families and their peculiar way of life, the life we briefly experienced, vanished almost overnight.' The interviewer had pretended to take notes, but he had only been interested in hearing about the murders...

'How many companies do these Three Hundred people own altogether?' asked May.

'I haven't counted them all. I was endeavouring to do so when you tipped up. It's rather hard to keep track of.'

'Here, let me give you a hand.' May pulled up a stool and began glancing through the text.

'Fine,' said Bryant, fishing in a top pocket for his spectacles. 'My eyes aren't too good this morning. We arrived late at the Gaumont last night and had to sit right at the front; it nearly blinded me. Stay and help.' He grinned. 'We can send Biddle on all the horrible running-about jobs.'

The checking process took over an hour. After a while, Bryant grew irrationally annoyed that May was more proficient with the new teleprinter keyboard than he would ever be, and went off to scrounge a packet of tea from the station next door.

'So, how many have you found?' he asked when he returned.

'I should have guessed.' May gave him a meaningful look. 'Exactly three hundred.'

'They own *three hundred* companies? Are you sure?'

'Some of them are very small. There's one listed here in Scarborough, a theatrical talent agency called Curtain Call Productions. I just rang them and spoke to the managing director. He was delighted to talk to me.'

'Could he tell you anything?'

'Only that Andreas Renalda, the big boss, lives here in London.'

'Handy. Ever hear of the Club of Rome? It's supposed to be an Anglo-American cabal of business managers and planners. It was first secretly assembled in the late nineteen twenties to form some kind of one-world government. That was based on something called the Three Hundred Club, which gets its title from a biblical passage, Romans, chapter three. Just before the Great War, Germany's Jewish foreign minister announced that the economic future of the continent was in the hands of three hundred men who all knew each other. They're also called the Olympians, following on from the Illuminati and the Cathars. It's one of those paranoid theories that suggests a small elite group runs the financial empires of the world.'

'I wouldn't go looking for conspiracies where there are none,' May advised, reading through the printed addresses.

'You've got to agree it's a bit of a coincidence that the group controlling the theatre company should be named after them.'

'It's a coincidence that doesn't make any sense,' said May heatedly. He was beginning to see where Bryant was going with the idea. 'Why would the owner of such a company wish to kill the cast of a play that's costing him a fortune to stage?'

'That's the question, isn't it?' Bryant smiled annoyingly.

'Don't you think there are enough crazy rumours about Nazi infiltration in British business without us adding to them?'

'If any lesson from war is to be learned, John, it must be always to prepare for the unexpected and face the unthinkable. There is no orthodoxy to follow now. Everything is in a state of flux.'

As if to emphasize Bryant's warning, a pebble knocked sharply against the windowpane. When May peered down into the street he saw Betty Trammel looking up at him imploringly. 'Your lady sergeant won't let me in,' she explained. 'I told her I simply had to see you.'

One look at her darkly swollen eyes warned him that the stifling dream world of the Palace was taking its toll on those who depended on it.

31

THE STRENGTH OF DAMAGED SOULS

Arthur Bryant sat in the flesh-chilling gloom of the marble foyer and wondered whether he should tackle the receptionist again. He had been waiting to see Andreas Renalda for forty minutes, and no one had appeared. The reception room of Three Hundred International, Horseferry Road, Victoria, was a dingy mausoleum filled with paintings of continental lakes, their frames criss-crossed with strips of tape to prevent injury from flying glass. Filling the entire wall opposite was an immense Victorian bookcase, the contents of which appeared to have been chosen by the yard. He had heard about companies buying up the stock of bombed-out booksellers. It irritated him that they were being used merely to suggest erudition. Bryant was considering the problem when the receptionist received a call and beckoned to him.

'Please go to the fourth floor, Mr Bryant, and someone will meet you.'

The young detective straightened the knot of his tie in the lift mirror. It had been his partner's idea to interview the head of the theatre company. May made a good impression on strangers, whereas Bryant's interview technique managed to be both obtuse and hectoring. In an attempt to learn from his affable partner, Bryant had insisted on handling the appointment, and had scribbled out a scrappy list of questions a few minutes before setting out from Bow

Street. He wasn't sure what he expected to find, but something told him it was best to start at the top.

John May had his hands full comforting his chorus girl, who had not yet recovered from her encounter in the theatre. Her lurid description of her assailant was exaggerated, no doubt, by an attack of blackout nerves and too much to drink. Bryant had suggested as much to May. He had not meant to sound callous; it was all too easy to joke about being scared nowadays. Everyone was scared. Nobody was given enough information. The newspapers were short of paper and short of news. Too many heart-warming stories about horses being dug out of collapsed stables and not enough analysis of the nation's long-term prospects. Perhaps that was the idea, Bryant decided; if people suspected the cold truth, they would give up right now.

Andreas Renalda's assistant was encased in a black wool dress and black stockings, and looked more like a theatrical performer than anyone he had met at the Palace. He was shown into a plush cream-shaded office overlooking a block of Edwardian apartments. It must seem odd, he thought, that pyjama-clad couples could find themselves separated from company executives by ten yards and two panes of glass.

'Peculiar, is it not?' came a strongly accented voice behind him. 'On my first day I arrived early and walked to the window to find a startled woman with no clothes on just a few feet away. Such a thing would never happen in my country. People have more respect for themselves.'

Bryant turned to face a stocky man in his mid-thirties with shoulder-length black hair and fierce dark eyes. As he set a lurching pace across the room, the detective realized that the man facing him was wearing steel calipers on both legs.

'I am Andreas Renalda.' The tycoon held out his hand. 'You must be Mr Bryant. Please take a seat. You will forgive me if I stand.'

Bryant tried to explain his look of surprise. 'I'm sorry to see you've been injured.'

'No, I was born this way. My legs are useless, but my brain is in perfect working order. So, you were expecting someone in good health and I was expecting someone older. Well, nothing lives up to expectations.'

'I assure you I meant no offence.'

'Of course you did not, and none has been taken.' Renalda waved aside the apology. 'I am at a loss to understand how I can help you, though.'

'I just wanted to learn a little about you,' said Bryant, shrugging with what he hoped was a look of healthy curiosity.

'There is nothing here to interest a policeman. The company belonged to my father, and he left a long shadow.' He gave a crooked smile, wagging his finger at Bryant. 'I have seen you before.'

'Oh? Where?'

'At the theatre. I am often there, watching the rehearsals.'

'Nobody told me.'

'That is because no one else knows. I do not want them to feel they should be on their best behaviour just because the man to whom they all owe their jobs is in the building.'

'Are you financing the entire production?' asked Bryant.

'One hundred per cent,' Renalda answered, leaning against the rear wall of the office in a position he presumably found comfortable. 'You have a particular question in mind?'

'What can you tell me about the Club of Rome?'

Renalda's smile cooled a little. 'Ah, that. Rather an embarrassment to us all. The Three Hundred.' He made a little gesture with his hand, as if to say, you understand. 'My father was not the most tolerant of men. For a while he kept an office in Berlin, and he created the name while it was there. We closed that branch in nineteen thirty-six. The company's history is rarely recounted with any accuracy.'

'Well, I'm a pretty attentive listener,' lied Bryant.

'We are Greeks, Mr Bryant. To be a success in Greece, you are connected with the sea. My father, Sirius, made his money in shipping. He understood the sea, and trusted no one but his immediate family. He had a son whom he considered worthless, and then his beloved wife gave birth to me. From the day I was born, I was chosen to run the business. Sirius was half blinded in the Boer War, but his handicap only made him fight harder. When he saw my withered legs, he took it as a sign that I would grow up to be a fighter too.

He believed in the strength of those who were damaged, saw it as a test of man's nature. My father was very superstitious. Sirius never understood women, but he valued his wife enough to take her advice. I remember a conversation he once had with William Randolph Hearst. "Grant the women some of your power," Hearst said, "they will always surprise you." He did not say whether he regarded it as a good thing.'

'And your mother took over the running of the company when your father died?'

'She held the reins of power in his lifetime, and maintained them until I was strong enough to make decisions.' Renalda winced, shifting his balance from one steel scaffold to the other. The device that granted him mobility was also the source of great pain.

'Why did he not consider your older brother worthy of taking control?'

'Perhaps he saw too much of his younger self in him.'

'But after your father died, your mother presumably could have shared his empire with her other son?'

'I really do not see that this can have relevance to your problems, Mr Bryant.'

'They're your problems, too. Two people died in your theatre this week. I'm sure you appreciate that where the loss of human life is concerned, we have to expand our investigations into areas we would not normally enter.'

'Indeed. And on a personal level, I must insist that you include me in your list of suspects. After all, I was in the building when Mr Senechal was killed.'

'You weren't on my list.' Bryant hated being caught out. 'Nobody told me you were there.'

'I have my own key to the royal entrance. It's more private. If I attempt the stairs with these things,' he banged the side of his leg, 'I clank like a steam train. People can always hear me coming.'

Bryant picked up his hat and rose to leave. 'You realize I'll have to ask you to close down the theatre if anything else happens.'

'You must understand the scale of our undertaking, Mr Bryant. This is not some little play that can weather bad reviews and closure after a week. Global capital is invested in this production. *Orpheus* has been designed to run for years around the world, changing the financial stakes for future productions everywhere. It is a golden goose that will lay eggs for years, in spite of your archaic censorship laws. Shutting down the production is not an action I would be well disposed towards.'

'Perhaps not, but if I thought it would protect lives, I'd order it.'

'I think you will find yourself with an interesting battle on your hands.' Renalda displayed an alarming array of teeth. 'The days of the British owning everything on their terms is coming to an end. Future fortunes will be made with the involvement of international cartels such as ours.'

'I understand very little about the workings of the business world,' Bryant admitted, remembering his father in Petticoat Lane. 'What do you intend to do about Charles Senechal? You've lost a first-class baritone.'

'I am sorry for his family, but there are plenty of other good voices. I understand you wish to place an order restricting access to the theatre's backstage areas.'

'That's correct. From now on nobody comes in or leaves without signing with my men. You'll appreciate that we need to know who is in the building at any time.'

'We have many people who need to hold meetings with Helena Parole and the production staff.' Renalda swung out his left leg and moved forward, standing free in the middle of the floor. The callipers gave his body a fragile sense of stability.

'Then they'll have to sign in with the front-of-house manager or be arrested.' Bryant stuck his hat on his head and tipped it back at a rakish angle. 'I've taken up too much of your time already.'

'If there is anything more that I can tell you, perhaps you will let me know?' Renalda's courteous smile closed over his teeth.

Bryant turned at the door and looked back across the room. This was Renalda's inner sanctum. Bare walls, glass coffee table, mahogany desk, cream blinds. No photographs, no plaques, no papers. Not a scrap of personality showed. There was damage in the family's history, enough to make a man hide his feelings. 'I'll make sure you're kept in the picture once our information has been verified.' He paused, thinking. 'Are you close to your mother, Mr Renalda?'

'My mother is dead, but yes, we were very close.'

'And I suppose your relationship with your brother—'

Renalda cut him off. 'I see no reason to provide you with further personal details unless you intend to charge me with an offence.'

'I'm sorry, I was thinking aloud, it's a bad habit.' He smiled, brushing his fringe back from his high forehead. 'I'll see myself out.'

'Mr Bryant.' Andreas Renalda swivelled to face him. 'I would prefer it if you would obtain all the information you need about my company directly from me in the future. It will save you telegraphing Zurich.'

Renalda was still smiling when he made the offer, but as he left the building Bryant couldn't help feeling that it had been a threat.

32

INFERNAL MORTALITY

For the next five decades, the two detectives made it their habit to walk along the south bank of the Thames around sunset, from the Houses of Parliament to Blackfriars, and if the weather was especially fine, all the way to Tower Bridge. After this the river grew too wide to cross as it made its way to the sea.

They argued about criminal psychology, endlessly revising their conclusions, but sometimes, when the sky was lower and the colours were drained from the Embankment buildings, they talked of women they had loved and lost, of plans made and abandoned, of outlandish ideas and unrealized dreams; often they just walked in comfortable silence, enjoying the lightness of air across the water, letting the sunlight fall on their faces.

On days like these they set each other questions about the city that, for all its faults—and there were an increasing number—they still liked best. Their second visit to the river took place on Thursday, 14 November 1940, and it was John May who came up with the first question, setting a course for years to come.

'Look at that.' May pointed to the damaged dome of St Paul's, fires smouldering behind it like the distant horizon of a forest. 'Still standing.'

'Only just,' said Bryant sadly. 'Most of the bookshops in Paternoster Row have been burned out. I spent many happy hours browsing there as a child.'

'I bet you don't know where you can see a second St Paul's Cathedral, a replica in miniature.'

'I do, as a matter of fact,' replied Bryant, who had dandified himself today with a silver-topped umbrella, a gift from his landlady. 'There's a big architectural model made of wood in St Paul's crypt.'

'I was thinking of another one,' said May with a grin. 'We've walked past it. Give up?'

'You've got me there, old bean.'

'It's held in the arms of one of the bronze female statues on Vauxhall Bridge.'

'Well, I never knew that.'

'I'll point it out to you next time.'

Bryant paused and looked out over the water, pretending to watch a boat, but May knew he had stopped to catch his breath. He had first noticed the problem when they had climbed the stairs together at the theatre. His partner had been panting with exertion by the time they reached the landing, and had made an effort to hide the fact. He charged about in a mad rush, refusing to give in to his heart.

'Two flamboyant deaths, the first without an audience, the second on stage before several people. Murders are prefaced by violence, John. They don't just come out of the blue. It makes no sense.'

'Does it have to make sense?' asked May kindly. 'Take Miss Capistrania. Whoever killed her must have wanted to humiliate her, carting off the feet like that. With Senechal, perhaps the killer just saw his chance and seized it.'

'Without a motive we have nothing. There can be no witness appeals, no knocking on doors, no one to pull in for questioning apart from the theatre staff and cast. The interviews I've dumped in Biddle's lap so far are among the most unedifying I've ever heard. We have a murderer acting in freefall, panicking, not caring who he strikes. I hate not finding a pattern.'

'There is a bit of one, though,' said May.

'Well, I'm damned if I can spot it.'

'Have you not noticed? He has only attacked during air raids. There was one around the time of Capistrania's death, another just before the globe fell, and another last night, when Miss Trammel frightened him away. Crowhurst took a look around on the roof

this morning while you were in Victoria, and found absolutely
nothing. Perhaps he can get into the theatre only during blackouts,
or when everyone is off the street. Judging from Betty's description,
people would certainly notice him if he was walking about in broad
daylight.'

'You've a point there,' agreed Bryant. 'Was it windy late last
night?'

'I can't remember. I can easily check. Why?'

'Just an idea I had about our ghost who walks through walls.
Let's find some shelter, I don't like the look of those clouds.'

The rain funnelled into iron gutters and rattled through drain-
pipes. The sky had a bare, washed-out look, as though the darkened world beneath it had been finally forsaken. The café that stood
beneath the brick railway arches of Waterloo Bridge looked closed
until they saw that the lights had been turned low.

'When I was a child I used to believe that bad people always
acted for a reason. Now I'm starting to think criminal behaviour
is inexplicable,' said Bryant, disconsolately stirring his tea. 'There
have always been individuals who are prone to murder. They're
methodical, but not logical. Look at Crippen, Wainwright, Seddon,
Jack the Ripper—they weren't driven by quantifiable needs but by
aberrant impulses. And now the world has become an irrational
place. That's why the Sherlock Holmes method of detection no
longer works; logic is fading. The value system we were raised by in
the thirties has little relevance. Beneath this stoic attitude of "business as usual" there is madness in the very air.'

'I don't know how you can think that.' May wiped a patch of
window clear with his sleeve and watched the sheets of obscuring
rain slide across the road like Japanese paper screens. 'Throughout history, human nature remains unchanged. The world's oldest
questions are still being asked. Medea, Oedipus, we're not adding
anything that the Greeks didn't already know. If you believe our
knowledge has no relevance, why have you become a detective?'

'I thought I could be useful, so long as I could prove it to
Davenport and the Home Office.' Bryant carefully set aside his teaspoon. 'You clearly have other interests apart from your work. I'm
not sure I have anything else. I think about what's going on all
about me until my brain feels as though it might rip itself apart.'

'Then you should find something else to concentrate on. If you imagine that without your job you have no purpose, you must find one.'

Bryant appeared not to have heard him. He absently tore at a Bath bun. 'Have you ever been to the Lower Marsh market in the middle of a workday morning? It's filled with old people. Half of them can barely walk, and so many are alone. It's like an English seaside town in winter. Everyone looks so cold and frail, as if death is already touching them. I wonder how they can be bothered to go on amid such devastation. It's a kind of courage, and I'm not sure I'd have it if I was in their shoes. When the war ends they'll have lost our generation again.'

'Oh, this is sheer morbidity. Don't spend all your time in the unit. Have you considered the option of regular sexual intercourse? I can't recommend it highly enough.'

'I'm no longer mentally equipped for spousal duties. My interests are too arcane. The Met boys all talk behind my back, you know. They think I'm obnoxious. They're waiting for our funding to be pulled away. They'll all have a good laugh then. I don't make friends.'

'Rubbish, Arthur. DS Forthright told me that you've made tons of friends, it's just that, well, you've befriended the kind of people nobody else talks to. Or even goes near.' He had heard about Bryant consulting the Deptford medium Edna Wagstaff and her flat full of stuffed tabby cats. 'In fact, from the sound of it you've made friends with people many others would cross the road to avoid.'

'You'll be able to adapt with the times, John. I'm already going in the opposite direction. At the age of seven I was reading Plato and Aristotle. By the time I was fifteen I had finished *A la recherche du temps perdu* in French. Academic enlightenment is a curse. It's certainly held me back with the fair sex. Forthright is the only woman I feel truly comfortable around these days, and that's because I tend to think of her as a man.'

'Maybe you should try a good nerve tonic.' May looked down at the brown Formica tabletop, resting his broad hands on the cool surface.

'I've tried them all. The unit is being given the difficult tasks to keep it out of the way. It's easier to separate out the problem cases than to explain to the Home Secretary why they aren't being investigated. We're a government expediency.'

'You think investigating murder is a waste of time?' asked May. 'Why, we could have great successes ahead if we learn to apply your ideas. All those listings in your contact files for spiritualists, clairvoyants, covens, cultists. Could they really be of use?'

'As much use as anyone so rational that they can eventually become a judge and sentence an innocent man to death. If we're going to run the unit together, you'll have to agree at least partially with my methods, otherwise you'll never sanction their use.'

'I already trust your instincts, Arthur, even if I don't understand you.'

'I don't believe in the innate goodness of people any more, John, if I ever did to begin with. Are you a Christian?'

'I was raised as one. I'm not sure what to believe now. I know you've got a theory about the theatre. Why don't you tell me?'

Bryant looked as if he was about to, then changed his mind. 'It's hard to explain. I think we're being presented with a challenge. I keep coming back to the Greek gods, the capricious ways they exacted revenge on mortals. We've been chosen to make certain that something happens, but I'm not sure what. There's a Greek god on the roof of the Palace, did you notice? Right at the pinnacle, a fragile-looking thing, still in one piece despite the bombing. I wonder they don't remove it. I can't place who it is, but there's something very odd about it. I believe somebody's playing a cruel game.'

'To what end?'

'I'm not yet sure. To spark an investigation into the workings of Three Hundred International, or to decimate the theatre company. Or perhaps the killer simply can't help himself. What is it that guides his murderous impulses? How can we know?'

'There are plenty of practical steps we can take,' offered May. 'Start by tightening security, putting men in the building round the clock. We need to be firmer with Stan Lowe, the stage door chap. Will he take notice of us, do you think?'

'He should do. They all should. I mean, we have government authorization, and you're over six foot.' Bryant bucked up. 'I suppose I'd better talk to Davenport about bringing in officers from another division. When I joined the unit I was promised a staff of twenty. We're down to half a dozen, and two of those are constables.'

'Let's finish the interviews so that Biddle can see if there's anything anomalous in their stories. Runcorn and Finch can liaise with Lambeth and pull in results from the rest of the forensic samples. We have to locate every entry point in the building to prove that nobody entered the theatre immediately before Senechal's death.'

Bryant dug a florin out of his coat pocket and placed it on the table. He admired the way in which May came up with plans, making everything sound ordered and rational.

'So, what did you make of the managing director of the Three Hundred?' asked May once they were outside.

'I found him rather intimidating.' Bryant unfurled his umbrella and raised it. 'I wouldn't like to be his enemy. But he does have a certain menacing charm.'

'What do you mean?'

'I don't know. There's something odd about him. I'd like to dig up some more on his background. Of course it'll be hopeless trying to get information out of Greece, but an old chum of my uncle's spent a couple of years in Athens as a correspondent for *The Times*. I'll give him a call. Are you around for a drink tonight?'

May looked at his watch. 'I'm sorry, Arthur, I can't tonight. I'm seeing Betty again. She was a bit shaken up, and doesn't want to spend another evening in the theatre.'

'Oh, right.' He sniffed and looked out at the water as they recrossed the bridge. 'Well, I should go back to the Palace, give Lowe a talking-to.'

'You don't have to,' said May, feeling guilty. 'Look here, you're welcome to join us tonight.'

'No, it's fine. I have my notes to catch up on, anyway.'

May watched as Bryant turned away and walked back along the Embankment, ducking beneath his umbrella as he skirted the stippled puddles. He would always see him like this, walking ahead, walking alone.

33

AS BAD AS EACH OTHER

Always ahead, always alone, thought May. If only I'd been friendlier from the outset...

He returned his attention to the retired pathologist.

'I haven't finished yet. I'm eighty-four,' continued Oswald Finch. 'I'm slowing down. When you get to be this old, it seems like everyone else is on Rollerblades.'

'I appreciate that, Oswald,' May insisted, 'but you must have removed most of the intact material by now.'

'Oh, we've removed it from the building, all right. Not that it's my job, you understand. I'm just here because, well, I have an interest in finding out what happened.' He pushed open the door of the evidence room. 'Nobody's had a chance to go through it all.' In front of Longbright and May were around thirty large clear plastic bags filled with chunks of charred wood, blackened files, sticks of furniture, bricks, pieces of broken glass and twisted metal.

'This is all that's left of the unit?'

'Pretty much so.' Finch lowered himself into a chair and grimaced. 'Stinks, doesn't it? Wouldn't be surprised if there were still bits of Bryant in there.'

May ignored his remark. The pair of them had never really got on. Even so, he was surprised and rather touched to find Finch in the building. 'Did you find any of our office equipment in one piece?'

'Not actually in one piece, but there are surviving chunks that were shielded by closed doors. Raymond Land thinks the explosion was caused by old hand-grenades, you know. Something about cordite striation patterns.'

'Surely grenades couldn't have done so much damage?'

'Well, they weren't all the same size, some were more powerful than others. The Mills grenade was really a small-barrelled missile containing up to three ounces of amatol. Modern blast sites smell different because they use more sophisticated chemical compounds. This was pure stuff. We found powder burns on the walls. The remains of your photocopier should be over there somewhere.' Finch pointed into a corner, and May and Longbright clambered across the bags in that direction.

'He was always playing tricks on me, you know,' called Finch as they went through the bags. 'Gluing my furniture to the ceiling, putting fleas in my briefcase, weeing into my rain gauges, getting my keys recut so that they only fitted the ladies' loo, replacing the fish in my tank with piranhas. Remember the tropical plant that made us all sick? A tarantula fell out of it and bit my wife. He had a very strange sense of humour. I suppose I'll miss him.'

'Over here.' May unzipped the top of a sack and peered in. 'This looks like it.'

'Let me give you a hand.' Longbright was as strong as her mother had been. Together they lifted out the buckled grey panels of the photocopier and set them on the floor. The quarter-inch plate-glass square was cracked, but had not shattered. Unfortunately, the plastic lid had melted tightly over the top of it, like Cheddar on a piece of toast.

'Give me your penknife.' May took the Swiss blade from Longbright and inserted it into a corner of the lid.

'You're tampering with evidence,' complained Finch, turning his chair round. 'I'm not a part of this, I'm not looking.' He couldn't stop himself from glancing over his shoulder. 'Aaah, you're not even wearing plastics, you're as bad as Bryant.'

May sawed the blade through the melted cover and gingerly pulled it away from the glass sheet. There beneath the cover was a single scorched sheet of paper. With the tips of his fingers he lifted it away from the glass.

'Looks like we've got it,' he told Longbright, grinning.

'You're not taking evidence away, it's illegal,' cried Finch. 'Sixty years I've had to put up with this kind of behaviour. Why me?'

'Oh, stop moaning, Oswald, you can just pretend you never saw us,' said Longbright.

'You're on the CCTV, I'm not going to lie for you and risk my job.'

'You're eighty-four, this is no time to worry about being passed over for promotion.' Longbright rose and carried the sheet to a bench by one of the side sinks. 'This is odd,' she said, after examining the scorched page for a minute. 'It's got Arthur's notes scribbled in the margins, but it's not a list at all.'

'What is it?' asked May.

'I think it's an architectural plan,' she said finally. 'Look at the stamp on the bottom. "Palace Theatre Revised Edition September nineteen..." Can't read the rest of the date.'

'He must have taken it from the archive room when he went back to the Palace. Then what did he do with the list of patients from the Wetherby clinic?'

'Maybe it was of no use, and he threw it away. He told you he'd been to the theatre, so he was either looking for this, or stumbled across it while he was researching his memoirs.'

'But what is it?'

'Dunno,' Longbright admitted. 'Oswald, is there a lightbox anywhere?'

They laid the scorched sheet on a fluorescent panel and May studied it. 'Looks like a layout of two long corridors, bisecting at one end. These shadings ... the wall cross-sections look completely circular. What's he written down the side?'

'Looks like a circumference measurement. You wouldn't normally build a corridor with round walls, would you?'

'I wonder if it could be part of a theatrical set design. It would help to have a complete date. The Palace might keep records of the struck sets.'

'We could check it against them,' said Longbright. 'That's what Bryant would have done.'

'We don't know what he was looking for. Anyway, I have a better idea.' May dug out his mobile. 'Arthur had an architect friend called Beaufort. I think we should get an expert opinion.'

'Wait a minute, you're not leaving here with evidence,' warned Finch, barring the door.

'Don't be daft, Oswald. No one will know unless you tell them.' May moved him gently aside.

'What you're doing is illegal,' Finch called as they left with the evidence. 'You're both as bad as him, you realize that, don't you?'

34

JUNO'S SON

It was still raining hard in Charing Cross Road. The deluge vibrated across the roof of the auditorium. Somewhere, water was dripping onto metal, like the beat of a drum. It was impossible to keep the weather out of a theatre as old as the Palace. There wasn't a Victorian building in London that didn't have a damp patch somewhere, and the cracks caused by the continuous bombing made it worse.

Stan Lowe and PC Crowhurst sat inside the Greek Street stage door, at the rear of the theatre, watching the rain fall. Spatters of water leaked over a handwritten sign that Bryant had made Lowe place on the wall. It read: 'NO VISITORS AFTER HALF-HOUR CALL OR DURING SHOW. DO NOT LEAVE THIS DOOR OPEN FOR ANYONE YOU DO NOT RECOGNIZE.'

For the first few weeks of the Blitz Stan Lowe had allowed the well-protected stage door area to be used as a first-aid post, but now he had been forced to add chains and a padlock. Most of the cast, orchestra and backstage crew had been signed in for the technical run-through. Crowhurst had taken names and addresses from everyone. He had heard the same piece of music, something Jack referred to as the 'Sleeping Chorus', echo through the backstage areas over a dozen times now, and was growing mightily sick of it.

'I suppose you know there's a ghost,' said Stan matter-of-factly, knocking out his pipe on the emulsioned brick wall at his back. 'You ain't got any tobacco to spare, have you?'

PC Crowhurst poked about in his jacket and produced a half-ounce of St Bruno Flake. 'You can have that and welcome,' he said. 'What sort of ghost? Not Dan Leno?'

'No, he haunts Drury Lane. Only time Leno's ever appeared here is in a newsreel.' He pushed a wad of tobacco into his pipe and returned the packet with a nod. 'This is some old Shakespearean actor. You know them bleeding great china dogs on the stair landing? They was his. This old cove was playing Polonius, and he gets to the arras scene, only the Dane's sword is missing its button, see, and when 'Amlet runs him through, he really runs him through, only nobody realizes because he's behind the bleeding curtain, isn't he, so they play out the rest of the scene, and it's only when he's supposed to get off the stage that they notices. Well, a'course by that time it's too late to do anything for the poor old bugger, so every time there's a new play coming on, he turns up as Polonius in a bloodstained doublet and hose, wandering about backstage putting the willies up the carpenters.'

PC Crowhurst looked sceptical. 'Miss Trammel says he looked deformed, like he'd done something terrible to his face,' he pointed out. 'She said it was like a mask of tragedy, you know, like a Greek mask. She was in a right state this morning.'

'His face was contorted 'cos he'd been run through with a bleedin' epinard,' said Lowe sagely. 'Actresses suffer with their nerves. That's why so many of 'em take to the drink.' He flicked out a match and drew hard on the pipe. 'Anyway, he was a bleedin' awful Polonius. I could shit a better lecture to Laertes than that.'

Onstage it was the beginning of act two, and the gods slumbered on Mount Olympus. Venus, Mars, Cupid and the chorus went through their paces, but there was no Jupiter. Geoffrey Whittaker, the stage manager, was on the company office telephone trying to organize transport to collect their new head of Olympus, who was stuck on the wrong side of a bombed railway line in East London.

Helena was tired and irritable. She wanted a break and needed a whisky, but Harry and Elspeth were tailing her around the building to make sure that she didn't find a way of breaking her contract.

The technical run-through was necessary at this point because an unusual amount of scenery had to be flown through the tableaux, and Mouse, Stan Lowe's boy, had been appointed to transcribe the complex stage manoeuvres in a movement programme as they progressed.

It didn't help that the performers were having to work around a central hole in the production. Few of the cast had known Charles Senechal very well, but his absence was acutely felt. The understudy baritone had been approved and cast at the same time as Senechal's appointment, but he didn't have the diction quality Helena required for the recitative passages, so she was anxious to give him extra coaching. Senechal's wife and child were holed up in a quiet Holland Park hotel, and had been visited by Andreas Renalda, who had dispensed with pleasantries and instructed the distraught woman not to talk to journalists. Luckily for him she spoke little English, and her interpreter was employed by the company.

With the arrival of the auditor, the company secretary and the treasurer's wife, Stan Lowe gave up trying to keep the area restricted. Happily, Helena remained professional. She'd coped with ranting producers, cheating financiers and lying managers, compared to which the gripes of cast members who found their dressing rooms too far away or their fellow performers impossible to deal with were frankly small potatoes. But, God, she wanted a drink.

Rachel Saperstein was just starting to cope with the idea of her son's success. She was proud of him, even though the Saperstein family name was apparently not good enough for Miles any more. She had been up to the apartment the company had rented for him, and had found the meat-safe in his scullery completely empty except for a bottle of vodka, which would only ruin his stomach in later life. Now she was seated at the front of the upper circle, watching him perform on the London stage, and her heart swelled with pride as he sang each note.

In the balcony of the theatre, above her, a young man named Zachary Darvell fidgeted in his seat and refined the tip of his hand-rolled cigarette with finger and thumb. 'Of course I'm proud of her,' he whispered across the seats. 'I couldn't do what she does, night after night. Trouble is, she doesn't think I can do anything.'

'So where's your father?' asked his best friend, Larry.

'He buggered off ages ago. He was selling defence bonds until the war started, and now he's a black marketeer. She rehearses all the time, so they were never together. I saw more of the baby-sitter than either of my parents.'

'Lucky boy.'

'Yes, it was pretty damned good.' He held sharp smoke in his lungs, then exhaled. 'Have the rest of this, I know you're down to your last Woodie. Try not to cough, I don't want her looking up and seeing me.'

'What do you care?' asked Larry, accepting the cigarette.

'If she sees me up here she'll throw a tantrum. Especially if she finds me with you.' Zachary was supposed to be in medical college, but he and Larry had cut classes, not that there were many to cut at the moment. Every student with the ability to hold a scalpel had been seconded to the local hospital unit, where their tasks largely consisted of helping to clean up bodies. Sometimes identifying marks had been so neatly blown off that the only way to tell if the victims were male or female was to check for a sciatic notch. Everyone smoked because it was the only way to get rid of the smell of dead bodies. Today the students had decided to hang out in the West End, cooling their heels on counter stools in a few bars, looking out of the windows, watching stockingless girls in tight business skirts dart through the rain.

Larry had asked where Zachary's mother worked, and Zachary had suggested going to see her. He wanted to show Larry how he could breeze into a major theatre and be recognized. The pair had gone up to the balcony, standing at the rear, so close to the top of the building that you could hear the rain. Now they were sitting in its front row, smoking and watching. Below them, Barbara Darvell, soprano, wife of Jupiter, waited for her cue as a pair of stagehands struggled hopelessly with a prop cloud.

'Must be peculiar, always being in buildings with no windows,' said Larry, drawing on the last inch of the cigarette. 'No night or day. You can't even hear the traffic outside. At least there's more room than in the shelters. I don't know how people can be bothered to go down there. All those mewling infants. You've just as much of a chance staying under your stairs.'

'My mother used to say that fire engines were the curse of the performer,' said Zachary. 'Now she's had to add dogfights, bombs and sirens to her list of interruptions. She goes all over the world, but I don't think she sees much outside because she's either rehearsing or performing.'

'Strange job.' Larry checked his watch. 'Let's go.'

'You haven't heard her sing yet.'

'I know what opera singers sound like, it's unbelievably horrible, no offence to your dear mama. Come on.'

'I just want to stay until she does her piece.' Zachary didn't want to make a grand thing out of it, and tried to sound offhand. 'I'll catch you up. Go over to the Spice and order me a gin and French. I'll meet you in the saloon bar.' He watched in annoyance as Larry threaded his way along the steep row to the exit. Back onstage, Juno rose to join in at the end of Mercury's song, but the sight of her was obscured by a gauze-covered purple cloud.

Zachary pushed the seat back up and stood in the shadowed aisle at the front of the balcony. He wanted her to know he was there, but the idea embarrassed him. His mother preferred the company of her own friends, theatricals who talked endlessly about themselves to the exclusion of everyone else, behaving as if nobody else was worth a damn. He would come home to their overheated house in Chiswick and find the place filled with thespians slugging her whisky and getting excited about Euripides. Surely it was meant to be the other way round, with her accusing his friends of being layabouts? In a few months' time he would be able to get to the front, then perhaps she would take notice of him.

Below, Juno was singing about making room for Mercury, a bouncy song but not exactly Henry Hall, and if Zachary leaned forward he could see his mother rolling her eyes at the rest of the cast and overacting wildly, except that it was an operetta so nobody seemed to mind.

Miles Stone's mother thought the woman was overacting too. Why didn't the director do something about it? It wasn't fair that she couldn't sit in the stalls. She had been told not to, because onlookers in the sightlines put the actors off. Juno was still shrieking away and waving her arms about like a demented windmill. Rachel felt like going down to the stage and giving her a slap. She was putting her son off his stride, anyone could see that. Rachel squinted back into the seats behind her, to see if anyone else had noticed, and her eye caught a glint of sharp light from the balcony above her head.

Zachary heard a sound behind him, a seat creaking, and turned as the occupant rose. At first he thought Larry had returned. Then he saw the hulking, twisted figure. The poor chap was deformed, and was trying to speak. His face was like something from an amusement-park mirror, a badly made-up villain from a melodrama. A terrible face, like one of the demons from the production below, hideously brought to life. Big hands, young hands.

'What's the matter? How can I—'

Zachary was going to ask him who he was. He wasn't afraid, until he saw the slim shine of the cut-throat razor as it folded open. Then he jumped back. He raised his hands in protest when the blade flew past. For a moment nothing happened. Then the skin of his palms split like opening eyes. By now the razor was returning at a higher level, passing his left cheek, the bridge of his nose, slicing flesh and muscle and bone, stinging across his throat, cutting deeper at his thyroid cartilage. Other red mouths were opening all over his face and neck. He could not see. A thick caul of blood dropped over his eyes, obscuring his vision. The hand darted forward again, and Zachary felt a far more terrible pain at his throat. A three-pronged fork had been pushed into his windpipe, sealing it. He stumbled forward but was pushed back, over the step, and over the low wall of the balcony.

Miles Stone had half expected Rachel to turn up at the theatre, but he hadn't counted on seeing her seated at the front of the upper circle watching his every move. It was enough to put him off his stride. They were halfway through the technical and Juno was upstaging him all over the place, and there was nothing he could do but ignore her and go on with his lines. Eve was watching from the wings. She knew that his mother was coming to town, although she had no idea that he had slept with Becky as recently as his Carnegie gala night in New York three weeks ago. It made sense for Miles to keep his mother and his new girlfriend apart—they would either be instant enemies or, worse still, form an alliance against him.

Stone could see his mother fidgeting in her seat. It didn't help that she was wearing a preposterous hat. He tried to ignore her and carry on with his recitative, but from the corner of his eye he saw her twist round and look up. She didn't appear to be watching the stage at all. Was it a criticism of his performance? He glanced back at Juno and realized that she had followed his glance to the upper circle. As he waited for the technicians to clip the cloud scrim back on its rollers, he looked over at his mother once more. She was still turned away from the stage. He was so intent on watching her that he missed his cue.

'Miles, when you're absolutely ready,' called Helena. 'I appreciate it's been a long day but I hate to keep everyone waiting longer than necessary.'

'Of course, sorry.' They had cut Eurydice's scene with Jupiter at the end of the third tableau and had skipped to the flight from Hell, but Public Opinion's rowing boat was now stuck in the flies, and the orchestra seemed confused about their entry point.

Between the late arrival of two woodwinds and the total disappearance of Jupiter, who had been replaced in the run-through with a hobby horse tipped on its end, Anton Varisich was close to walking out. The sudden noise in the balcony made the conductor cut his orchestra off in mid-note, although someone had trouble stopping, because there was a piercing howl from one of the instruments. For a moment he thought that somebody had thoughtlessly banged the seats up again, and in an afternoon of stops and starts, Varisich's legendary temper was about to make itself felt.

'*Miss* Parole,' he called to Helena, referring to her so formally that it showed disrespect, 'would you be so good as to join me at the podium for a moment?'

Helena Parole allowed a beat of defiance to pass before complying with the conductor's request, then made her way to the side of the stage. She had worked with Varisich before and had survived his angry outbursts often enough to know that he was relatively easy to mollify. It was a matter of letting him see that she appreciated the subordination of the stage performance to the music. Text was updated and retranslated at regular intervals, but the music remained sacrosanct. So long as she respected this rule, they would work well together. She tried to imagine a tall glass filled with Glenfiddich, and donned her most quenching smile. Varisich was going to complain about the presence of outsiders at the run-through, and about the levels of noise they were creating, but now somebody was yelling. On stage, several members of the chorus were pointing into the centre of the building.

It wasn't until they ran towards the screaming woman in Row A of the upper circle that they looked up and saw the man, now a twisting, bloody blur, flail and fall from the edge of the balcony.

35

MANIFESTATION OF GUILT

Zachary Darvell's nose had been pushed into his skull by the fall. His face was a crimson mask. The segmented flesh was efflorescing with bulbous bruises, pink jelly the colour of an infected gum protruding through slashed skin. His jawbone was exposed in a shockingly severe white line. The iron fork was sticking out of his gullet. He looked like a prop demon removed from the set after a particularly arduous run. His left arm hung at an unnatural angle to his body. There was a member of the St John's Ambulance Brigade in attendance, uselessly armed with a tin box full of crêpe bandages, calamine lotion and smelling salts. Barbara Darvell had rushed up from the stage and was cradling her son's head.

'What happened?' asked Bryant, who had just entered the auditorium in time to hear Juno's son plummet noisily from the balcony.

'He's dead.' Barbara Darvell swallowed thickly. 'I looked up and saw him. He had his back to me. Someone was standing behind him. A tall man. I could see his arms moving. I couldn't make sense of it from where I was.' She pointed feebly down at the illuminated set of Hades. Droplets of blood had spattered the artificial carnation that still stuck from Zachary's jacket lapel.

'What's that?' Bryant pointed to the fork handle protruding from Darvell's throat.

'Aristaeus' fork. It went missing from the prop box.'

'I've just been up in the balcony. It's deserted.' Geoffrey Whittaker dropped to his knees and tried to catch his breath. 'Let's get everyone back to their dressing rooms for a few minutes,' he suggested. 'There was no one else up there, no one at all.'

'How do you know?' yelled Barbara Darvell. 'How could you look everywhere? We can't see in this damned gloom!'

'I was in the stairwell and ran in,' Geoffrey explained.

'I certainly didn't see you,' said Harry.

The assistant's remark took Whittaker by surprise. 'What are you saying?'

'Just that I know who was in the stairwell and you weren't there.'

Whittaker was angered by the idea of having to defend himself. 'If you must know, I'd gone upstairs to get something from my office, and stood at the back of the balcony for a moment. Mr Darvell was sitting in the front row by himself. I left the auditorium and was coming back down the central staircase when I heard a shout and a crash from the floor below. Then I ran down to him. He only just missed landing on that lady over there.' He pointed at Miles Stone's shocked mother.

'He landed a seat away,' gasped Rachel. 'I nearly died.'

'Then the person who pushed Mr Darvell must have passed you on the staircase,' Harry insisted.

'No one passed me.'

'I don't see how you could have missed him, Geoffrey.'

'My son is dead, could you show some restraint?' cried Barbara Darvell.

'Perhaps we should leave the matter until the police have finished searching the building,' Harry suggested.

'You can manage here, can't you?' Bryant strode along the row of seats and raced down the stairs to the stage door. There he found Lowe and Crowhurst looking puzzled.

'Has anyone left in the last few minutes?' he asked, trying to get his breath back.

'No, sir. Only the gentleman Mrs Darvell's son came in with. What's going on?'

'There's been another one,' Bryant explained. 'You'll let me know if anyone tries to leave?'

'Of course, sir, I—hang on, that's the royal entrance.' Beyond them came the muffled slam of a door.

Bryant stuck his head out into the street and saw a broad figure in a shiny black raincoat divorce himself from the shadow of the royal entrance. He turned and saw John May walking from the other direction, towards the stage door.

'John!' he shouted. 'That's our man! Stop him!'

The dark figure started and broke into a run, instantly followed by May. Night had fallen and the blackout was once more in full force. Shaftesbury Avenue, blurred and smeary with rain, was almost deserted as they turned into it.

I've got him, thought May, watching the figure ahead as it hit a thicket of parked motorcycles belonging to the army despatch riders. There was something round the man's neck, a raised collar or hood that obscured his head. He looked to be around six feet tall, but in the gloomy drizzle of the early evening it was hard to make out any further detail. To May's horror, the raincoated figure vaulted the first motorbike and landed hard on the kick-start, firing up the engine. The army engineers kept their Matchless bikes in racks beside the road, ready to take them to emergencies. May grabbed the nearest machine and mounted it. He knew how to ride, but with the lights of London extinguished and the roads wet, he wasn't sure whether he would be able to give chase. The engine barked into life on first kick, and he released the handlebar valve lift as he took off, slamming into the road so closely behind his quarry that their wheels almost touched.

The motorcycle in front fishtailed sharply and skittered across the oncoming traffic in the direction of Piccadilly Circus. May felt his back wheel slip as he followed, and was able to keep the bike upright only by hammering his boot along the tarmac and forcing the machine into a vertical position. He concentrated on the black square of the numberplate in front, LR109. The figure hunched low as he throttled up, the engine's roar deepening as he passed between a pair of unlit taxis. May forged ahead too, trying to draw alongside, but the bike was pushing beyond a safe speed. They passed the side of the London Pavilion and the darkened cinema opposite, hitting the Circus traffic at such speed that buses were forced to brake and swerve. The electric advertising hoardings that had become such an area landmark were extinguished, lending the buildings a drab, derelict air. LR109 cut the wrong way round the boarded-over fountain and shot into Piccadilly with May in pursuit. A policeman, visible only by the white stripes on his cuffs, raised his hands and ran towards them, then backed off when he saw that neither bike was going to stop. The sound of his whistle was quickly lost as the pair raced on past the Royal Academy into oncoming traffic.

Bryant's going to kill me if I don't catch him, thought May as he accelerated. The young detective felt chill rain pitting his face as the wheels lost their purchase on the slippery road, found it again and pushed him on. The buildings on either side were great grey blocks, no light showing anywhere. Ahead, just beyond Green Park, a bomb had heavily cratered the middle of the road, and rubble-removal trucks indistinctly lined its edges. As they came closer, May saw that the entire causeway was cordoned off. He can't get through, he told himself, watching in disbelief as LR109 pounded up over the kerb and into the long portico under the Ritz. May felt the kerb slam his tyres as he followed, the back wheel juddering as he shot beneath the arches, his engine reverberating in the tunnel as he scattered the shrieking evening-gowned women who were exiting the hotel.

At the end of the colonnade, the bike in front swung sharply to the right off the main road and thundered into the maze of narrow streets that constituted Mayfair. May tried to close the gap between them, but was forced to slow in order to turn the heavy machine. He could hear LR109 revving and braking, but caught only glimpses of its brake light as the machine raced ahead of him. At Curzon Street the lead bike was forced to slow as pedestrians ran for safety, and May gained a few yards. As they turned into the dark chasm of Bruton Street, the detective saw the thick brown earth and bricks strewn across the road, and knew that his tyres would not cope with them. The other bike had bypassed the mess by mounting the pavement. He hit hard, the Matchless's handles jumping out of his hands as the machine jerked from his control. He knew that if it went over now it would trap his leg beneath the engine, and forced himself to roll backwards, leaving the bike seconds before it toppled and slid along the street in a shower of sparks, to vanish over the side of an unfilled pit.

Bryant ran round to the foyer and checked on the FOH box office. He doubted that May would be able to track their man for long in the blackout. Elspeth was almost asleep when he knocked on the glass, startling her so badly that she nearly fell off her stool.

'Did you see him come past here?'

'No, no one's been through.' She straightened her cardigan, embarrassed. 'I'm afraid I was having forty winks. The phones are down. Seamus told me they've found an unexploded bomb across the road and the Heavy Rescue people have severed a line getting to it.'

'Who's Seamus?'

'Our milkman. He was dropping off some rhubarb from his allotment.' She held up a paper bag full of purple stalks. 'I said it would be nice to see a banana again but there are limits to his powers.' She patted a stray lock of hair into place and smiled vaguely. By the entrance doors, a heavyset woman in a pinafore rose from her mop bucket and came over to the detective.

'Did you just wake her up? Poor lady was trying to have a rest.'

'She's been here with you?'

'All the time. You're one of them detectives, ain't you?' she asked. 'Several of the chorus girls are talking about a phantom roaming the theatre, have you heard? Apparently it's got hands like claws and eyes that glow red in the dark. And Miss Betts said it followed her up Tottenham Court Road, wearing a mask.'

'I need to use your phone,' said Bryant.

'I just told you, the lines are cut. And you don't want to listen to her silly gossip,' warned Elspeth, raising the tone of her voice by half a social caste. 'Actresses get such first-night nerves, it always shows itself in silly stories.'

'Where's the nearest call box?' asked Bryant.

'That'll be the other side of Cambridge Circus. Oh, it's quite the norm, lurid imaginations working overtime. During the rehearsals for *No, No, Nanette* one of the saxophonists dropped dead, and rumours went around that he'd been cursed by Negroes because he played late-night sessions in a jazz club and owed them some money. People get such funny ideas.'

'Yes,' agreed Bryant uncertainly, heading for the door. He nodded to the cleaner. 'If you hear any more talk about a Palace phantom, you'll let me know, won't you?'

'He'll be back,' she said cheerfully. 'Not that he worries me. I've got nothing to fear.'

'Oh? Why not?'

'He's not real,' the char explained, hitching up her bolstered bosom. 'It's just guilt. These young girls, they're a bit loose, a bit wild, living for the moment, running around with boys and getting up to God knows what in the dark. Extroverts and introverts, it's all in their collective unconscious, a manifestation of guilt, if you ask me.'

'Well, your manifestation of guilt just killed someone with a cut-throat razor,' he snapped.

Bryant had not expected an earful of Jungian theory from the charlady. He stepped carefully over the wet marble and stood on the step outside, looking up at the sky. A pall of brown smoke hung over the buildings to the east, most likely dust from building clearance. The clouds were starting to break now, giving the bombers a clear path into the city. He wondered what terrors the night would bring this time.

Poking the last of his tobacco into his pipe, Bryant headed off in the direction of the phone box, a theory shifting uneasily at the back of his brain. The globe, the compass, the flute, the wind, the mask of tragedy, the statue on the roof of the theatre, Stone's mother, the flower in Darvell's lapel, things he could not make sense of without sounding deranged.

If he was wrong, it would not just be the finish of a promising career, it would end the credibility of the unit for good.

36

THE BROADER PICTURE

'What on earth happened to you?' asked Bryant. His partner was covered in streaks of mud, his jacket torn from shoulder to waist.

'Came a bit of a cropper on an army motorbike,' May explained, examining himself. 'Our man moved like a bat out of Hell. I lost him in the back streets, didn't Biddle tell you?'

'He said you stole an army emergency vehicle and smashed it up. Don't worry, I'll square it with them later. Are you all right?'

'Took the skin off my hands, no real damage. What are you doing?'

Bryant was standing on an upended metal milk crate in the car park of Bow Street magistrates' court, preparing to throw a muslin-wrapped leg of pork onto an iron sheet that was balanced on a pile of masonry rubble. 'I'm testing out a theory,' he explained, swinging the leg and letting it go. 'Bloke fell out of the balcony. I suppose they told you. Slashed to bits with a straight razor. Not one of the cast, though.' He climbed down from the crate and bent over the joint of meat, which had landed squarely on the metal sheet. 'It's all right, condemned black-market pork, quite inedible, but it's about the same weight.'

'As what?' asked May, bemused.

'As a pair of feet, obviously.' Bryant threw him an old-fashioned look as he hoisted the leg for another swing.

May had no time for such foolishness tonight. He was starting to wonder if his partner was all there. 'Mr Davenport's waiting for us in your office,' he warned. 'At least, I assume it's him.'

'Raw-boned, red-faced man, tufts of grey hair coming out of his ears, staring eyes, lots of broken veins in his nose, reeks of chewing tobacco?'

'That's the one. I hope he doesn't see your plant.'

'What plant?' asked Bryant, his eyes widening in innocence.

'Don't pretend you don't know. That one with the serrated leaves. Chinamen dry them out and smoke them. Reefers. Used by Limehouse dope fiends.'

'Are you accusing me of being a dope fiend? Actually, it's an old herbal remedy.'

'Well, I've hidden it under your desk just in case.'

'Thanks, old man.' Bryant grinned. 'You're a sport.'

Farley Davenport stared with distaste at the mouldering Tibetan skull surrounded by African juju charms that inhabited Bryant's bookcase. 'Perhaps one of you can explain what's going on at the Palace Theatre? Someone just wrote off an army bike, another one is still missing.'

'Mr May here was in pursuit of our murderer. We're lucky he's still with us. I've asked for an apprehension on the other number plate.'

'Who was this bloke who died?'

'He shouldn't have been allowed inside the building,' Bryant explained, in that way he had of not answering the right question. 'I requested an access restriction, but the company's director overruled me.'

Davenport was finding it hard to make the detectives understand why he was so angry with them. He ran his hands through his thinning grey hair and made a frightening face. 'I asked for all visitors to be signed in and out. That should have been enough.'

'That's exactly what we did,' said Bryant, 'but somebody still got hurt. We shouldn't have been allowing any visitors in at all. There are people wandering about all over the place. It's like Hyde Park on a bank holiday in there.'

Davenport grunted with disapproval. 'I had a phone call from some mad harpy named Parole, typical bloody showbusiness type, complaining to me about areas of the theatre staying shut. She couldn't seem to tell the difference between a real-life murder and a staged drama.'

'I'm sorry, sir. I told her we needed exclusive access to certain areas for forensic examination, but she refused point blank to close off the rest of the building. Apparently it's beyond her control because there are two separate companies involved, hers and the management who own the theatre.'

'This bloody war is giving everyone an excuse to defy the law.' Davenport's nose looked redder than ever. 'I tell you, when it's over all these women will go back to being bloody housewives and we'll be able to get on with running the nation again.'

'Miss Parole answers to a board that's determined not to allow anything to hamper the production.'

'It's going to be hampered a bloody sight more when Westminster shuts it down,' snapped Davenport. 'If this had happened in peacetime the building would have been cleared without question. Good Lord, three people dead, ghostly sightings and what have you, people frightening one another with stories about phantoms that walk through walls. It's the Palace Theatre, not Borley Rectory. Do you want to tell me how it happened?'

'I'd like to, sir, but we're not sure ourselves. Mr Darvell, the boy who was attacked in the balcony, is the son of a member of the cast. He and a friend were watching the run-through. The friend left, Darvell was seen to stand up at the front and turn his back to the stage, he was cut and fell over the parapet. It's a low rail, and the floor slopes steeply. The fall broke his nose, his jaw and his collarbone, he lost too much blood and died. The person he nearly landed on, Miles Stone's mother, glimpsed his attacker from below, and what she saw matches the description of the man Miss Trammel gave last night. This is the man who got away on the stolen bike.'

'What a bloody nightmare. It wasn't Darvell's friend?'

'He was already in the pub when it happened.'

'I suppose you know that the press has got the story now.'

'We kept it back as long as we could,' said May, 'but the chestnut vendor was discovered by the *News of the World*. Luckily that particular rag only comes out once a week.'

'You really are a dunderhead, Bryant,' Davenport complained. 'Half their stringers do double duty with the *Daily Sketch*. There's bound to be something in tomorrow's paper.'

'I think you're overestimating the *Daily Sketch*'s interest in theatre,' Bryant protested. 'Coverage of *Orpheus* is too intellectual for their readership.'

'You think a murderer loose in an old music hall is too intellectual? "Hellfire Show Summons the Devil", that sort of thing, a bit too brainy for the masses? You may be academically on the button but you're not much good at understanding people, Bryant. I suggest you go down there,' he slapped his hand against the window, 'and see how the ordinary man in the street is passing his days. There's a typing pool sitting out on the corner of the Aldwych in the pouring rain, working under a makeshift shelter of corrugated iron because the roof's been blown clean off their office. You're telling me they don't want to have their minds diverted by a juicy murder?'

Chastened, Bryant fell silent. It seemed to May that their superior might have a point.

'The partially digested meat in Miss Capistrania's stomach showed positive for hemlock,' he pointed out. 'There was an empty sandwich tin in one of the wings, and hers are the only prints on it. Nobody seems to know where she got her food. Quail is not the sort of item you often find outside of Simpson's in the Strand these days. We've checked with all the butchers' shops in the area. There's a place in Brewer Street that sells quail, but they don't recall serving her, and besides, they're noted for carrying out stringent quality checks on their meat.'

'Anything new on Senechal?' asked Davenport.

'The cable ends were examined under a microscope and came back with an open verdict on them.'

'What do you mean? Either the wire was cut or it wasn't.'

'Dr Runcorn thinks there's a possibility that it sheared under its own weight. He reckons the cable had been reused so many times that it was probably full of stress fractures. But if it was cut, the person who cut it had to be standing on the gantry at the time in order to judge the moment for the globe to hit Mr Senechal.'

This news made Davenport far from happy. He liked the unit's cases to be tied up neatly so that he could present them to his superiors as solved and closed, another job well done. He wanted someone to blame. He would have put everything down to sheer bad luck if it wasn't for this latest attack. And, of course, there were the feet.

'How the hell did they get onto a chestnut stand?' he asked again. 'Come on, Arthur, you must have an idea by now.'

'I do, but you won't like it much.'

'Try me.'

'I think they were thrown into the cart from the canopy of the theatre.'

'What on earth makes you say that?'

'The evening was dry, and the vendor had griddled his fire before the air-raid siren called him away. On the morning of the discovery, PC Crowhurst noted that the coal dust on the pavement was unmarked by any footprints. Mr May and I saw it for ourselves. There are several sets of small mullioned windows above the canopy. One on the second landing has a pane missing, and another has a broken hasp. They're not big enough for a person to climb through, but you could stick an arm out of them. I think somebody dropped the feet out of the window, intending them to land on the canopy. Instead, they rolled off and fell onto the chestnut stall, which happened to be standing by the kerb below.'

'You mean the Turk just left it there and scarpered?'

'He was obeying the law, sir, getting himself to a place of shelter. Obviously, the blackout was still in effect when he returned, so it's feasible he didn't notice that anything had been disturbed.'

'Have you checked the canopy beneath the window for blood spots?'

'We didn't find anything swabbable, but it has rained since then.'

'I'd like to be able to tell Miss Capistrania's father that his daughter's death was a bizarre but unfortunate accident.'

'I don't see how you can do that.'

'In case it's escaped your attention, Mr Bryant, there are no motives. Capistrania hardly knew anyone in London. Senechal was universally admired. This last chap isn't even directly connected to the production, for God's sake.'

Davenport lowered himself into Bryant's chair and attempted to straighten his legs beneath the desk, but something was in the way. He peered under the desk. May gave his partner a grim look.

'Worse still, if Capistrania's death could have been mistaken for food poisoning, why would someone make it look like a murder by throwing away the bloody feet? And why attack a boy who's got nothing to do with the theatre? There's no sense in it, is there? I bloody give up with you lot.' He reached beneath the desk and pulled up Bryant's marijuana plant. 'What on earth's this?'

'Ah,' stalled Bryant, 'so that's where it is. Evidence. I'll bag it.'

'What evidence?' asked Davenport suspiciously.

'Ah, the Leicester Square Vampire. Dr Runcorn wanted some items removed from his house for examination.'

Davenport was thrown off guard. 'I didn't know we'd caught him,' he said.

'We haven't,' countered May as he gently drew the plant away from Davenport. 'He's a suspect. A, um, Lithuanian botanist experimenting on rare plants with, er, horticultural grafting techniques. I'll get rid of that for you.'

'You're telling me the Leicester Square Vampire is an experimenting Lithuanian botanist?' Davenport rose and walked to the door, vaguely troubled. 'Do you think I'm completely stupid? I've been fielding hourly calls from Albert Friedrich, Capistrania *père*, who, you'll be pleased to know, is staying at the Austrian ambassador's house this weekend, where he'll be receiving no less a personage than George VI himself for tea. I'm seeing the Home Secretary on Saturday morning. I want your written conclusions about this investigation presented to me no later than six o'clock tomorrow night. And give me rational solutions, none of your psychological supernatural mumbo-jumbo.' He slammed the door behind him.

Bryant stuffed the plant into the top drawer of his desk. 'I think that went quite well, don't you?'

'No, I don't, frankly. Have you come to any conclusions?'

'Well, there's a madman on the loose, obviously. Someone who hated Capistrania enough to have her mutilated, who had Charles Senechal killed in full view of his peers, who slashed a young man to death just because he was close to a member of the cast. We'll test the bike for prints when it turns up but I don't suppose we'll get anything.'

'He was wearing gloves.'

'Then there's the Greek aspect of all this. Which reminds me, we need to find out who gave Zachary Darvell the flower.'

'What flower?'

'The silk carnation. Stan Lowe says he'd never seen the boy wearing a buttonhole before. Not his usual style. Don't those gypsy women in Piccadilly press them on you as you pass? I'm sure they're not made of silk these days, though, unless someone's cutting up parachutes. And then there's the business with the flute.'

'You've completely lost me,' said May, exasperated.

'Anton Varisich halted the orchestra when the accident occurred, but his first flute released a high-pitched note of alarm. Except of course he couldn't have, because two of the woodwinds, of which the flautist was one, had failed to turn up that morning—so who played the note?'

'Arthur, I have absolutely no idea what you're talking about.'

'I'd like to tell you,' said Bryant, 'but I think I'd better make sure I'm right first. While I'm doing that, you might pause to wonder why Davenport's so anxious to keep this out of the newspapers.'

'I imagine he doesn't want the unit made to look foolish.'

'Nobody knows about the unit,' said Bryant. He raised his voice. 'Come in, Mr Biddle. Don't hover outside.'

Sidney Biddle looked defiant. 'I wasn't listening,' he said at once, thereby confirming he was. 'I was coming to see you.' He warily ventured into the cluttered sepia office.

Bryant threw his partner a questioning look. 'Oh? What's on your mind?' Biddle's tie was knotted so tightly under his collar that it appeared to be choking him.

May stretched back in his chair. 'Why don't you take a seat, Sidney?' he prompted.

The young man twisted awkwardly round to look at each of the detectives in turn. 'I want to transfer out of the unit, Mr Bryant.'

'You've only just got here. Can we ask why?'

Biddle looked uncomfortable. 'I don't believe I'm suited to this kind of operation.'

'Could you be more specific?' asked May, sensing what was coming.

'Mr May, my aim was to get inside the Home Office end of the London force, reach the important stuff, and I thought I'd hack it by working for an SIO. I knew Serious Crimes only handled murder cases. I was told how different this unit was to anything else currently available. I didn't realize working practices would be so—not how things are supposed to be.'

May peered at him in what he hoped was a manner of surprise. 'Would you care to give me an example?'

'Even the most basic procedures aren't followed. Take custody of evidence.' Biddle began to grow heated. 'I was taught to maintain continuous control over crime-scene evidence from signing and dating of possession to court introduction, keeping copious notes throughout the process. Mr Bryant walks into Dr Runcorn's lab and pokes about, and takes whatever he likes out of the property room. Half the time he doesn't even secure it as he leaves. When I remind him of protocol, he shouts at me, or he laughs.'

'So this is about Mr Bryant,' said May solemnly.

'Yes, sir. I was always warned that we would have to work reactively on suspects, eliminate or associate them according to the likelihood of their involvement in a crime. Mr Bryant doesn't do that, sir. He doesn't share information, and he starts with the unlikeliest scenario. He won't cold-type fingerprints or correlate his data with colleagues. He starts writing up reports before he even receives blood-typing results. Mr Finch should have run epithelial cell checks on the lift doors, the globe cable and the balcony seat backs by now, but Mr Bryant doesn't even seem interested. It's like he thinks he's above the law.'

'I understand your concerns. You must bear in mind that no fingerprints other than the victims' have been found at any of the three crime scenes. Still, sometimes Mr Bryant fails to respect the fact that criminology is a modern science.'

Bryant was keeping quiet. He had known this moment was coming, had seen it in the boy's disillusioned eyes.

'I'm sure Mr Bryant does not consider himself above the law,' May continued. 'His mind just takes him off the beaten track.'

'Think about why this case came to us,' suggested Bryant, relishing Biddle's discomfort. 'Does it appear to involve any of the elements present in your college case histories? Domestic violence, burglary, spousal assault, alcohol-related crime, pick-pocketing, grand larceny?'

'No, sir.'

'You see, Biddle, our cases get prioritized for the wrong reasons: they have a higher profile, meaning there's an influential relative somewhere in the background, or there's a more complex political element involved, or they're a publicity risk, or they're against the public mood. Most importantly, they're cases that can cause damage to public morale during a time of conflict. Thanks to Hitler, we are no longer living in a world that cares about the death of someone because they were loved in the past. It cares only if that death can do damage to the future. It's a grim truth, Sidney. Like Orpheus leaving Hades, we are rushing headlong into the light of a terrible new world.

'There is a way of providing accountability, though. You get a grant from the Home Office to run an autonomous unit like this, one that siphons off the publicly embarrassing cases during wartime and takes the heat, and you head it up with men whose operations run so contrary to traditional methodology that once in a while they produce the goods. That's what everyone's baying for now, the press, the state, they're only interested in culpability. Take a look at the witch-hunting that's going on out there, most of it whipped up by rumour and conjecture. We lump everyone we don't like in with the Germans, most of whom are probably as decent as you or me, and God help you if you disagree, because you'll be tarred and feathered along with them.' Bryant fumbled about in his waistcoat for some matches. 'Tell me, Sidney, are you aware of the recent troubles in Greece?'

'Greece?' Biddle looked thrown. 'No, sir.'

'Last week some British soldiers got into a fight on a border checkpoint that they had no right to be on in the first place. It ended up with a local man being tortured and killed. The man was a Greek national suspected of collaborating with the Italians. When that happened, his family was shipped off and his private property was seized. The victim was probably innocent, but he was travelling without the right papers, and had bribed our boys to let him through. The British ambassador to Greece extradited the men, and the blame for the death was placed on an extremist Turkish national group. There have been quite a few violent incidents in Greece inspired by Turkish national activity, and relations between the two countries are poor. Meanwhile, we have a British building programme going on in Istanbul. Is this starting to make sense to you?'

Biddle stared furiously at his hands. 'No, it isn't.'

'Let me spell it out. The *Orpheus* production company is owned by the son of a Greek shipping magnate, and has its headquarters in Athens. The closest thing we have to a suspect is an illegal immigrant who happens to be a Turk. What will the Foreign Office's position be if it can be proved that a powerful Greek company deliberately framed an innocent Turk for murder?'

'You're telling me that this is about keeping building contracts in Istanbul?' asked Biddle.

'Add to this mix a powerful Austrian with Mosleyite connections in London, a man whose only daughter has died in mysterious circumstances, and a theatrical production, of all things, that simultaneously demonstrates international solidarity and co-operation while challenging the nation's moral dignity. Is it any wonder that the matter is attracting attention in high places? You see, Biddle, you have to look at the broader picture. Four days and three murders on, we're no further forward than when we started, so I'm going to handle the case in the manner I think fit. I know I'm an unlikely-looking subversive, but it's people like me you have to watch out for. I won't toe the party line and I don't have to cover my back against losing a court case over technical irregularities—'

'You're talking about contaminated evidence, failure to observe—'

'—because,' Bryant cut across him, 'our cases get solved before they ever reach a public court, something you'd have realized if you'd studied the unit's history a little more thoroughly instead of worrying about logging procedures on trace evidence.'

He rose, bringing the meeting to an end. 'Now you may want to reconsider your transfer. You seem like a smart chap. Put your talents to good use. Check out the spot where Darvell was butchered.

Ask Runcorn about the blood patterns in the aisle. Forget the paperwork and get stuck in. That's where you'll be best used. Don't let your ambitions pull you in the wrong direction. I know you asked Davenport down here today. But think about what I've said. You can let me have your answer by tomorrow morning.'

'Thank you, sir,' said Biddle, looking at Bryant as if he was mad, 'but my mind is made up. I'm requesting a transfer from the unit at the first available opportunity.'

He's angry that John saw action and he didn't, thought Bryant suddenly. He wants to be out there rugby-tackling the villains. It was all he needed to understand to get Biddle back on track.

37

THE VOICE OF THE ABYSSINIAN

Arthur Bryant stood outside the café lost in thought as the rainwater slipped through its blast-damaged canopy, dripping onto the shoulders of his gaberdine. Some office girls dashed across the road with newspapers held over their heads. A taxi splashed past with a dirt-smudged child sitting on the running board. A tramp in a torn cardboard hat was carefully stepping in and out of a large puddle at the kerb, his head bowed in concentration. The safe canopy of inclement weather had brought life back to the night streets. Bryant checked his watch again, and decided to give Elspeth five more minutes.

Like Geoffrey Whittaker, Harry, Stan Lowe and Mr Mack, Elspeth belonged to a brigade of workers whose lives were lived in darkness, a perpetual night divided into sections that ran concurrently from one production to the next. Bryant was surprised how little they knew of the world beyond their own circle. They were the real theatre angels, happy to remain in the shadows beyond the footlights, only tangentially attached to the stage, essential to its survival.

He checked his watch again. She must have known that she'd be too busy to break for supper; that was why she had insisted on meeting him outside the café. She had not wanted to hurt his feelings by refusing him outright. He pulled his scarf a little tighter round his neck and sniffed the cold air. For a brief moment he thought he had been given a shot at finding himself a new girl. But it was clear where Elspeth's loyalties lay. After repeatedly choosing work over women, he felt as though he was getting a taste of his own medicine.

At moments like this, the memory of Nathalie returned. He missed her so badly that he wanted to cry. As he stepped back into the foggy drizzle, he decided to avoid the theatre in order to spare Elspeth embarrassment, and walked off into Soho to buy himself a mug of cocoa.

When he reached the corner, something made him stop and glance back at the theatre. He looked up at the pairs of mullioned windows, and had the briefest impression of being watched through the mist. A pale twisted face, a fleeting presence, like the fading heat of a handprint on glass. It dipped back from the window, and the thought of his aberrant imagination chilled him. He was starting to believe that buildings held ghosts.

'There's something in there I don't understand,' he told May later. 'I want to take someone in with me after dark.'

'Don't say it,' warned May. 'Don't tell me you want to go ghost-hunting in a theatre at midnight with one of your clairvoyant pals.'

'That's exactly what I'm going to do, how did you know?' asked Bryant innocently. 'Edna has a good sense for these things.'

'Not your alternative theologian, the woman with the cats,' groaned May. DS Forthright had told May about the eerie afternoon she had once spent with Bryant and Edna Wagstaff in a run-down slum flat filled with feline familiars.

'We're lucky she's had a cancellation and can fit us in so soon. She doesn't normally make house calls.'

'You've already spoken to her? What have you arranged?'

'She's meeting us outside the stage door at midnight tonight.'

'No, Arthur, you promised Davenport you wouldn't. No mumbo-jumbo, he said.'

'I think she might be able to do some good. Sensations of pain and harm are as visible to her as the walls around us. She doesn't charge, but I usually drop her something. Mrs Wagstaff is tormented by her gift. Past, present and future are all the same. Everything crosses over. The only way she can relieve the pain her gift causes is by using it to help others.'

'And you really believe this?' asked May.

'With all my heart.' Bryant's pale blue eyes were so wide, so honest that he had to be telling the truth.

'I'm sorry I'm late. The blackout and the fog. I had to follow a tramline to get here, and then I followed it too far.' Tall and ascetic, wrapped in a frayed black coat and carrying a cat box, the old lady looked considerably more frail than when Bryant had last seen her.

'Hello, Edna,' he said jovially, 'I hear you're still living on the Isle of Dogs.'

'Oh yes, Arthur, one of the last. I've been bombed out twice now, and I lost my Billy, my proud boy, at Dunkirk. At least he saw service.'

'I'm so sorry,' said Bryant, taking her hand.

'He was happy to be mobilized. The air force and the navy have no chance to stop and think because they stay on duty around the clock. My boy spent so much time confined to barracks, he was so terribly bored with the endless drills. At least it was an active end.'

'But how are you?'

'Oh, they keep trying to rehouse me. I had people round from the council, telling me my cats were insanitary. I explained they were all dead, what harm could they do? How could you catch fleas from them? They were sprayed for parasites when they were stuffed. They want me to go to a home in Stepney. That's miles away.'

'Can't your daughter take you in?'

'She's gone to the WRNS. I'm very proud. I wouldn't want to bother her.' She made her way up the stairs with awkward slowness. 'You know, I haven't been to the theatre in years.'

'Edna, this is my new partner, Mr May.'

She reached over and shook his hand, then hastily released it.

'I do beg your pardon, Mr May. What a jolt. I get very strong feelings from some of the people I come into physical contact with, mostly the young ones.'

'Oh, really?' said May, rubbing the static shock from his fingers with some embarrassment. 'What did you get from me?'

'Best not to say, just in case I'm wrong,' said Edna mysteriously. 'Let's not dwell on what hasn't happened yet. I brought Rothschild with me. He's an Abyssinian, the lion of cats.' She raised the cat box high.

'Are you sure this is a good idea?' whispered May.

'Edna sees things.'

'And I can smell something.' May grimaced. 'I think it's her.'

'I just need to pick up the psychic scent,' she called over her shoulder.

'I don't know how she'll do it, she's wearing so much of her own. She needs a bath, Arthur. And she's got her wig on back to front.'

'You're a sceptic, Mr May. I don't mind.' Edna gave a throaty chuckle. 'The world will need sceptics after the war is over. Too many people are ready to believe anything they're told. Where do you want me?'

Bryant led the way up the painted concrete staircase until they reached a set of red double doors. 'The dress circle will do,' he told her, 'there are—'

'Four floors, yes, I know, upper circle and balcony above us, stalls below.'

'You can sense the building's layout?' asked May.

'No. I saw *No, No, Nanette* here. I'll go down to the front, if I may. Perhaps one of you could carry Rothschild.'

May reluctantly took the cat box and waited as Bryant showed the old lady to the front of the balcony. He raised the box to eye level and peered inside. Something glittered blackly back at him.

'Do you still have your familiars, Evening Echo and Squadron Leader Smethwick?' asked Bryant, seating her on the aisle.

'Sadly no.' Edna arranged the folds of her coat about her. 'The German bombers come right over my house and interfere with the signals.'

'You make it sound like tuning in a wireless, Mrs Wagstaff,' said May.

'Well, it's not dissimilar,' said Edna. If she detected the scepticism in his voice she gave no sign of it. 'Ever since they put a barrage balloon at the end of the street I've been getting terrible reception.'

'From your spirit guides?'

'No, on my wireless. I keep missing *Gert and Daisy*.' She leaned forward and looked about. 'Of course, London theatres are filled with ghosts.' She smiled, patting Bryant's arm. 'Mostly just echoes of emotional experiences, drawn out by the intensity of performance in such buildings. Any actor will tell you. They're terribly vulnerable to mental distress, you know. Unstable pathologies so often lead to cruelty and suicide. You know about the "Man in Grey", I suppose.'

'He appears in the Theatre Royal, Drury Lane, just before the run of a successful production, doesn't he?'

'That's right, dressed in a three-cornered hat, a powdered periwig and a grey riding cloak. He always follows the same route along the back of the upper circle, starting from the bar and vanishing into the far wall. Even the firewatchers have seen him, and they're not as prone to nerves as theatre folk. Workmen supposedly found his corpse bricked into a wall on the Russell Street side of the theatre. He had a dagger in his ribs. You can read about him in any cheap guidebook. I don't suppose there's much truth to the story, but there's no denying the fact that such houses attract collective hysteria and magnify the emotions. After all, that's what they're intended to do.

'There are lots of lesser-known spirits, though. The Haymarket has the ghost of the dramatist John Buckstone. Margaret Rutherford had to spend the night there once during a rail strike, and found him in the wardrobe. Or hasn't that happened yet? Time plays such tricks on me.' She thought for a moment, relaxing her watery green eyes.

'We're more interested in sensations, Edna.'

'I understand. Could there be another animal in the building apart from Rothschild? A tortoise, perhaps?'

'Yes, there is,' said May, looking at his partner in puzzlement.

'I thought so. I was getting a distress message.'

'He has insomnia,' explained Bryant.

Edna stroked her knuckles restlessly, anxious to help. 'There's so much humanity here. So many people have passed through. There are few public places left in London that are as psychically rich as its theatres. The interiors don't change. The walls absorb. I wonder if you'd get Rothschild for me?'

Bryant brought over the cat box and opened the wire door.

'I must be careful with him,' said Edna, 'he's getting rather fragile.' Her long, tapered fingers felt around the edges of the cat and pulled him out. Rothschild was a leonine sandstone-coloured Abyssinian, and had been stuffed in crouching position, as if watching a mouse. His ears were tattered with handling, one glass eye had sunk back into his skull and there was sand coming out of his bottom. She carefully set him on the edge of the balcony, facing the stage.

'Is there any way of lowering the house lights a little?'

May had arranged to have them left up, mainly because he was worried about the old lady tripping over.

'I'll see what I can do,' he offered, heading back along the balcony.

'There are plenty of friendly spirits here, but then there should be,' she chattered on to Bryant. 'First-time performers are sensitive to them. Sometimes they help newcomers to forget their nerves and remember their lines, or they redirect them to better positions on the stage. Actors sometimes speak of being guided by unseen hands. Oh, there is something here.' She became silent, and seemed to fall into a light sleep. The house lights dimmed and May quietly returned, taking a seat behind the medium.

The detectives listened and waited. The faint, high voice that emerged from Rothschild startled them both. At first it seemed little more than the sound of a draught whistling under a door. Gradually they were able to make out a few words. 'Not the actors, the actors are adored.' The voice reverted to a thin wind. 'Someone has been ignored and forgotten. No hatred... only desperation... desperation. History repeats.'

May studied the old lady's face. She didn't appear to be throwing her voice. Something prickled the base of his neck.

'It's not his fault, you understand...' Now the voice was Edna's, so alone, so melancholy. 'Selfish and blind. Medea... Calliope... goddesses of the theatre, so very sad.' A tear ran down her left cheek and trembled on her chin. 'The poor tortured soul is here, right among us now. A painted world is so confining. There must be a way to set such a trapped spirit free. The cruelty of the moonlight, so far beyond reach.'

Just as May was peering into them, Edna's eyelids lifted, startling him. She sat up and wiped her chin. 'I'm sorry,' she apologized, 'I didn't mean to get so upset. It's being in a theatre. A house of the emotions. Did you hear the voice?'

'Yes,' said Bryant enthusiastically, nodding at his partner. 'Who was it?'

'I rather fancy it belonged to Dan Leno, the clown. This used to be a music hall, didn't it?'

'I believe so.'

'Dan's ghost often used to appear in the halls. There were many recorded sightings at Collins' Music Hall on Islington Green, and in Drury Lane. He would appear to give advice to the actors. Sometimes they heard him performing his clog-dancing routine. A very reliable source. What did he say?'

'Something about a forgotten tortured soul and a painted world, and history repeating,' said May irritably. 'Greeks. It could mean anything.'

'You're looking for a little child,' said Edna firmly. 'A child so desperate to be set free that it must hurt people. I feel that very strongly.'

'You make it sound as if we're supposed to be searching for a ghost.'

'I rather think not,' said Edna, lifting the cat back into its box. 'This is not someone reaching from beyond the grave. The person you seek is real, and dangerous when cornered. Medea murdered her sons to take revenge on their father.'

'But we're looking for a killer, not some Greek woman,' said May, exasperated. Edna did not appear to have heard. She looked up at the ceiling, listening to her inner voices. 'Edna?' He turned to Bryant with his palms outstretched. 'Look at her, she doesn't know if she's at the park or the pictures.'

'Come on, Edna,' said Bryant gently. 'Let's get you home.'

He helped her from her seat, and for a moment the house lights flickered out. They waited in the oppressive darkness, halted by the foot of the stairs, listening to the old woman's laboured breath. Then the auditorium filled with light. May wanted to complain that the visit had been a waste of time, but something stilled within him as he watched the balcony curtain lift and fall in the sighing draught that blew beneath the doors, as though the spirit of the theatre had departed with them.

38

RENALDA'S WAR

On Friday morning, the city awoke to the terrible news.

Despite the presence of a bombers' moon, as close and cold as death, London had passed the night unscathed, and instead, the city of Coventry, Luftwaffe target no. 53, had suffered the full force of Germany's squadrons in a devastating *Mondschein Serenade,* a 'Moonlight Serenade'.

Nearly five hundred bombers had delivered high explosives and incendiary bombs in eleven hours of dusk-to-dawn raids that had obliterated the heart of the city, destroyed its cathedral, killed over five hundred inhabitants, seriously wounded nine hundred more.

The night had been clear and frosty, providing perfect visibility. London was a metropolis large enough to weather such a disaster, but Coventry, with a population of just under a quarter of a million, had been almost eradicated. The residents who survived were dazed and terrified. Gas, water, electricity and transport systems stopped. Twenty-one of its factories—twelve of them tied to the aircraft industry—had been heavily hit. Radio reports made no attempt to make light of the attack; the news spread like bushfire. The lines to the city were down. It was impossible to discover if relatives were dead or alive.

Listening to the Home Service made John May late for work. He hurried to the unit and found his partner seated at the teleprinter, checking several yards of paper.

'You've heard?' May asked. 'Christ, we should be there instead of here.'

'There's nothing you or I can do for them,' muttered Bryant, barely raising his eyes. 'I want you to meet Andreas Renalda. He's the only Greek we know, and Edna mentioned Greeks. When I looked into his eyes I caught a glimpse of something.'

'He's probably upset about spending a fortune on a show that may never open. According to Helena Parole, updating *Orpheus* was all his idea. Anyway, didn't you already get everything you could out of him?' May was finding it increasingly hard to concentrate on Bryant's theories when, just a short distance from London, the bodies of so many innocent civilians were being dragged from the smoking ruins of a town. Their case seemed absurd and almost pointless by comparison.

'He might be different with you. Talk about whatever comes into your head. Keep him off guard. I want you to study him. You're better with people than I am. I'm still missing a link, and I keep wondering.' Bryant sucked at his pipe pensively. 'Suppose Renalda thinks he's betraying the ancient gods of his homeland by staging such a controversial production? He says his family is superstitious. What if they think he's going against the mythical protectors of Greece? He may have accidentally inspired someone to seek revenge. That would make him responsible for what's happened, wouldn't it?'

May gave a sigh of annoyance. Bryant's thinking seemed so far removed from his own, so unrelated to the cause-and-effect crimes of the real world, that he could not find a response. Instead, he went to see Andreas Renalda.

The tycoon was on his way to a board meeting but agreed to collect May at Piccadilly Circus and let him travel in his limousine as far as Hyde Park Corner. The sleek black Rolls-Royce was a vision of lost elegance. It glided to a stop beneath the vast 'Dig for Victory' banner that hung across the fascia of Swan and Edgar, and the chauffeur, liveried in black and red, the colours of the family guild, opened its passenger door to admit the detective. Renalda was sprawled across the back seat, his steel calipers holding his useless legs to one side.

'I have arranged a telephone call in order to speak to the board in Athens tonight,' Renalda explained, after introductions were made. 'My fellow directors have received news of our troubles, and require assurances. I was the one who convinced them that we should adopt such a high-risk venture. Our people, Mr May, are conservative individuals. They do not approve of my show, but they like the thought of the revenue it could generate. I have to assure them that we are not facing some kind of moral crusade. Harmful reports are appearing in your newspapers, suggesting that we have brought misfortune on ourselves, that we deserve what we get for bringing continental sex into venerable British theatreland. What your journalists are really saying, in their own charmingly circumspect manner, is that we are unwanted foreigners.'

'Not all of us share the views expressed by those newspapers,' May said, sinking back into the polished opulence of the leather seat. 'Since you've raised the subject, I was wondering about your enemies.'

Renalda peered at him coldly over the top of his rimless glasses. 'I don't recall discussing my enemies with your partner.'

'Forgive me, you're running a company that, according to *The Times,* is venturing into a market it knows nothing about. Your father was known to be a hard negotiator, and you told Mr Bryant that you take after him. You may well have offended someone. Your rivals have good reason to want to see you fail in this enterprise.'

'I am sure they do,' Renalda admitted evenly, 'but the wars of my father are not mine. You might credit me with more sophistication. At the end of the nineteen twenties my father's company had few remaining assets. Its debts were converted into equity that is still held by the other trustees.'

'How do they feel about your plans to leave the world of shipping?'

'Most of them consider me foresighted.'

'Most but not all?'

Renalda folded away his glasses with a sigh. 'I have known the board's directors all my life. You are looking in the wrong place.' Something in his voice suggested this was not necessarily so.

'This is a very important week for you,' said May, watching the grey window-boards of Selfridge's drift past.

'It's the culmination of a lifelong project that has not been destroyed even by a world plunged into war. My mother was a free spirit, but my father's house was her prison. Sirius would not allow the curtains to be opened because the sunlight damaged his paintings. When I was a boy my mother used to play Offenbach's music and dance alone through the still, dark rooms. It was the only time she was ever really happy.' The Rolls-Royce pulled up at traffic lights. The red, amber and green lenses had been covered with black tape so that slits formed narrow luminous crosses. 'I cannot afford to make any mistakes, Mr May. There are too many people watching me.'

'Who, your directors? Your rivals?'

'There are others who are closer.' Renalda seemed about to speak further, but stopped himself.

'We may be able to find enemies you can't,' May suggested. 'But you have to tell us who you suspect.'

'These are family affairs,' said Renalda finally. 'If you cannot protect my company, I will have to take care of the problem myself. I do not trust the officials of your government. They happily take my money and make promises, then do something else.'

May wondered if Renalda had bribed civil servants connected with the Lord Chamberlain's office.

'I think you're right,' he told his partner later. 'Andreas Renalda isn't telling us the whole truth.'

'Perhaps we haven't asked him the right questions,' suggested Bryant. 'I need to know more about his family.'

'I can probably get the company records opened, but it'll take a few days.'

'I wasn't thinking about the official records. I'm more interested in where Renalda grew up, what the rest of the family was like, what his neighbours thought of him.'

'I don't see how that will help,' said May.

'You don't? No, I suppose you don't. I'm sure I read somewhere that Andreas Renalda was raised on one of the smaller islands to the south, Santorini, I think. Interesting, isn't it, that he chooses to honour his family with a play that mocks the mythology of his homeland? My uncle's friend at *The Times* wrote an article about the Renalda empire, but when war broke out the piece was spiked. I have a feeling Renalda has been generous with his war donations.'

'You still haven't told me what's on your mind.'

'Be patient for just a little longer.' Bryant knocked out his pipe and squinted into the bowl. 'I have to be absolutely sure.'

'Arthur, this has been an unusual week but even at the worst of times—'

Sidney Biddle put his head round the door. 'There's someone here to see you both.'

He pushed the door wide and DS Gladys Forthright walked in. Her hair had been dyed blond and cut in the style of the film star Alice Faye. Bryant leaped up from behind his desk and slapped his arms on the policewoman's shoulders.

'Forthright! Bless my old socks! What are you doing back here? You're supposed to be getting hitched and living with the land girls.'

The sergeant pulled off her jacket and gloves, and threw them into a corner. 'I had a bugger of a time getting here. The trains are up the spout. I slept in Chatham station last night.' She sighed. 'At least I didn't get around to posting a wedding list. It would have been embarrassing having to send gifts back.'

'What happened?'

'He didn't want to go through with it.'

'The absolute bastard,' cried Bryant, barely able to conceal the pleasure in his voice. 'What reason did he give, if I may be so bold?'

'Oh, the war, of course. He says it's not right to be thinking about ourselves when there are so many in difficulties all around us. We shouldn't bring babies into such uncertain times, et cetera. It was me who wanted to make us legal. I didn't want to risk dying a spinster. We drove down to his parents' on the last of his petrol, and I suppose I did talk about work quite a lot. We had a bit of a row, and finally came to an agreement. He promised not to mention his constabulary so long as I didn't talk about the unit. But I couldn't stay where I wasn't needed, like some kind of evacuee. I rang the

unit to explain and spoke to Mr Biddle. I wanted to warn you that
I was coming back.'

'He didn't tell me,' said Bryant indignantly.

'That's odd. How's he working out?'

'He's not. Look at this, I'm making my own tea from reused
leaves.' He fished a half-dissolved sugar cube out of his mug with
the pointy end of a dart. 'We have to make one lump go around
the whole unit because it's against Biddle's principles to buy black-
market demerara. His trial period ends today, thank God. He wants
to leave us and go back to the Met, and the feeling's mutual. Here, I
kept your mug just in case.' He poured her half his tea.

'Arthur, did you put him off?'

'I bent over backwards to make him feel welcome, the ungrateful
little sod.'

'How's the case?' asked Forthright.

'I'll have to take you back, I suppose. Just until you can get yourself sorted out.' Having answered an entirely different question, he
turned to the window and warmed his hands round his mug, smiling to himself.

'I thought you'd need me,' Forthright said, 'what with this latest
development.'

He turned, the smile fading. 'What do you mean?'

'I picked up the call just as I was coming in. Something strange
has happened again.'

39

THE ABDUCTION

The house in Lissom Grove was set back from the road and surrounded by battered birches. The hedge leading to the front door was so overgrown that it soaked May and Forthright as they passed. They were met by PC Crowhurst, who appeared from the shadowed porch and unlocked the front door for them.

'When was she last seen?' asked May, stepping into the gloomy Lincrusta-papered hall.

'The evening before last, sir. The girl she shares with was away for the night, but the next-door neighbour saw her coming in with shopping bags. She didn't turn up for rehearsals yesterday. They thought she was taking a day off sick, but when she failed to show again this morning, the other girl who boards here rang the police. I came round and found—well, you'll see.'

'Who is she?'

'A member of the chorus, name of Jan Petrovic. Sixteen years old. This is Phyllis.'

A slender girl held out her hand. She had ragged blond hair cut to her jawline, and was wearing a man's rowing sweater several sizes too large for her. 'Hello, you'd better come through.' She held open the door to a front room that was cluttered with the possessions of young girls living away from their parents for the first time: dinner plates, stockings, magazines, half-burned candles, a radiogram, some dance records out of their cardboard sleeves.

'In there, next door,' said Phyllis, wrapping her thin arms round herself. 'I can't bring myself to look.' Her voice had a soft Wiltshire burr. In the kitchen, a back door led to a small yard. The window above the sink had been shattered. There were several small drying spots of blood on the wooden draining board. May turned and found himself confronted by a shocking crimson smear that arced across the whitewashed wall.

'When did you last see Jan?' asked Forthright.

Phyllis chewed her lip nervously and stayed in the doorway. 'Two days ago. In the morning. I went to visit my boyfriend in Brighton. He's studying at Sussex College. Jan was getting ready to leave for her rehearsal.'

'How did she seem to you?'

'Pretty much in the pink. We talked about what we were going to do this weekend. She was fed up, but that's because she's worried about performing in the show. She's talked about leaving it before the opening night.'

'Why would she do that?'

'The schedule's too hard on her. I mean, she's just a kid, and she bluffed her way into the part. She didn't think she could handle it. Then this week's goings-on have been the last straw for her.'

'Have you known her long?'

'No, only a few weeks. I don't think Petrovic is her real name. She doesn't like people to know where she's from. I wondered if she might be Jewish.'

'Do you have a photograph of her?'

'No, but I think they took some publicity shots at the theatre.'

'John, look at this.' Forthright pointed into the corner behind the sink. Two halves of a cup lay in shadow. Beside them stood a short, wide-bladed knife, its tip stuck in the tiled floor, its handle darkly smeared. The DS stepped out of the kitchen, called the unit and asked to speak to Dr Runcorn. 'I'll get someone from FS over right now,' she told May, her hand over the mouthpiece. 'You'd better make sure Phyllis is all right.'

May gingerly stepped out of the kitchen's narrow corner and returned to the lounge.

'I've been calling her aunt's number, but there's been no answer,' said Phyllis, pacing along the edge of the carpet. 'She sometimes goes there when she gets fed up. I didn't know what else to do. Her mother rang to speak to her and I just couldn't say where she was.'

'When did you first think she was missing?' asked May.

'I tried calling her when I arrived in Brighton, but assumed she had gone to the theatre. Then when I got back and went into the kitchen I saw the mess.'

May took another look inside the kitchen. 'Odd. The break in the window isn't big enough to let anyone in, so why are there signs of a struggle? It's not near enough to the back door for anyone to be able to reach in and undo the latch.'

Forthright tested the lock. 'The door's still locked.' She carefully turned, studying the walls. 'Maybe he was already inside and she was trying to get out, away from him.'

May returned to the front room. Phyllis was seated with her hands pressed on her thighs, staring blankly at the floor. 'When you came in,' he asked, 'did you have to unlock the front door from the outside?'

'Yes. The latch is faulty, so you have to double-lock it as you leave or it comes open by itself.'

'What about the back door? Have you touched it?'

'No. I took one look at the kitchen and backed off. Then I called the police and was put through to your department.'

'When was this?'

'About two hours ago.'

'Hang on.' May called his constable in from the front garden: 'Crowhurst, come in here for a second.'

'Sir?'

'How did this get put through to us?'

'The station rang Miss Petrovic's work number, sir. As soon as they realized it was the theatre, the call was transferred to the unit.'

I bet it was, thought May. They couldn't get rid of it fast enough. He looked at the chaotic front room, at Phyllis, who seemed close to tears. 'Would you care to show me the other rooms?'

'Of course.'

Two small bedrooms, bathroom and toilet. An attempt had been made to brighten them up, the bedrooms painted a hopeful yellow, the bathroom pink, but the flat needed more than a lick of cheap paint to make it comfortable.

'Which one is Miss Petrovic's bedroom? No, just show me, don't touch anything.'

An unmade bed, socks and a sweater lay on the floor. A crumpled bath towel at the foot of the eiderdown. Stacks of books, undisturbed. If there had been violence, it hadn't reached here. He made a slow tour, checking the window frames and door handles. The flat reminded him of his own room.

'You think she's been abducted?' asked Phyllis, following behind him. 'Something terrible's happened to her, I'm sure of it.' She wiped her nose on the back of her hand. 'I should have been here.'

'We'll have to see what turns up from the kitchen,' May replied. 'We're going to have to take some items away with us.'

When he caught Forthright looking at him, he saw the same question in her eyes. If she's been abducted, her look said, how did he get her out of the house without opening any of the doors or windows?

The pattern, such as it was, had been broken, yet felt strangely consistent. There was the same kind of arrogant theatricality; the evidence of the abduction reminded May of the blocking rehearsals he had witnessed. It's deception practised in public view, he thought as he left the house. The interpretation of gestures, wasn't that what acting was all about?

But who was providing the direction?

40

GROUND ZERO

The interpretation of gestures, May recalled as he unfolded the architectural plan from his pocket. It all happened so long ago, the other end of a lifetime. We've learned a lot since then. Then he remembered there was no more 'we'. He was alone now. He would never adjust to the awful singularity. There was no one else. His wife and daughter were dead. His son lived in a commune in southern France and refused to speak to him. April, his granddaughter, had suffered a nervous breakdown and could not bear to leave her house. Only Bryant had given him hope.

'John, are you all right?'

'Oh, I suppose so.'

'Then show me,' said Stanhope Beaufort, holding out a pudgy hand. The architect was uncomfortably perched on a glass stool at a glass bar with a glass counter, surrounded by glass walls, a glass floor and a glass ceiling. Hundreds of tiny silver bulbs reflected from hundreds of square mirrors. It was so bright that nobody could see a thing.

John May handed over the building plan he and Longbright had rescued from the debris of the burned-down unit and waited for his analysis. He had tracked Beaufort, one of Bryant's old contacts, to the new Hoxton bar, and was hoping that he could explain the meaning of the page. The roar of street traffic entered the bar and bounced off the vitrine walls, vibrating everything and making it difficult to hear. Dust sifted in and settled on the shining surfaces like radiation fallout.

'I'm sorry to hear about your poor partner.' Beaufort tipped the paper into shadow so that he could read it. 'Old Arthur was a bit of a one-off.'

'He was at that,' agreed May.

'What do you think of this place, by the way?' Beaufort asked, as a waiter blundered into an indiscernible column with a tray of drinks.

'It's very—glass,' said May diplomatically.

'Glass is the new steel,' Beaufort explained. 'They all want it, it's so seventies. I've lost count of the number of accidents we've had here so far. The staircase is glass, too. One of the waitresses went arse over tit down it this morning. Cracked a step and knocked out her front tooth. She's been locked in the bog all day, crying her eyes out. You can see her if you want. The toilets are transparent. The owner complained that it's like a hall of mirrors, and I said, "That's because it *is* a hall of fucking mirrors, it's what you asked for." Wanker.'

'But you must like it if you designed it,' said May, puzzled.

'No, mate, it's just a commission. The secret of design is re-interpreting what was popular thirty years ago. Everyone wants the things that remind them of childhood. I just re-imagine them with the materials of the present.'

'So this isn't your taste?'

'What, New Britain? Fuck off. I live in an unfucked-about-with Georgian house in Islington with nice big comfy sofas. I'm not going to split my shins on a chrome coffee table shaped like a fucking rocket. I've got three kids. I don't want them running around covered in dents. Same with the clothes. I don't dress like this at home, I wear jumpers. This is just for the clients.'

Beaufort was wearing black tracksuit bottoms and a T-shirt that read: MUTHAFUCKA. 'It's like those singers who bang on about teen rebellion so they can buy homes in Hampstead. This is all wrong, by the way.' He turned the sheet of paper round and held it up. 'See the calibrations down the side? They're in feet and inches reading left to right. That tells us two things. Pre-metric, post-war.

LCC stamp here, see? And it's not a ground plan, because the central corridor wouldn't be measured off from a single left-hand starting point, it would have a single width measurement.'

'So what are you saying? What is it?'

'A depth measurement, calibrated from ground zero going downwards. That's why it's shaded to indicate round walls. This isn't a corridor, it's a shaft.'

'What are the broken lines at the bottom?' May pointed at the base of the diagram.

Behind them, there was a small scream and a tinkle of glass.

'It's the architectural symbol used to indicate water. Looks to me like you've got yourself a well.'

'And the passageway off to the side?'

'Overflow escape. It's artesian; the water rises through natural pressure. If it rains heavily the excess drains off through the side passage and prevents the well from overflowing.'

'Where would the overflow pipe surface?'

'Oh, somewhere outside the building in the street, probably.'

'I need to get an indication of scale,' said May. 'Could a person fit down it?'

'Looking at this, the main shaft's got to be six feet across, so you can reckon the side vent is four feet, easily large enough to hold a grown man. The Victorians loved stuff like this. They built their drains big so they could shove children down them with brooms and shit shovels. They were great designers, but had no thought for the poor bastards who had to use their buildings.' Behind him, a waitress winced as she sponged blood from her sliced elbow with a cocktail napkin.

'Not like nowadays, then,' agreed May.

As he headed for Old Street tube, it began to rain. The area looked every bit as derelict as it had just after the war. How was that possible? May thought of the London that might have been, the abandoned plans, the failed dreams. Once, a causeway of buildings had been proposed for the centre of the Thames, a vast triumphal arch of Portland stone suggested for Euston Road, a grand national cemetery attempted on Primrose Hill, a Piranesian entry gate blueprinted for Kensington. Gothic towers, pyramid morgues, elevated railways, none had come to pass. The grand social schemes had collapsed in favour of piecemeal sale to private interests. It all could have been so beautiful, he thought sadly.

May pulled the backpack from his shoulder, removed his mobile phone and rang Longbright at home.

'You said there was no one left alive from the Palace,' he told her, 'but you're wrong. Believe me, I know how it sounds, but I think our killer is still around. Arthur recognized the diagram for what it was. A possible escape route.'

'It's a bit of a long shot, don't you think?'

'We know Arthur went to the theatre to research his memoirs. I think he discovered the blueprint and realized the implications at once. Then he did the most obvious thing. He ran a search. Combed the city's mental institutions and checked through hospital records looking for further signs of survival.'

'You're saying he traced this aged lunatic and found him in residence at the Wetherby? Why would he do that?' Longbright sounded sceptical.

'You know how Arthur always hated loose ends. He went galloping off to the clinic, made a nuisance of himself, questioned the nurses, poked about in their records and ended up with a shortlist of former patients.' May ducked through a grey wall of stalled trucks, heading for the tube. On the pavement ahead, a tangle of red and white plastic tape cordoned off a vast pile of roadwork rubble, more haphazardly arranged than any wartime bomb debris.

'He was only going to write up the story for his memoirs, but suddenly found himself back in the case. That's why he wanted me to go with him. He warned me he could get into trouble.' May was forced to shout into the cellphone. 'He found what he was looking for, then probably drove around to the poor bloke's house. You know how insensitive he could be.'

'The newspapers of the time called him the Phantom, didn't they? He was probably rather upset to be tracked down again.'

'Enough to follow Arthur back to the unit and plant a bomb,' May replied. 'From what we know of him, it would make perfect sense. A case of history repeating, a farewell performance. Finch said he thought the explosive material was old.'

'Yes, but sixty years old? Where on earth could he have been keeping it?'

'Who knows, he could have buried it in his back garden and re-turned to dig it up. I think seeing Arthur brought back everything that had happened, and ignited his desire for revenge.' May paused while the trucks juddered past. 'Listen,' he bellowed, sticking his finger in his ear, 'I need you to track someone down for me.'

'Of course, who do you need?' Longbright asked.

'Bryant's dentist. I know he's left the practice, but they must have a contact number. It's very important that you locate him.'

May snapped the phone shut and gave one final glance at the rain-filled sky before stepping into the clammy warmth of the tube station.

41

RUNNING TO DAYLIGHT

'You realize we're an hour away from tonight's dress rehearsal, and that we open tomorrow?' asked Helena Parole, lighting a cork-tipped De Rezske and fanning the smoke through the opened window in her office.

The young detectives were seated with her. Bryant listened as he cleaned out his pipe bowl with a pickle fork that he kept in his coat for just such a purpose.

'How am I expected to feel? I've got an under-rehearsed cast that's too panicked to concentrate on the score, a violinist who's more used to playing in Leicester Square for a hatful of pennies, a musical director who fights with the conductor over every note-change in the arrangements, fifty-year-old mechanical equipment that refuses to control several tons of lethal scenery, a replacement Jupiter who has never performed in the West End, a cleaning lady who's trying to scrub blood out of the balcony seats, and now some kind of women's temperance league is picketing the theatre. Stan and Mouse are spreading rumours about ghosts walking through walls. Benjamin got punched on the nose by a woman who says we're the spawn of Satan. I nearly broke my leg in the foyer after Elspeth's tortoise pulled rhubarb leaves all over the floor. And you're telling me we have an abduction on our hands.'

'How important is Jan Petrovic to the show?' asked May, attempting to look unfazed.

'She's just part of the chorus, not featured at all. I replaced her the minute she failed to show for the rehearsal. That's not the point. I have to be sure that you can protect my boys and girls, otherwise I can't go out there and convince them that everything's fine.'

'We're doing as much as we can. I'd prefer to see the production suspended rather than place anyone in danger, but Mr Renalda has every intention of ensuring the show goes on.'

Helena's voice rose a notch. 'This is no reflection on your abilities, Mr May, but in view of your *extreme* youth, I wonder if a senior officer might not be available now.'

'I'm afraid there is no one else available, Miss Parole,' he replied politely.

'They've spent a fortune on advance advertising and publicity. There's not a bomb site in London that's not been plastered with the posters. To Mr Renalda, a missing chorus girl is less important than an outraged review in the *Telegraph*.'

'Obviously we're all hoping that Miss Petrovic turns up safe and sound. We found signs of a struggle in her apartment, and several small spots of blood that may be hers, but no unaccounted-for fingerprints. What appeared to be a large smear of blood on a wall turns out, rather oddly, to be nail varnish. Beyond that, we know very little.'

'It seems to me you know very little about what's been happening at all. I suppose all the good detectives have been taken by the war effort. It's not your fault, you just lack experience. God knows who I'd blame. I certainly wouldn't listen to any of the cast.'

'Why not?'

'They're actors, for Christ's sake, they exaggerate everything. Have you talked to them all?'

'Pretty much.'

'What about those crazy women outside? Don't you think it could be someone who's taken the show as a personal affront to decency?'

'I think plenty of them are doing that. I just can't imagine anyone being so upset that they would break into a theatre and start murdering the performers.'

'Don't be so sure. The Nazis are on the lookout for signs of dissatisfaction and unrest. It said so in the paper. They're infiltrating groups and stirring up trouble, just like they did in the thirties.'

'I don't think we're under attack from German spies,' said Bryant firmly. 'My spiritualist mentioned Medea and Calliope.'

'Your spiritualist,' repeated Helena.

Bryant nodded, patting his pockets for a light.

'I'm surrounded by blithering idiots.' The artistic director rose to leave. 'If you'll excuse me, gentlemen, I've a show to rehearse.'

'Calliope was the mother of Orpheus,' Bryant explained once he and May had returned to their offices behind Bow Street. 'He got his musical talents from her. Perhaps we should take a look at the original legend, not Offenbach's version of it.'

'We're not looking for a mythical creature, Arthur, even your Mrs Wagstaff agreed about that.'

'We need to find a motive, John. Aristaeus tried to rape Eurydice, and she trod on a serpent as she fled. The poison killed her. Hemlock is a poison that was known to the ancient Greeks. Orpheus followed her down to Hades, and suspended the tortures of the damned with his music. Orpheus was instructed not to turn round to look at her until she had reached the light of the sun. Eurydice made her way through the darkness, guided by the sound of his lyre. As he reached the sunlight, he looked back and lost her for ever. Various reasons have been given for his behaviour. Some say he was frightened by a clap of thunder. Others reckon he was pushed in the back by Jupiter. Our Jupiter is dead, and can no longer stop the flight of Orpheus, running to daylight. Edna talked of ghosts, unseen hands guiding, pushing at the actors' backs. The girl, Jan, she's not been seen anywhere?'

'It's impossible to find out. The stations are still full of evacuees and servicemen, people moving around all over the place.'

Forthright looked in. 'Arthur, the article you requested from your journalist pal, Peregrine Summerfield. He's managed to find you a copy. He's sending a lad over with it right now.'

Several minutes later, a boy arrived with a brown envelope under his arm. May gave him sixpence from the petty-cash tin and tore open the accompanying letter.

'What appalling handwriting.'

'Give it to me, I'm used to reading his scrawl,' said Bryant, snatching away the letter.

Dear Arthur,
There was a lot of interest in this at the time, but the paper
wouldn't run my article because Andreas Renalda got wind
of it and threatened The Thunderer *with a lawsuit. The*
family was based in Calliste ('Most Beautiful'), also known
as Santorini. I managed to locate his former home on the
outskirts of Thira, but couldn't gain admittance to the estate.
Everyone on the island knows the family, but nobody was
very happy talking about them. I tried mentioning them in
one of the local bars and the locals all clammed up, it was
like one of those scenes in a cowboy film where the stranger
comes into town. However ...

'Is there another page to this?'

'Sorry.' May handed the sheet to Bryant.

... I wrote a profile and was even paid, but the damned thing
never appeared in print. Andreas Renalda has made my life a
living hell ever since, ringing up publishers and complaining
about me. His old man employed half the island, and a lot of
loyalties still survive. I suggest you read the article and form
your own conclusions.

For the next few minutes no sound was heard in the office, save for the familiar double clang of a distant tram.

'You wanted a motive,' Bryant said finally. 'It looks like we've got one. Listen to this.' He balanced his legs along the edge of the desk. 'Peregrine called his piece "Orpheus Ascending". Sirius, Renalda's father, lost an eye at the battle of Modder River, and was employed as a mercenary under General "Backbreaker" Gatacre during the Boer War.'

'That's not what I'd call a motive,' said May.

'Don't be so impatient. His wife, Diana, bore him two sons.

Andreas came along in 1905, when his brother Minos was five. His legs were too brittle to support him, so Sirius had his workers build steel calipers that would enable him to walk. He had lost an eye before finding his own strength, so thought Andreas would also turn disability to his advantage. He gave Minos, his other son, an allowance, but reserved his empire for Andreas. He dismissed the missus to a wing of the house and took a series of mistresses. Diana stopped attending church and raised her son in pagan ways in order to afford him protection from enemies. Superstitious lot, eh? Andreas became the keyholder to a shipping fortune and Minos turned into an embittered drunk who couldn't touch his brother for fear of reprisals.

'Andreas married a young English girl called Elissa. He inherited the Renalda estate on his father's death, and it will be given to Minos only if his entire family dies.' Bryant swiped the papers with the back of his hand. 'Now *this* is where it gets interesting. A week after the old man's funeral, while Andreas was attending to business on the mainland, bad brother Minos told Elissa that he wanted to make amends for his behaviour. He took her out to a taverna, but only the brother came back. Nobody knows what happened. Elissa was seen with Minos on the jetty late that night. She supposedly slipped and fell into the water. It took a month for her body to wash up on the beach. Andreas took the case to the local magistrate, but no evidence of murder was found. The tycoon was convinced that his brother had killed his wife, but had no proof. Andreas moved to England, and Minos's whereabouts are unknown. Well, we wanted a suspect.'

'Andreas's brother. You think he could be here?'

'I suppose he could be using any name.' Bryant called in Forthright. 'We're going to need a recent photograph of Minos Renalda,' he explained. 'We have to talk to Andreas again. Have you got any tea rations left? We've used ours up.'

'Certainly.' Forthright paused in the doorway. 'Did you hear? The other army bike has turned up. No prints on it, though. I heard about Mr May's little adventure.'

'Where did they find it?' asked Bryant.

'Right outside the theatre, back with all the others.'

'I can't believe it. The audacity—he went right back. Gladys, what are you hovering about for?'

'May I just say that it's a pleasure to be working with you again?'

'No, you may not. Get on with your work.' Bryant smiled poisonously at his partner. 'I knew those two would never last,' he said.

42

MR MAY PRESENTS HIS THEORY

The follow-up to Coventry's night of terror was a bombing raid on London that proved almost as devastating as the attack of 15 October, when the city seemed to combust with over nine hundred fires. On that occasion all railway traffic had been halted, and the shattered Fleet sewer emptied its poisoned waters into the train tunnels at King's Cross.

On Saturday, those who survived the night arose to find great chunks of the city alight or simply gone. Hospitals, schools and stations had been hit, and doctors cut their way into unsafe buildings to administer morphine to the injured. Pumps and water towers were drained to fight the raging blazes spread by incendiary bombs. Because the city's water was routinely turned off at the weekend, the fire hoses had run dry, so riverside cranes were used to drop trailer pumps into the Thames from offshore barges.

Looters struck, risking their lives to pillage from the ruins of shops and houses while residents took cover, but most of the cases went unreported for fear of harming morale. A deep crater had been blown in the centre of Charing Cross Road, exposing the underground trains to daylight. In Farringdon, a fish shop was hit by a bomb that loosened a great girder, causing it to fall on a queue of housewives. Not even gangs of men could move the beam, and the women had to wait and die while a crane was sought.

Brick dust settled across the roads and buildings as thickly as falling snow, a pale cloak of mourning. All sounds were deadened. People moved quietly through the ashes like determined ghosts.

John May had spent the night under the stairs at his aunt's house in Camden. The noise had been deafening and almost constant, the explosions preceded by the droning of aircraft, the thunder of anti-aircraft guns and the ghostly wail of the sirens, one of which was mounted on the roof of the primary school opposite. The early fog was so dense, and the blackout still so effective, that May could see no more than a few feet ahead as he walked into Covent Garden, listening to the fall of masonry, accompanied by the chinking tumble of London bricks. The rescue squads were pulling down cracked chimney stacks and walls.

In Long Acre the atmosphere changed; the costermongers were still in fine voluble form, singing and bellowing jokes across their wicker stacks. Many offices asked their exhausted workers to handle extra shifts. With so many lines of communication cut, the daily push and pull of commerce slowed. But the size of London worked in favour of its population. No matter how much havoc had occurred in the night, it always seemed there was another way to get things done.

Bryant had spent the night in the office and needed to clear his head with a walk beside the river. He felt close to the truth and wanted to talk to Andreas Renalda, but nobody knew his whereabouts. There was no answer from the telephone at the tycoon's Highgate home, and his office was shut for the weekend.

The premiere of *Orpheus* was still planned for tonight, come incendiary bombs, hellfire murders or the Lord Chamberlain himself. The day was grey and dull, the skies louring with the threat of rain. Everyone was praying for a deluge to dampen the fires, and for clouds to hide the city.

An *Orpheus* lyric rattled around in Bryant's brain. 'The Metamorphoses Rondo', in which Cupid sings, 'What do these disguises prove? Only that you find yourself so ugly that whenever you want to be loved, you daren't show yourself as you really are.' If Andreas Renalda's brother was here, he could have adopted the identity of anyone. Tonight the theatre would open for the grand premiere, and the invited public would be admitted. How much harder would it be to spot a rogue face in the crowd?

Bryant studied the water, watching the chromatic petrol ripples of a passing boat blossom on the surface in diseased ziggurats. Then there was the matter of the missing girl, lost in a city of missing people. If Jan Petrovic had been kidnapped, why had no one heard from her abductor? What was to be gained from removing someone so unimportant to the production? He thought back to Edna Wagstaff's nervous chatter about the ghosts of the theatre, and how they walked through walls. How had someone been able to enter and leave the Palace unnoticed? When the building wasn't locked up, the two entrances had staff posted at them. There were two pass doors between the backstage area and the front of house, and one of those was kept permanently locked. The doors to Petrovic's flat were also locked from the inside. It was as if . . .

Edna had spoken of desperation, but someone desperate to do what? The police at Bow Street and West End Central were far too busy to help the unit. Sergeant Nasty-Basket Carfax next door had laughed in his face when he had requested assistance. Suppose Minos Renalda had infiltrated the staff of the theatre? He would be forty now, which eliminated quite a few members of the orchestra, about half of the cast and all but one of the house staff. Forthright was checking the ages of the backstage crew.

Bryant let his mind roam loose. In 1922, the Palace had premiered *The Four Horsemen of the Apocalypse.* Gilbert and Sullivan longed to trump Offenbach, and set *Thespis* among the gods of ancient Greece, but *Thespis* was now lost. The painting in the Palace Theatre's foyer was *The Concert,* a Greek revival subject. Offenbach's hero helped Jason to find the Golden Fleece. The brown interiors of the Palace were rubbed gold by the hands of patrons. Mythic links but also Masonic links, the compass and the globe. Orpheus's mother was Calliope. The Maenads tore Orpheus limb from limb for preaching male love, and his head floated down the River Hebrus still singing. Which Greek goddess carried a scythe? Wasn't a scythe like a razor?

His mind was reeling with impossible associations. But there was a more prosaic possibility. The show was already being accused of blasphemy, indecency, blatantly unwholesome sexuality. Could some guardian of moral standards really have become so incensed by its perceived perversions that they were prepared to kill? The idea didn't sit well with him. The crimes felt passionless, almost accidental. It was as though anyone could have died in place of Capistrania and Senechal.

'I thought I'd find you here,' said May, laying a hand on his shoulder and passing him a silver flask. 'This'll warm you up.'

'I'm trying to think, old bean. Am I to be allowed no privacy?' Bryant grumbled, but unscrewed the cap and took a swig. 'This business is giving me the pip. If I had to paint a picture of the person we're looking for,' he said, passing the flask back, 'I'd reckon we were up against an older male, middle class, with some kind of grudge against the play itself.'

'Why do you say that?'

'Traditional theatre, by which I discount the music halls and picture palaces, is largely ignored by working-class youths. It's not really a public place but a sealed arena. Unless you're a paying customer or a member of the production, there's no easy way in or out of the building. Our killer acts with the kind of confidence that comes with experience. He's male because of the sense of distance from his victims. He's unemotional. Statistically, women make passionate murderers. He has a grudge against the play because the players themselves are unimportant to him. There's a plan, and we haven't seen its culmination yet.'

'Do you see any way of stopping it?'

'The theatre opens its doors tonight. The time for deciphering clues is over.'

'All we can do is be vigilant,' May agreed. 'Every attack points in a different direction.'

'Do they, though? Couldn't our killer be fulfilling a ritual? Orpheus faced the rigours of Hell before he was allowed to climb towards the light. I believe true evil is dispassionate, faceless, selfish. A game is being played out right before my eyes. Our perpetrator knows this and is unconcerned, or is so blinded by the need to take action that he's prepared to take risks.'

May had not seen his partner in this fugue state before. 'I think you're wasting your time with all this mythological stuff.'

'Oh?' Bryant turned to look at him. 'Do you have a better idea?'

'I wouldn't say it's better, but I do have a theory.'

'Would you care to share it with me?' Bryant jammed an absurdly large briar pipe in his mouth and waited for May to give him a light. He had misplaced his regular pipe. May would spend the next sixty years locating lost objects for his partner.

'Renalda's brother is implicated in the death of the tycoon's wife. Now he's missing, possibly here. Who would he want to strike at most? At Andreas himself. So he attacks the theatre to destroy his brother's empire.'

'But then he gains nothing financially.'

'What if it has nothing to do with financial benefit, but is simple revenge?' May leaned on the balustrade, watching the red fireboats pumping water.

'Why would he have waited until now to take action?' Bryant checked his watch. 'I have to find Andreas. He can't be far from the theatre. Let's have him removed directly to the unit for questioning, show him we mean business.'

'That's more like it.' May looked up at the dark, scudding sky. 'Listen.'

Bryant cocked an ear. 'What? I can't hear anything.'

'Neither can I.' May grinned. 'Wonderful, isn't it?'

43

MERRY HELL

'I have no time to talk to you,' said Helena Parole impatiently. 'When we hit our half-hour call in around one hundred and thirty minutes, the backstage area is sealed until the performance ends. Only the audience can enter and leave. Have you ever been backstage before the start of a first public performance? It's a nightmare, people running in every direction, and there's barely a corridor more than two feet wide in the entire building. You saw the understage area. Imagine it filled with actors waiting for their stage-lift cues. As far as I know, nobody's heard from Petrovic. Got a snout?'

John May dug a packet of Three Bells from his jacket and offered her one.

'We're not supposed to smoke back here either.' She flicked a cigarette between crimson lips. 'All these timber struts. But with buildings ablaze all around us these days, what's the difference? God knows there are enough fire buckets scattered about. Geoffrey fell over one by the grave trap and nearly broke his ankle. Quite how a bucket of sand is supposed to put out a raging fire is anyone's guess. The truth of the matter is, anyone caught understage would be fried alive. A theatre's no place for claustrophobics.' She rubbed smoke from her eye. 'This tastes like it's got vegetable shavings in it.'

'Mr Bryant got them for me.' He examined the strangely misregistered lettering on the packet. 'I don't think they're kosher, not at a shilling for twenty. He has a theory that Petrovic's abduction is somehow separate from the killings. You can't think of anything that would single her out?'

'She filled in the same employment forms as everyone else. We don't check their backgrounds. Right now, we're grateful to find anyone at all. I suppose it's possible she had another identity. Have you seen her rent book?'

'Yes, and I spoke to her landlord about her references. Nothing unusual there.'

'You know we have a full house tonight. How are you going to keep a check on the doors?'

'The only admittance to the auditorium is via the front of house. The ushers, bar staff and ticket tearers have to sign the book, and everyone else needs a ticket.'

'You've been around the building, you realize there are a thousand places to hide, and this maniac could be in any of them.'

'I know that,' admitted May. 'We can't search them all. We've only been allocated two extra PCs. Andreas Renalda insists that he's keeping the production open whatever happens.'

'I'd better get going. He'll be here soon.' Parole finished the cigarette and checked her watch. 'God, these things burn up fast. What do you make of him?'

'Seems very determined. A bit of a cold fish.'

'I just wish he'd keep his distance. He thinks we don't hear him, but we do. He gives me the creeps, thumping about in his leg-irons like the captain of an ancient vessel. This isn't just a financial enterprise for him, it's more personal.'

'What do you mean?'

'He's had one of the entresol dressing rooms converted into a sort of chapel, and spends twenty minutes in it before he watches rehearsals. We're short of space here, John—may I call you John?—there's nowhere to put anything and there aren't enough dressing rooms, yet he's had one turned into a shrine. Doesn't count as normal behaviour in my book.'

'Is there bad feeling about that?'

'About that and everything else, Charles's death in particular. It was the one event witnessed by several people, and it's got everyone disturbed. You try standing in a dark corridor with ten other performers waiting to go on, and see if the atmosphere doesn't get to you. They fairly race out of here after rehearsals. No one wants to be the last to leave.'

'Who'll be last out once you start the run?'

'Elspeth, I suppose, although she's FOH, so actually it would be Stan Lowe at the stage door. He can't leave until the last of the backstage staff has gone. After the evening performances the actors invite friends up to the dressing rooms, but they're supposed to be out by eleven. Now that the run is starting, they'll go over to the Green Room, one of the actors' clubs off the Strand, or to Macready's in Covent Garden. You have to be an Equity member or working in a current production to get into such places. Absolute dens of vice, but I suppose they're a lot more convivial than staying here, drinking out of chipped mugs as the heating goes off.'

'Well, I'll let you get on,' said May. He stopped at the top of the stairs and turned. 'My colleague wanted me to ask you—the statue on top of the building, in the centre of the roof. You don't happen to know who it is?'

'I think she's a Greek goddess. There's some kind of odd story about her. She's holding a flaming torch, but she's not supposed to be, or something. There was an accident of some kind. I think she's bad luck.'

'You're superstitious, then?'

'Me? God, no. If you want to know about the statue you could try the archivist, although I think he's moved out of London for the duration.'

'Do you know where I can find him?'

'Mr Cruickshank has a desk in the archive room, although you'll have trouble spotting it. It's buried under newspaper clippings and old building plans. You should speak to him before you start moving anything. Elspeth might have his new address.'

'Thanks.' He paused on the stair. 'And good—'

'Don't say it!' yelled Helena. 'No whistling, no well-wishing.'

'I thought you weren't superstitious.'

'I'm not,' she said defiantly, 'but obviously there are limits.'

'I'm glad we were able to run you to ground. Have a look at this.' Bryant smoothed the creases from the article Summerfield had penned for *The Times* and slid it across the table to Andreas Renalda. The tycoon was furious at being brought directly to the unit instead of being taken to his Highgate home to change for the theatre. He peered angrily out of the dusty windows as if searching for a means of escape. May called his attention to the document.

'What is this?' the tycoon asked, gingerly touching the edges of the pages.

'A history of your family,' Bryant explained. 'You were reluctant to talk about your background, so I took the liberty of digging it out.'

Renalda flicked the sheets aside in disgust. 'We sued over this damned article. There were dozens, and we took every one to court. They were appearing all over the world.'

'You won this battle without going to court. The piece was never published.'

'It was the last thing our shareholders would have needed to read about at that time, a public washing of dirty laundry. This man had no right to write about my father, but at least he was one of the few to suggest my brother's guilt. Things were very difficult for me personally. I had lost my beloved wife, the light of my life.'

'You still believe she was murdered by your brother?'

'He said he took her out dancing as a gesture of reconciliation. My Elissa, out dancing, with her husband away on business! In our culture, this is not done. She did not know the island, and she had hardly ever had a drink in her life. They passed the evening in a taverna, and at midnight they walked along the harbour wall together. Ask anyone in the town and they will tell you that my wife was deliberately drowned. Every night, before I go to bed, I blame myself for being away in Athens on a trip that I could have easily delegated to one of my staff. Minos was waiting for me to leave.'

'But you have no proof.'

'There are some things in life you do not need proof to see.'

'You don't think that your wife—'

'Mr Bryant, I hope you are not about to suggest that she was in any way attracted to my brother. That would be an insult to her memory.'

'May I ask how your mother died?'

'In hospital, from cancer.'

'You've never feared for your own life?'

'Of course not.'

'I don't understand. If you're convinced that your brother is capable of murder, why are you so sure that you're safe?'

'My mother let everyone know that her religion protected me. Minos believed in the old gods enough to avoid angering them. Now I think I have answered all your questions.'

'But you,' persisted Bryant, 'do you really believe in the old gods?'

'It is how I was raised. I would sit in the cliff garden and see my ancient protectors seated all around myself and my mother.'

'And do they still protect you?'

'Of course. The events of my life are beyond my control, just as yours are. I must get to the theatre.'

'I'm sorry to have kept you.' Bryant rose to his feet. 'I was wondering...'

'Yes?'

'I'm fascinated by your mythological beliefs. I wonder if you'd care to take lunch with me tomorrow. The theatre has no performance, and you can tell me more about them.'

'I don't think that would be a good idea, Mr Bryant. I'm a little too old to fall for such obvious tricks, don't you think?'

'I assure you, I intended only to be sociable.' Bryant was flustered, mortified.

'It's all right, I suppose in your clumsy way you mean well.' He gave a sour laugh. 'You have a lot to learn, I think. I can take care of myself without the help of the damned police. I worry more for my friends at the Palace. My theatre is under attack, my staff are being killed and injured.' He struggled to his feet and swayed so violently that for a moment Bryant thought he was going to topple backwards. 'The Palace is being assaulted by Christian moralists, your courts are trying to close me down before we even open and the press is denouncing me as a filthy foreign pervert out to corrupt the innocent, plucky islanders. This is no time to attack cherished national institutions. Well, we shall see who survives and who falls, but I know one thing: the show will go on, come hellfire, Blitz or the Lord Chamberlain. If people think I am the devil, we shall have a merry Hell.'

And with that declaration of war, Andreas Renalda swept from the cluttered office with as much force as his crippled legs could muster.

'Interesting,' said Bryant after the magnate had been helped back into his car. 'He's hiding something about this brother of his. But he'll only answer direct questions, and I'm clearly not asking the right ones.'

'Then let's run with your instincts,' said May. 'Take a chance.'

Bryant shook the idea from his head. 'We have to uncover the truth about Minos before we start accusing anyone. Come on, it's time for curtain up.'

44

LOOKING OUTSIDE

'They've put together an e-fit of your culprit.' Liberty DuCaine waited for the printer to finish running off a hard copy of the monochrome JPEG, then passed it over to May and Longbright. The annexe of Kentish Town station was experiencing an eerie lull in the battle-stations activity that had been surging around them all day. Officers sat making quiet phone calls, wearily nursing plastic cups of coffee.

'What's it based on?' asked Longbright, examining the face on the desk.

'A couple of bouncers from the Camden Palace were walking past Mornington Crescent tube station, heading for their car. They saw this geezer come out of the door to the unit just before the bomb went off.'

'These things are about as much use as old Identikit posters,' May complained. 'He looks like a character from a video game. How can you identify someone from that?'

He studied the picture more carefully. It was the blurred face of an old man with staring alien eyes and abnormally large teeth. This wasn't Bryant's murderer. May was sure that the man seen loitering outside his flat had also stolen his partner's dental records. The infuriating part of it was, May knew his identity. But they had met only once, and had not seen each other in over sixty years. You could study the face of an old man and find no vestiges of his youth.

DuCaine's e-fit bore no resemblance to that wartime killer. Time wrought great changes. How would he ever recognize such a person now?

'These two guys couldn't even agree on how he was dressed,' warned DuCaine. 'They'd been smoking a bit, and when I say a bit, I mean a lot.'

'This looks more like Arthur than our mad bomber. So much for technology. Did nobody see him turn up at the unit?'

'If they did, they haven't come forward.'

'What about the CCTV cameras?' asked Longbright.

'Nothing on that side of the road. We've got a shot from a supermarket camera further along the pavement, someone standing outside the entrance. Trouble is, the time lapse on the footage lets him simply disappear. All we've got is a distant figure in a grey coat.'

'You couldn't tell if he was carrying anything?'

'Not from the back. Nothing identifiable at all. I'm sorry.'

'That's all right,' sighed May, running his hands through his white hair. 'We weren't expecting a breakthrough. I'm told they want to use you here for a few days.'

'Yeah, I was going to ask you about that. I mean, the unit's got nowhere to work from, and they've got all this shit going on. Kids running around, taking each other out with activated replicas.' DuCaine felt guilty, but he was too valuable a resource to waste. His restless energy needed to be applied, and May wasn't about to hold him back.

'Someone around here is bringing Ingram Model Ten sub-machine guns in from the U.S. and converting them into working firearms. It's the accessory of choice for would-be gangsta rappers. I've got some contacts, I can help—'

'There's no need to explain,' interrupted May. 'Do what you have to do. Longbright and I will figure this out.'

'Well, what do we do now?' asked Longbright as they walked towards the tube station.

'Something I should have done earlier,' May replied. 'I have to start thinking like Arthur. If he could do it, track down someone after six long decades, why can't I?'

'How do you propose to do that?' How much weight he's lost, she thought. This could be the last thing he ever does.

May thought for a minute. 'When I first met Arthur, he'd already suffered a tragedy. I didn't know it at the time, of course. It was your mother who told me what had happened. Later I realized it was what made him look beyond rational explanations. It drove him to solicit the advice of outsiders. In a way, it was what made him the man he became. It locked him out of the normal world.'

'You make it sound almost like a good thing,' said Longbright, stopping.

'Sometimes it almost was.' May gave a rueful smile. 'It could also be disastrous. That's why he needed me. To balance him.' He gave the detective sergeant a gentle pat on the elbow. 'I've been too sensible for too many years. It's time I learned the lesson he was always trying to teach me. Come on.'

45

IN THE DEVIL'S COMPANY

The audience was resplendent in evening dress, but most members were carrying gas-mask boxes. They were as Helena Parole had predicted, culturally more diverse, livelier and younger than the lethargic Home Counties brigade who usually attended operettas—perhaps reflecting that this was not in any sense a classical production. Eurydice's opening striptease and virtually naked seduction by an outrageously priapic Aristaeus saw to that.

The single intermission occurred between the second and third tableaux, and listening to the exhilarated hubbub in the building's bars, Bryant judged the production to be a hit—more, a sensation. The crowd made him feel claustrophobic. He descended the grand staircase and wandered out into the lobby. The bow tie he had donned for the occasion was strangling him. Few playgoers had ventured down here because the night was so cold. He nodded to PCs Atherton and Crowhurst, who were meant to be acting as security on the entrance but found themselves holding back a ragged line of irate demonstrators. Rain was falling hard from dark, low clouds, and that meant a cloak of safety for the theatre.

'We're going to need more men if this goes on every night, sir,' warned Crowhurst.

'They've got their own security people coming in on Monday.' Bryant studied the placards pinned to the steel barriers. BAN THIS PAGAN SHOW NOW. THOU SHALT HAVE NO OTHER GOD

BUT ME. And more peculiarly, LESS LUST THROUGH LESS MEAT AND SITTING. This makeshift placard was displayed by a soaked young man in a corduroy cap who looked as though he would rather be somewhere else, preferably in a pub.

A mobile anti-aircraft gun had been placed on the opposite corner for the last two days, but now this reminder of danger from the skies had been moved away to higher ground. The theatre had been banned from spotlighting its exterior, and was forced to content itself with displaying a large OPENING TONIGHT! banner.

'They're all out this evening,' sighed Bryant. 'I'm surprised we haven't got any Band of Hope ladies.' Temperance women were known to turn up at any public event to extol the evils of alcoholism.

'There were a couple chucking eggs here earlier, sir,' said Atherton. 'One lady punched Mr Woolf on the nose and called him a dirty darkie. None of 'em has gone in to the show, they just heard that saucy bit about it on the wireless. You'd think they'd have something better to do with their time.'

Bryant strolled over to the box office, where Elspeth was closing up for the night.

'Have you heard from Miss Petrovic yet?' she asked anxiously, hauling a bagful of leeks from behind her counter. She had permed her hair into an unflattering helmet of Medusan curls for the occasion.

'Not a word.'

'I do hope she's all right. There's been talk about sea mines being dropped by parachute down the Old Kent Road. Sea mines! Apparently they blow up sideways and take out all the houses. I feel sorry for anyone over there tonight.'

'It seems quiet in town,' said Bryant, 'what with the rain.'

'I'm worried they'll shut the production down. The Archbishop of Canterbury says we're all going to go to Hell, and that the only practical solution is to pray.'

'Oh, he always says that,' said Bryant. 'The moment he finds something people enjoy, he's on the wireless faster than a cat up a Belgian, telling us all to stop doing it at once. Is everyone accounted for from your side of the house?'

'It would appear so, although I can only check the ushers and FOH staff. You'd have to go back to the stage door and see

Stan about the sign-in book, but I think they've got a full complement.'

'No unfamiliar faces, then?'

'No, we know everyone. Mr Mack had to locate two more stage-hands because a lot of the scenery has to be shifted manually. They're a father and son team who know the understage area well. He bribed them away from the Duke of York's.' She locked the box office and pocketed the keys. 'We're having drinks up in the balcony green room after the performance. You're welcome to join us.'

'I thought everybody had to be out quickly.'

'Yes, but it's traditional on opening night.'

'You know, I've walked around this place for a week now,' said Bryant, 'and the running of it is still a mystery to me.'

'Some people never get used to it. I've been at the Palace most of my life and I still get lost. I never venture down to the lower levels because the lights are scattered all over. You have to keep trying different switches as you make your way across, but half of them don't work, and you need to know where they are in the first place. Then of course there's the well. Everyone knows it's hazardous so they just stay away from the area.'

'Are there any parts of the building you haven't visited?'

'I've never been to the upper gantry levels, and certainly not to the grid. You can only access that via a drop-ladder, and I've no head for heights. Hardly anyone has been up there in years, but a couple of the stagehands had to get up there to refurbish the block-and-tackle system. You forget how big the Palace is. It's hemmed by three roads and a circus, all exactly as it was when Mr Sullivan was here.' A bell sounded above them. 'That's my signal. I'm not keeping the box office open once the second act starts, no matter what Mr Renalda says.'

'He wanted you to keep it open?'

'Until the end of the performance and for twenty minutes beyond. I told him absolutely not. We never have in the past, and he has no authority to change my hours because we work for different companies.'

'Of course, you're with the theatre management, not the company production,' remembered Bryant. 'Tell me about the pass doors again. You said there are two of them.'

'Yes, but as I explained, we lost the keys to the left-hand one. The right side still works, but not many people use it. There's no need, when you can go around to the stage door and access the backstage area that way.'

'But you'd have to pass at least one permanently posted member of staff to do so,' said Bryant thoughtfully. 'Who has a key to the pass door?'

'There are two, but they have to be signed out by Geoffrey Whittaker. He keeps hold of both of them.'

'Are you aware of him signing them out at all?'

'Not to my knowledge, but you'd better check with him. Are you going to watch the rest of the show?'

'Thank you, I saw it earlier in the week.'

'Yes,' Elspeth agreed, 'but you haven't seen it with the applause in.'

'My partner's prowling around the building with his henchmen, so I suppose I could spend a little time in the devil's company after seeing Mr Whittaker.'

'You can slip into the rear stalls box,' she said, leading the way. 'It used to be a cigar booth before it was converted to hold chairs. The sightlines are pretty poor because the ceiling of the dress circle cuts so low. We didn't open it tonight because Geoffrey's storing stuff from dressing room two in it. We'll have to, though, if *Orpheus* proves popular.'

'I think that's a pretty safe bet, don't you?'

'It's bad luck to discuss it before the reviews appear, but yes, I have a feeling we're in for a very long run indeed. Mr Renalda will be able to make good on his promise.'

'What promise is that?'

'Why, to run on right through the war.' Elspeth looked at him oddly. 'I thought you knew. He came round to tell us that he's done a deal with someone in the Home Office, not to let the bombs close us down. It's going to be good for public morale. "Britain Can Take It" and all that. That's why the Lord Chamberlain won't touch us. Apparently, Miss Parole will cover up a couple of the girls, take out some of the ruder lines, but we'll stay open right through to the bitter end, barring a direct hit.' She smiled nervously. 'You could say it's the first time theatre folk have ever prayed not to have a hit.'

46

FALSE IDOL

'As you can imagine, I'm rather busy,' said Geoffrey Whittaker, unsnagging his cardigan from a nail and racing ahead. 'Can't Madeline help you?'

'It's you I need to talk to,' said May, ducking beneath a low pipe as they passed along the narrow corridor at the head of the orchestra pit.

'It's the assistant stage manager's job to know everything I know,' Whittaker called over his shoulder. 'Mind out.' They passed a set of ten vicious-looking steel costume hooks, part of a quick-change area that had not been altered since the theatre's construction.

'This won't take a minute. I was wondering about the keys to the pass doors. I understand you're the only person who gives them out.'

'That's right. The left door got painted over, and then the lock broke. It was never much used because the company office and the stalls-level dressing rooms are to the right.'

'I need to know who you've given the keys out to this week.'

'That's easy enough. I can tell you from memory. Miles Stone asked for one a couple of days ago.'

The day the boy fell from the balcony, Bryant noted. 'How long did he have it?'

'A couple of hours. He wanted to store a suitcase, and it was too heavy to take the long way around. Helena borrowed the other one because she was shifting stuff out of dressing room two to make room for Mr Renalda's memorial thing. Sometimes it's quicker to do a job yourself than wait for the stagehands to do it.'

'How long did she have the key?' asked Bryant.

'She's still got it, as far as I know,' Whittaker replied as he vanished through an arch. 'She wears the trousers around here.'

Bryant stepped back and trod on Biddle's foot. 'Do you need me here, Mr Bryant?' Biddle asked. He looked very fed up.

'While you're still under the unit's jurisdiction, Mr Biddle, you remain on duty until we're through. Do we understand each other?'

'How can I help when you haven't told us what we're looking for?' asked Biddle angrily. 'I'd be more use filing DS Forthright's interview slips.'

'I realize it's boring for you.' The boy's attitude exasperated Bryant. 'Perhaps you'd rather be sitting in front of a nice big pile of paperwork. A lot of our tasks are the same as you get in any police unit, foot-slog stuff, standing around and waiting. It requires a sharp eye for detail, a good memory and an ability to judge character. But we have the power to leap off the rails of traditional thought and head into darkness. Once you've done it a few times you'll be hooked. Now go down to the floor below and watch out for anything unusual.' Considering there was a ten-foot-high three-headed purple dog god growling on the stage above their heads, it was a little like asking a clown to keep an eye out for any funny business.

Eurydice was imprisoned in Pluto's palace with her gaoler, John Styx. Jupiter had called for the three judges of Hades, and set about questioning Cerberus, Hell's doorkeeper. The gigantic six-eyed dog owned by Hecate was a mechanical device winched up onto the stage in three sections that slotted together as they met. It was a feat of engineering to rival the construction of a Spitfire, but with less practical purpose.

John May scanned the darkened auditorium through the velvet curtains and spotted Andreas Renalda seated in the royal box with several middle-aged men in smart black suits, who were busy ogling the chorus girls' exposed thighs. The front rows were filled with corpulent broadsheet critics taking notes, writing without removing their eyes from the stage. The orchestra performed beneath their steel mesh cage, a precautionary measure taken because the apron had been brought out to the edge of the pit, and some of the dancers came very close to the edge, much to the pleasure of the woodwind section.

May left the corridor and made his way to the rear of the stalls. He could see Bryant's tufted head poking over the parapet of the converted cigar kiosk.

'I thought you were keeping an eye on the backstage area,' Bryant whispered.

'There's nowhere to stand without being in the way. Did somebody check the fly wires on Senechal's replacement?' In the next part of the tableau, Jupiter was due to turn himself into a bluebottle in order to squeeze through the keyhole into Eurydice's cell. This involved him being swung out over the heads of the audience on a rig.

'I mentioned it to Geoffrey Whittaker this morning. They're using a double rig with a second set of cables attached. Did you hear about Senechal's wife suing the company for negligence?'

'Can't say I blame her. Gladys said she'd get in touch if she had any news on Petrovic. The girl Phyllis is adamant that she's been abducted. I'd like to know how her kidnapper got in and out of the house.'

'The same way he got in and out of here,' Bryant muttered. 'Maybe he's a magician.'

Onstage, there was a fiery explosion as Jupiter vanished through the floor and reappeared as a rather overweight insect. He rose from the ground and gracefully swung out across the front row of the audience, his wires glimpsed in the beam of the spotlights. Bryant held his breath, half expecting something terrible to happen, but the god made it safely back, flapping across to down right in order to duet with his lover. Bryant watched John Styx exiting the stage left centre with a silver hoop of prison keys in his hand.

'Tell me, who's got the keys to the top-floor offices?'

May thought for a moment. 'You'll probably find them in the box in the company manager's office. Why?'

'Something I've been meaning to do,' Bryant whispered, bypassing May's question. 'I'll use the pass door to the lift, I'm not facing all those stairs with my ticker.'

'Can't you get Biddle to run up for you?'

'No, I have to find it myself. Hang on here and enjoy the show. It's nearly the end of the scene.' Bryant felt his way out of the booth as a swarm of human flies invaded the stage and buzzed into a sprightly chorus.

The curtain fell at the close of the tableau, and reopened as the applause died down. Now they were at Pluto's orgy on the banks of the Styx, and once again the stage had filled with cavorting golden-breasted women. There were worse things, May decided, than guarding a theatre on a cold winter's night.

Bryant tried the lights, but nothing worked on the top floor. The oppressive darkness increased his heart rate. He pushed open the door to the archive and shone his torch inside. Beneath the photographs and programmes he found Cruickshank's desk. Beside it were piled damp-swollen books of building plans, blueprints filled with intricate arabesques of the understage structures, technical designs for a mechanized age too complex and cluttered for practical use. Bryant wedged the torch between his knees and flipped through the volumes, setting them aside one after the other. Finally he came to the volume he had been hoping to find, the one containing details of the building's exterior.

There, at the pinnacle of the roof, was the statue and a set of accompanying notes. Her designation, the name that had eluded everyone, was Euterpe, and suddenly everything began to fall into place.

He had been fooled—who wouldn't have been?—by the flaming torch she held aloft, because it wasn't supposed to be there at all.

According to the typescript pinned beside the picture, the statue was a copy. The original figure had been removed by the impresario Émile Littler, who had wanted it for his garden, but it had been smashed to pieces on its journey. A replacement statue had been commissioned, but a mistake was made. Euterpe was holding a flaming torch instead of her traditional double flute. Bryant shook his head in wonder.

Euterpe, the Muse of lyric poetry. He found himself a sheet of paper and began hastily scribbling notes in the torchlight.

47

DEADLY DEPARTED

Euterpe and the flaming torch.

He recalled Bryant's theory about the statue as he made his way through the crowded Camden streets. Euterpe had survived the war and was still cemented in place on the roof of the Palace Theatre, over half a century later. Not much else was, when you looked around the city. The Palladian stucco, the elaborate wrought-iron railings, the secluded courtyards and mysterious alleyways in permanent shadow, the absurd flourishes that gave the metropolis its character had mostly been removed, demolished, stolen. Developers had reinvented the future so ruthlessly that the London of his youth had disappeared. Offices were revealed behind glass walls, as though they had to offer proof of their profitability to pedestrians. There was no room in the modern world for anything unnecessary. At least Camden hadn't changed as much as people said. The layout of the streets was exactly as he had always remembered it.

The rain had eased, but the damp air invaded his leg muscles and made walking a chore. May wondered if he was being followed by the fanged man. He checked the pavement behind him. Camden was filled with students and tourists wandering between the market stalls. Every tribe and fashion was represented; nose-rings, navel piercings, velvet hats, leather jackets, Goths and God-Squaders,

skinheads and Sex Pistolettes. A permanent carnival atmosphere
had settled across the area. May was the oldest person on the street.
Outsized sculptures of a spacecraft, a tank, a Dr Marten's boot, a
rocking chair were suspended from the first floors of the high-street
shops like toys discarded by a giant child. Camden Lock survived as
a polyglot arrangement of stalls selling clothing, jewellery, incense,
noodles and furniture. The pavements were dirty, noisy, chaotic,
but alive in a way that the poplar-lined avenues of the suburbs
could never be.

May felt bad about dismissing Longbright, but this had to be
done alone. He stopped in front of the door leading to the flat
above the World's End pub. A chunk of floorboard had been nailed
over the letter box, giving the entrance an air of dereliction. A
scuffed steel plaque on the lintel read:

COVEN OF ST JAMES THE ELDER
North London Division
No Hawkers or Circulars

Below this, a photocopied sheet read:

Suppliers of Equipment to the Spiritualism Trade
Wholesale Only

The woman who answered his knock had a square, friendly face
framed by ragged curls of bleached hair. She appeared to have
missed when applying her lipstick, and missed again with her eye
shadow, so that she looked more like a confused plump poodle than
a white witch.

'John, thank God, I was beginning to worry,' Maggie Armitage
cried, propelling herself into his arms and hugging him fiercely. 'I'm
sorry I didn't come to Arthur's funeral but the vibrations would
have overpowered me. Isn't it awful? I mean, I know it's a great adventure for him, navigating a pathway into the celestial beyond, but
I'll miss our monthly piss-ups. Sorry about the front door. Drunks
kept being sick through the letter box. Don't talk to me about
care in the community. Come on up.' She led the way into a tilting

dark passage. 'Neema wanted to host a leave-taking ceremony for Arthur, but I couldn't bear the idea. She's a Muslim and I like to use dry sherry in the ritual, so we fell out.'

May followed the little witch into her front room, a riot of busy purple seventies wallpaper, battered Formica counters and plastic orange lamps. The thunder of a heavy metal band playing in the pub below was shaking the crockery in the kitchenette.

'What exactly is a leave-taking?'

'The idea is you summon the departing spirit with madrigals and conduct a ceremony to send it on its journey, but Neema's Yamaha badly needs a service.'

'She rides a motorbike?'

'No, her electric organ. It sounds so awful that decent spirits won't answer its call any more. The last time she performed the ritual she summoned an Icelandic incubus, and we had to burn incense-soaked cloths to clear it out. Unfortunately, she also set fire to the sofa and we all nearly wound up on the other side. Flammable kapok. I called *Watchdog* and lodged a complaint.'

Maggie's amber necklaces rattled as she threw herself down into a broken-backed orange armchair. 'There are only five of us left, you know. We had a membership drive for the new millennium but it's dropped off.' She waved a dismissive hand in the direction of the street. 'You'd think that lot out there would be curious about spiritualism, but they're more interested in shopping. Olive, the lady who used to conduct our séances, had to pack it in because she can't get up the stairs. She only attends the Hendon branch now because they have a ramp. Nigel and Doris have both passed over, and unless I use a spirit guide I never get to see them.'

'Do you still have Edna Wagstaff's cat?' asked May, looking around for the Abyssinian.

'I use it as a doorstop,' Maggie admitted. 'I fear its days as a source of spiritual succour ended when it got the moth. Of course I can't throw it out, because I have nothing else to remember Edna by, and she doesn't answer the Call'—Maggie pointed at the cracked Tibetan bell that hung above the fireplace—'because she's a lost soul. Either that or she's gone deaf. You've lost a bit of weight. Are you dying?'

'God, I hope not.'

'God's not got much to do with it any more. You're not coping well without Arthur, are you?'

'I'll manage,' May replied wearily. 'Do you have anything to drink?'

'I just made tea. You can have a shot of whisky in it.'

'What brand?'

'PG Tips.' She made her way to the kitchenette and rinsed a mug. 'I suppose you want "closure". That's the buzzword these days, isn't it? When will people learn that there's no such thing? Life and death are open-ended. Everything begins and ends in the middle.'

'Not this time,' said May, accepting the mug. 'I know who killed Arthur. I just don't know where he is.'

'Perhaps I can help you there. Hang on a minute.' Maggie crossed to the window and shut the curtains. 'Did you remember what I asked for?'

'Here.' May withdrew a plastic bag from his overcoat pocket and emptied the contents onto the coffee table before him. 'You said bring something that belonged to him.'

'What is it?'

'A souvenir of our first case together. It belonged to a tortoise called Nijinsky.'

Maggie picked up the tortoise shell and peered through its leg holes. 'What did you do with the body?'

'I guess it just, you know, decomposed or something. Bryant was given the tortoise because it wouldn't hibernate in the theatre. It lived right through the war, although its nerves went towards the end.'

'It's a bit Steptoe-ish, but it'll have to do.' She lit a pair of candles and set them at either end of the tortoise's earthly remains. 'Rest your fingertips on one end of the shell.'

'Which end?'

'It doesn't matter.' She seated herself opposite and extended her fingers to touch the tortoise, then began breathing deeply through her nose.

'You think you can really contact him?' May could hardly believe that he was doing this, after all the times he had given his partner grief about believing in the afterlife.

'As long as it's an object he touched many times in the past.'

'Oh, he had many happy years with Nijinsky.'

'Good. Now shut up and let me concentrate.'

May watched in the half-light of the front room as Maggie rolled back her head and fell into a light trance. After a few minutes, she started snoring. May wondered whether he should wake her. He leaned forward and reached out his hand, but just as he was about to touch her, she spoke. 'Do you remember the first time we met, John? What a sceptic you were in those days?'

'I still am,' he whispered.

'I can't be right all the time.' Her eyes remained closed. 'But you—I was right about you. You always did have a very power-ful aura.'

'That's what Edna Wagstaff once told me.'

'So you do, and it's that which enables the sensitively gifted to read from you. You're a bit of a tuning fork.'

The wind breathed around the sashed windows, pulsing them in their casements. The sound faded from the street, and time was gently suspended. He remembered his first visit to the flat in 1942, when Maggie had just passed her nineteenth birthday. The sur-roundings were more elegant; she had fallen on hard times since then. But the flickering candles were the same, and so were the oddly shadowed corners of the room. He remembered the settling silence of the street outside, the suspiration of the wind, and the strange visions she had described to him.

'Oh, we're like hypnotists,' said Maggie, her slack mouth barely moving. 'Nobody believes in our effectiveness until some time later. You and I have known each other for over sixty years, and you still don't really have faith in me.'

'I wouldn't say—'

'There's no point in pretending, John. We're both far too old for that.' She drew a long breath, her trance state deepening. 'I am speaking now to the owner of this shell.' She tightened her eyelids, focusing her thoughts. 'He is dead, but present,' she explained casu-ally, 'here in the room with us, right now. He is standing between us, silently watching.'

A chill lifted the hairs on May's arms as he shifted uncomfortably in his seat. 'Arthur?' he called, searching the shadows.

'He can't speak, poor man, he's dead. His injuries are terrible to behold. I can barely bring myself to look. He's put on quite a bit of weight. There is something he must communicate, but it's so difficult, so painful...'

I must be daft, thought May, sitting in darkness above a London pub, listening to the ramblings of a mad old woman. This is doing neither of us any good.

'He wants to show you what he feels, but to do so he must cross the divide between the spiritual and physical worlds.' Maggie raised her arms in a creaky gesture of prestidigitation, like an elderly magician's assistant. May had started to rise from his armchair when, to the surprise of both, a low rumble shook the room. There was a sheen of metal in the kitchenette, and something shiny shot between them. When May glanced down, he realized he was looking at a kitchen knife, and that it was sticking out of his calf. He sat down sharply in shock.

'Why on earth would he become violent?' asked Maggie, examining the cut on May's leg. 'That's not like him at all.' She found a length of crêpe bandage and unrolled it over the cut. 'It's not deep,' she consoled, 'but I'm surprised by his behaviour. It's rare for spirits to react so violently.'

'It was the underground,' said May, wincing. 'Just a passing train. The vibration made your breadboard fall over and it flipped the knife from your drying rack, that's all. This bandage isn't very clean.'

'Well, you can choose a rational explanation if it makes you more comfortable.' Maggie poured herself a generous tot of Scotch. 'You never were much of a believer.'

'Not when the alternative is believing that my dead partner just tried to kill me. This is crazy. I'm being trailed by a man with werewolf fangs, and now this.' May rose and collected his coat. He saw what a mistake it had been to come here. 'Thanks for the drink.'

'But how are you going to find Arthur's killer?' Standing in the middle of the faded rug she suddenly looked lost and frail. This was how it would end for her, he realized, alone and bewildered, stranded by the world racing ever faster past her window.

'I'll think of a way,' he promised, taking a card from his wallet and handing it to her. 'That's my new address. If you need me, please call.'

It was the least Arthur would have done, he thought as he headed back down the stairs to daylight.

48

FALLING INTO HADES

'Hymn to Bacchus, we're missing someone, who's late?' Helena Parole checked behind her as she strained to hear the commentary on the backstage speaker. Pluto's party girls were arriving onstage in a hail of artificial flowers while the gods of Olympus and Hades caroused around them in various stages of undress.

'Goddesses are all on, Helena.' Harry checked the clipboard he kept on a string round his neck. 'The rest of the chorus are at the traps.' There were five narrow iron staircases on the first understage level leading to hatches on the stage, the centre of which was known as the grave trap because Hamlet had jumped into it during his graveyard scene. 'Everyone's present, they're just bunched up,' he explained.

'It's going to look awkward if the ends of UR and UL have to duck their heads exiting.' Helena checked the peephole at the rear of the stage, but the image it presented was so confusing that she could not tell who to move.

'Why didn't we see that in the technical?' she whispered over her shoulder to Madeline Penn, the ASM, who was trailing behind her with a pad and pencil, keeping notes on all the changes that would have to be made after the first night. 'Go and see if they've got the same problem over the other side, because there are a lot of flats coming down in a minute.'

The final tableau was long, and the full cast remained onstage throughout. Before they reached the cancan, additional chunks of scenery were to be brought up from under the stage and flown down from the flies. This left only a narrow strip for the girls to dance in, but the cancan was performed in a series of lines, with the girls yelling and pushing through each other, their ruffled dresses covering any awkward motions. It was a highly disciplined routine that was designed to give a look of wild, spontaneous sexuality.

Helena knew which of her dancers were weak, and had placed them in the second line. She was hoping that the attention of the audience would be focused on the bare white thighs of the girls and the high-cut French knickers they were wearing instead of traditional British bloomers. She knew that the reception accorded Offenbach's finale at the Gaîté-Lyrique in 1874 had never been topped, but she was hoping to beat it tonight.

Now Cupid, Eurydice, Jupiter, Diana, Orpheus and Pluto were onstage with assorted gods, goddesses and chorus members as the fiery crimson walls of Hades, great tilting shards of fractured glass, rose in panels, segmenting them off into different parts of the stage, ready for the revolve to begin its rotation as Orpheus commenced his ascent.

Sidney Biddle had started his tour of the building, working from the roof downwards. He pointed his torch up at the ladders leading to the grid, but could see little apart from a confusion of ironwork, suspended steel girders and cable drums. A pair of stagehands were balanced on rails in the gloom, listening for their cue beside the drum and shaft mechanism. Several more were waiting on the sides of the carpenter's bridge at the top of the three gantry levels, uplit in yellow and pink, like characters from a French Impressionist painting.

At this height the combined sound of the singers and orchestra passed upwards through the distorting baffles of the theatre's fifty-year-old mechanisms, creating strange discords that vibrated the cablework and hummed forlornly in the grid, dislodging ancient cobwebs.

Biddle walked down a floor to the area behind the balcony, past the offices to the fly and loading galleries. The scene was the same here: staff waited for cues, immobile, then burst into sudden movement for a few seconds before returning smartly to their positions. It surprised him that the backstage personnel were as disciplined and concentrated as the performers. He stayed out of the main backstage area, away from the gantries; he had no designated position to occupy, and was in the way wherever he stood. Consequently, he found himself relegated to the corridors and passages, unable to see much of the stage or the audience. He longed to be away from the whole rigmarole, to be useful somewhere, in an office of order and precedence.

To the right-hand side of the balcony, he could see the floor's electrical engineer watching for cues, and, for want of something better to do, went to join him.

'How much longer to the end of the act?' Biddle whispered.

The engineer held his forefinger to his lips, checked the stage and counted off fifteen minutes. 'Including encores,' he mouthed.

Sidney sighed and leaned back against the wall, frustrated.

Arthur Bryant pushed his unruly fringe from his eyes and folded the paper into the top pocket of his overcoat. He redirected the torch and shoved the catalogues of drawings back in their places. After the death of Orpheus at the hands of the Maenads, his severed head prophesied until it became an oracle more famous than that of Apollo at Delphi, at which point the sun god bade him stop. His limbs were gathered up and buried by his mother's sisters, and his lyre was placed in the heavens as a constellation, so that his life began and ended at the same point in a great cycle.

Bryant was angry with himself for failing to recognize the symbolism earlier. He reached the door of the archive room and tried to open it. As he attempted to do so, he caught a glimpse of an angry white face in the gap. Someone on the other side wrenched the door shut and turned the great brass key. Footsteps thumped away along the hall. He pulled on the door, but the lock was set in thick oak and remained immovable.

He ran through to the adjoining chamber, but it contained no exit, only a half-boarded window that looked down to the street four floors below. With his heart thudding erratically in his chest, he watched as the torch beam flickered and began to fade.

John Styx took Eurydice's hand as Orpheus led them through the labyrinth of Hell. In front of the group, the earth's surface beckoned in the form of the single piercing beam of a par lamp, a lighting effect used to simulate daylight. At their head stood Public Opinion, Valerie Marchmont's face concealed behind a grotesque mask of tragedy. The procession walked forward against the revolve, appearing to climb towards the surface, as Public Opinion warned Orpheus not to look back for fear of losing his wife for ever.

To John May's mind, Eve Noriac was looking worried. He was not familiar with this part of the production, but even from the side of the stalls he could tell that something was going wrong. Eurydice stopped and nervously tried to pull free of John Styx's hand. May followed her eyeline up to the flies, but the gantries were concealed by the lurid decorative border that stood in for a proscenium arch.

At that moment, Jupiter was goaded into action, and sent a thunderbolt, in the form of an electrically ignited flash, across the stage. Orpheus looked back and Eurydice, now on her mark above the grave trap, vanished in a mushroom of white smoke. The scene changed as Eurydice—in fact a life-sized puppet cast from her nude body—was seen falling back to Hell, and a pair of great curving skycloths were flown down by the same drum and shaft device that hauled up the backcloths.

As he watched it swing lower, May realized that not all of Orpheus's group had moved clear of the revolve. Public Opinion, with her great trailing skirt, was still on the turning disc. The edge of the skycloth, weighted with a steel rod, dropped down sharply, moving towards Valerie Marchmont. Before May could do anything, it had swung down to her face, shattering the china tragedy mask she wore and yanking her off the stage like Eurydice's doll, but the audience noticed nothing because now the long-awaited cancan dancers were pouring on, screaming and high-kicking their way onto the extended runway of the stage.

May ducked out of the stalls' side entrance and ran towards the pass door, but it was shut tight. He hammered on it until someone pulled the handle on the other side, then pushed his way through to the rear of the stage. Behind the fallen skycloth, Marchmont lay on her back, her skull smashed through by the iron pole. Blood pumped from her severed carotid artery across the floor to the rear wall, pouring down into the run-offs that led to the main drain.

May looked around for Sidney Biddle and saw the young officer scaling his way along the iron-rung ladders that led between the first and second gantry levels above the stage.

Sidney had seen something from the corner of his eye, a blurred bluish figure strobing beneath the coloured lenses of the lights, but as he scrambled across one of the stage bridges, feeling it sway beneath his weight, he suddenly lost his sense of direction. The stage lighting distorted shadows, throwing them at mad angles across the scrims.

The dancers were screaming and whooping beneath him, a shimmering mass of white flesh and crimson silk. Above his head a shape shifted, knocking over a coil of cable, sending it unravelling down the side of the wing. Biddle ran forward, but the end of the bridge was blocked with equipment. There was no way of reaching the far side. He lowered himself over the bridge and swung his feet out until they touched the next gantry. Once he had established a foothold, he threw the upper half of his body forward and stretched out his arms, but even as he did so he felt the bridge beneath his feet kick away beneath his police-issue boots.

His right hand seized the railing of the gantry, but his left missed. He swung violently out above the stage.

As he hung from the bridge, his fingers slipping slowly from the rusty iron rail, the figure above him disappeared, a wraith returning to a realm of prismatic red and blue shadows.

The muscles in Sidney's arm betrayed him, and with a cry he fell to the level below.

49

THE PROTECTION OF THE GODS

The house lights were fully turned up in the stalls, giving the auditorium a shabby, melancholic air. Runcorn had taped off the rear of the stage. Wyman, a photographer from West End Central, was testing his flashgun on the blood spatters covering the backstage floor. The two halves of Public Opinion's white mask lay cracked in a coagulated crimson pool. It was now five minutes past midnight, and all unnecessary members of staff had been dismissed.

In true theatrical tradition the show had not been interrupted by the death of Public Opinion. The main purpose of the continuation was to buy the unit time before the news spread through the audience. Valerie Marchmont's body had been removed through the royal entrance on Shaftesbury Avenue and taken to University College Hospital in an unmarked van, the fourth they had used in a week.

'Has anybody heard from Arthur yet?' asked May anxiously.

'We've got him, John. He says somebody shut him in one of the rooms upstairs.' Gladys Forthright had slipped PC Crowhurst's rubber police cloak over her sweater. She had put her own coat down in the rush to help Biddle, and had lost it among the racks of costumes that hung like shucked carapaces behind the stage. Biddle had fallen onto a pile of folded backcloths but had split the cartilage in his left ankle, the tissue swelling so quickly that the theatre's medical officer had been forced to cut off his sock and boot with the blade of a pocket knife.

Arthur Bryant appeared to be in a state of great anxiety. 'I got locked in the archive room,' he said excitedly. 'He struck again, didn't he?'

May pointed to the rear of the stage. 'Public Opinion. Surprise meeting with a steel pole, fractured skull, killed instantly.'

'In front of everyone? How could that have happened?'

'One of the backdrops—dropped.'

'It came down right on cue,' said Mr Mack. 'Weren't our fault.'

Helena looked distraught and ready to sink a bottle of Scotch. 'The revolve should have carried her clear, but it halted suddenly. She was the last one off the stage.'

'One of the skycloth rods slipped out of its mooring,' May explained. 'It went right through her head, like a spoon hitting a soft-boiled egg, punched her backwards into the wall behind. Most of her brains are still on the bricks.'

'She must have felt the revolve stop. Why didn't she move forward?'

'Because the procession had to file offstage in a single column,' Harry explained.

'It's not my bloody fault,' exclaimed Helena, furiously digging through her bag for cigarettes. 'There wasn't enough room to take everyone off any faster. Getting into the wings is a tricky business. You have to wait your turn. Bloody, *bloody* hell, who's got a cigarette?'

'What happened to our cuckoo?' Bryant indicated Biddle, who was lying across two stalls seats having his ankle fitted into a wooden splint.

'Fell off the blooming gantry,' said Biddle. 'I saw someone standing near the drum cable looking down, and tried to reach him.'

May turned to his partner. 'What were you doing in the archive room?'

'I had an idea,' said Bryant conspiratorially. 'I need to discuss it with you in private. I think I have enough to make an arrest.'

'You found someone up there?'

'In a manner of speaking. Greek legends percolate through our lives and live in our collective subconscious. You'd think knowing about the misfortunes of the gods would keep us from repeating their mistakes and go some way towards protecting us, but we're too blind.'

'What in God's name are you talking about?' May exploded, shocking everyone. 'We've just had another death, that's four to date, with one more missing presumed dead and one of our men injured, and you're lecturing me on Greek mythology?'

'You know my conclusions are, ah, well, tangentially approached,' stammered Bryant, taken aback by his partner's outburst. 'I can't follow your operational procedures, I warned you about that.' He blinked steadily, as though facing bright daylight for the first time, and scrunched his hat onto his head.

'Where are you going?' May demanded to know.

'To talk to—to—find out if I'm—I know who's on the list, the death list. There are still another four to die, they must die before the thing can be broken, that's the whole point.' He turned, holding on to the back of the seat in front of him. 'I can't believe you have no faith in me.'

'I didn't say that, but if you knew then why the hell didn't you do something?'

'How could I?' cried Bryant. 'I was locked in the blasted room upstairs. I couldn't get to the stage.'

'Wait,' said May, 'let me get someone to go with you.'

'No, leave me alone, I'll be fine.' Bryant turned, stopped in confusion, then walked off up the aisle.

'John, go after him,' urged Forthright. 'Just call in when you get to wherever he's going. I'll clear up here and get the archive door dusted for prints.'

May caught up with his partner on the steps outside. The rain had stopped and the night had turned bitter. Their breath distilled in the frozen air. 'I'm sorry I shouted at you, Arthur, it's just that...' He tried to give shape to his frustration. 'How can I be expected to help if you don't tell me what's inside your brain? Do you appreciate how dangerous things have become around here?'

'You'll think I'm mad,' said Bryant quietly, leading the way across Cambridge Circus, 'but I've got proof. If you believe in evil, you have to believe in devils. I mean the kind that live in your mind, the ones that are put there by people with the best intentions.' He unlocked the door of the Wolseley from the Bow Street car pool and levered himself inside, reaching across to pull open the passenger handle.

'I'll come with you, but let me drive,' May insisted. He could hear his partner's chest wheezing. Bryant was sweating hard, wincing in pain. 'Come on, out. You've had a shock. Sit back and get your breath. Then you can tell me where we're going.'

Tottenham Court Road was in total darkness. Someone had hit the traffic lights by the police station opposite Heal and Son and had knocked the pole to a forty-five-degree angle. Bryant prised open a window and drew in some cold night air. 'We have to get to Andreas Renalda.'

May spun the wheel to avoid the damaged post. 'You think his life's in danger?'

'No, not at all,' said Bryant, peering sadly through the smeared windscreen of the Wolseley. 'We have to arrest him before he kills anyone else.'

50

GRECIAN MOCKERY

The Wolseley pulled up outside the sandbagged gates of Andreas Renalda's Highgate house just as it began to rain again. May tried to use the windscreen wipers, but the Bakelite control knob came off in his hand. He chucked it onto the back seat and stared out of the window, impotent and furious.

'Helena says Renalda's Rolls left immediately after the performance to bring him back here,' Bryant explained anxiously. 'If he's innocent he shouldn't know what's happened yet, unless someone's managed to telegraph him.'

May pulled up the handbrake and climbed out. Bryant loosened his tie and fumbled with the passenger door until May yanked it open. 'I'm rather nervous about doing this,' he admitted. 'You know—accusing someone.'

'I suppose I'll have to support you,' May sighed. Being angry wasn't going to solve anything. 'How's your chest?'

'A little better, thank you.'

'Renalda has a very good reason for wanting to sabotage his own production.' Bryant clutched at his partner's sleeve. 'Wait, before we go in, listen to me. The whole thing starts with his brother Minos. Something bothered me when I read Summerfield's article: if Minos murdered Andreas's wife, why did he stop there? Because their mother had made him believe that Andreas was protected. She wanted Minos to think that he couldn't harm Andreas without hurting himself.'

'I'm with you so far,' said May, turning up his collar.

'To do this, she had to make her crippled son believe it, otherwise he would have made them both vulnerable. From the day Sirius decided that this child would own his empire, Diana filled the boy's head with tales of old gods, and Andreas grew up believing in his protectors. He's even built a shrine to them in the Palace Theatre. That's why he chose the Palace, because of the statue of Euterpe on the roof. It was a sign to him. The building was guarded by a Muse.

'I hadn't realized who the statue represented at first, because nobody in the theatre could remember, and I was misled because the statue is wrong. Euterpe has a flaming torch in her hand instead of a flute. The original figure had been smashed, so it had to be rebuilt from scratch, but the delicate instrument she held, hard to see from the ground, and much less dramatic, was replaced with a burning brand. This much I know. But now I see how everything fits together.'

'For God's sake, let's get back in the car until you've finished. It's falling like stair rods out here.' May settled back into his seat and turned on the Wolseley's heater. 'Come on then, give me the rest of your hypothesis.'

'Which gods did Renalda's mother believe in?' There was excitement in Bryant's voice. 'Euterpe was one of the nine Muses of Greek mythology. Diana summoned the Muses to protect her son. These nine sacred goddesses nurture and inspire, bringing continued wealth and good fortune. But if you've ever studied mythology, you'll know that every request made to the gods exacts a price. The price for this protection was losing Elissa, Andreas's wife. Andreas believes that everything in his life has been decided by the Muses his mother invoked. Now that Diana is dead, Renalda is exorcizing his guardian spirits, getting rid of them one by one. He no longer has need of them. Worse, they've become his gaolers.'

'What do you mean, his gaolers? I thought they were helping him.'

'My guess is he doesn't want their help any more. He wants to prove himself, to make his own way, just as his father did. So what does he do? First he negates Euterpe's power by daring to stage a sacrilegious play in her temple, the building over which she presides in the form of a debased statue.

'Then he chooses Offenbach's version of the Orpheus legend, because it's a cruel mockery, and because it will give him access to all the representatives of the Muse. The mother of Orpheus was Calliope, one of the Muses, remember?

'After this, the removal of his gods begins in earnest. He drugs Tanya Capistrania with hemlock, a poison his mother would have taught him how to use, but panics when he can't tell whether the drug has worked. He isn't sure the dancer is dead, so he drags Capistrania's feet through the trellis of the lift to make certain. Tanya, a representative of Terpsichore, the Muse of dance, loses her feet, you see?

'Next, Renalda impales Charles Senechal, a perfect living example of Urania, Muse of astronomy. How better to kill him than with a giant planet? Urania is usually depicted carrying a globe and compasses.'

May shook his head, trying to free it from the clouds of Bryant's madness. 'But surely Senechal was the wrong sex to represent a Muse.'

'Come on, John, gender is virtually interchangeable in Greek legend. So, where are we? Ah, yes.' Bryant nodded vigorously. 'Andreas watches and waits for his next opportunity. Nobody knows when he's in the theatre, he told us that himself. He spots Zachary Darvell, the son of the performer representing the Muse Clio, proclaimer of history, smoking up in the gods. He waits until Darvell is alone and attacks him with a razor he has taken from one of the dressing rooms, pushing the body over the balcony.

'Why Darvell? Because in ancient mythology, Clio's son was murdered. Renalda nearly got two for the price of one, because the real-life mother of the stage Orpheus—Calliope, the chief of the nine Muses, represented by Miles Stone's mother, Rachel—was seated in the dress circle underneath. But Zachary yelled as he fell, enough for her to look up and get out of the way.'

'Do you have proof for any of this?' asked May, shaking his head sadly.

'I bet you anything that we'll find out Zachary is, you know, a confirmed bachelor. Clio's son was murdered by his male lover, and a flower sprang up in the blood he shed. The blood-spattered silk carnation in Darvell's buttonhole, remember? Whoever gave it to him is implicated in the murder, but we don't know where he got it. Which brings me to the woman he missed, Stone's mother. She had time to get clear, and it's ironic that she was alerted by the shrill blast of a flute, because it's the sound that always accompanies Calliope in Greek mythology.

'Andreas partially failed this time, but he can't allow himself to stop, so he must go on removing the power of each Muse, moving towards the day when he will be free of them all. Thalia, one of the three Graces, represented by Jan Petrovic, is missing presumed dead, then Melpomene, in her mask of tragedy, represented by the figure of Valerie Marchmont, Public Opinion, gets flattened. Five Muses down, four more—Erato, Polyhymnia, Clio and Calliope— still to go. Then he'll finally be liberated from his mother, and free to act for himself.'

'He's a cripple, Arthur. He can barely manage to get out of a chair.'

'For a man who makes a noise like a pile of saucepans falling downstairs when he walks, we still had no idea he was attending re-hearsals. He knows every inch of the theatre. Everyone keeps telling you the building is filled with hiding places. It's a mechanical hall of mirrors.'

'I don't know—he doesn't sound like the person Betty Trammel saw when she stayed overnight in the theatre. How could he have vanished from the roof right in front of the firewatcher? And how could he have got in and out of Jan Petrovic's flat without being seen? Anyway, why is it so damned important for Andreas Renalda to be free of his protectors?'

'Because they prevent him from doing the one thing he longs for most of all.'

'Which is what?'

'To take revenge on his brother for the death of his wife. Revenge, John—that most classic of all motives in mythology. He can't do it so long as he thinks the Muses guard him. So he's show-ing them who's boss. He's humiliated them and now he's sacrificing them. The whole play has been set up just to do that.'

'And the Muses will let him without striking him dead with a thunderbolt? What about the creature? The terrible face? Others have seen it at night in the theatre.'

'Masks and make-up. The prop room is filled with disguises. They're used in virtually every scene of the production. They must be lying around all over the place. A Greek tragedy mask? Bit of an obvious touch, that.'

'Do you know what I think?' said May, his voice cracking with anger. 'You're deranged. In a week of utter lunacies, you've finally lost your mind. Do you have any idea how insane all of this sounds?'

Bryant's eyes widened even further. 'That's why I didn't want to tell you, not until I was sure my theory was watertight.'

'I think *you're* tight.'

'No, no. I have you to thank for seeing clearly. You're part of the maieutic process.'

'The *what*?'

'Socratic midwifery.' He shook out his fingers in frustration. 'You know, the easing out of ideas. You help things out of my head, things that were already there but unformed. It's because you're so sensible, you're like the control part of an experiment.'

'All right, let's confront Andreas Renalda and you'll see how crazy this—delusion of yours is.'

At the top of the drive, the magnate's housekeeper had heard the car doors slamming and now stood in the doorway to the entrance hall. 'Mr Renalda is getting ready for bed,' she warned as they approached. 'He won't want to see anyone.'

'We'll wait downstairs while he dresses,' said Bryant, loosening his scarf and walking into the hall. 'Can we get some strong tea? It's been a long night.'

After a few minutes Andreas Renalda entered the lounge. He was dressed in a blue silk dressing gown, and was drying his neck with a towel. The steel calipers were still fitted to his legs, and May saw now that they were bolted through the flesh of his shins, deep into the twisted bones.

'It's late and I'm very tired,' he warned. 'I thought we had finished speaking.' Renalda's housekeeper helped him into a seat opposite the detectives. He looked thunderously from one face to the other. 'Good Jesus in Hell. What has happened now?'

'Public Opinion. The stage revolve jammed and she was hit in the head.'

'Is she hurt?'

'Um, actually she's dead.'

Renalda swore in Greek. It sounded as though he said 'God in a gondola'. 'Did anybody see her die?'

'Quite a few people. The stage was full—'

'I mean in the audience. Did the audience see anything wrong?'

'No, the cancan number covered it.'

He thought for a moment. 'I am not without heart, you understand, but I must think of the show.'

'I think I understand very well,' said Bryant.

'There have been mechanical problems with the traps and flies ever since my company moved into the theatre. The equipment had not been touched in half a century. We cannot get any new parts. The company that made them is now making armaments. Every spare scrap of metal is going to the war effort.'

'Whatever caused Miss Marchmont's death, the theatre is closed as of this moment,' Bryant warned.

Renalda's face set. 'I think not.' He hurled his towel aside. 'Until you come up with proof that these misfortunes are the result of negligence, I can promise you that I have the necessary paperwork to keep the show open.'

'You're insured, so what difference does it make?' asked Bryant. 'I'll let the press in and turn the case over to Westminster Council. At that point, your personal involvement in this will surface.'

'What do you mean?' asked Renalda, his anger growing. 'You know I have nothing to do with these tragedies.'

'Arthur, are you sure you want to do this?' asked May, wincing.

'I'm fine, John.' Bryant drew a deep breath. 'Andreas Ares Renalda, I am arresting you for the murders of Tanya Capistrania, Charles Senechal, Zachary Darvell and Valerie Marchmont, and for the abduction of Jan Petrovic.'

Renalda's face transformed from anger to amazement. A nerve in his neck blew some kind of synaptic fuse and started making his mouth twitch.

Breathing ever more deeply, Bryant explained his hypothesis. It took him a quarter of an hour to do so, and when he finished he sat back, exhausted from the effort. He waited for Renalda to explode.

'All right,' said the tycoon, in a suspiciously affable tone. 'This is most amusing.' He wagged tanned fingers at Bryant as though he was pointing a loaded revolver. 'The true part of your—what shall we call it?—fable is how my mother protected me from my brother. He was not a bright man, Mr Bryant, no sharper than the average police detective. He believed he could not touch me for fear of something terrible happening to him.'

'And that's why you're taking revenge on him now.' Bryant was sticking to his guns, May had to give him that. It took guts for a twenty-two-year-old detective to accuse a middle-aged millionaire of multiple murder and abduction.

'No.' Renalda laughed politely. 'Of course not.'

'Can you prove that?'

'I do not have to prove it.' He stared defiantly at Bryant, and a slow, terrible smile spread across his gaunt face. 'Even if I wanted to take revenge on Minos, I have no way of carrying it out.'

'Oh, why not?' asked Bryant.

'It is common knowledge. Even the most stupid Greek policeman knows about it.' Andreas Renalda shrugged theatrically. 'Minos, my brother, is dead. I buried him myself.'

51

THE END OF THE ROAD

'You honestly thought I would destroy the *Orpheus* production and ruin my company's reputation to take some kind of warped revenge against my dead brother?' said Renalda. 'British police. Too much Agatha Christie, no?'

Bryant wasn't about to give up without a fight. 'Can you tell me how you know that Minos is dead?'

'Well, I saw his eyelids and mouth stitched shut with catgut, and I saw him nailed into a coffin and placed in the ground, then the earth put over the top of him, and the shovels flattening down the earth, if you think that's proof enough.'

'How did he die?'

'He was killed in a car accident near Athens two months before the war started. He had been drinking all day. He lost control of the car and went off the road into a canal. He drowned, and so my wife, in some strange way, is avenged. I saw his body pulled from the wreck and buried in the family cemetery.'

'It doesn't make sense that Minos is dead,' said Bryant, staring down at the floor in confusion.

'I'm sorry it doesn't fit your theories. I suppose you can arrange to have his grave reopened if you like—you wouldn't be able to make yourself any more foolish. My brother's death is well documented.'

'Why didn't you tell me?'

'Why should I? If you had any connection with your police friends in Europe instead of keeping to yourselves on your funny little island, you would know how many times the press has told the story.'

'I thought you said you sued them all.'

'All the ones I knew about, but there were plenty of others. "The cursed family, the child protected by ancient gods." Journalists scaled the walls of the house to take my picture, they tried to bribe me, harassed me so much that I moved here, where I thought things would be different. The English, so private, so aloof, so secretive. They would leave the memory of my family alone. But no, along come you two, the music-hall comedians. Yes, I am sure that Minos killed my wife, but I am not glad that he suffocated in the filthy waters of a drainage ditch. He was blood of my blood. And I will not allow his memory to be defiled by young men who think too much about the wrong things.'

'I didn't mean to imply—'

'I know exactly what you meant. In your own clumsy way you suggest we are nothing but ignorant pagans. Our private beliefs have been raked over in your *News of the World*. You think I would slaughter my own cast and wreck my production, you arrogant little boy?' The veins were pulsing in his temples, and he began to shout. 'You pious English Christians, always so right, what do you know of the world that you have not read from your precious books? Do you know how many times I have heard these idiocies since my wife died? Her death was a godsend to your journalists, another tragedy in a rich family, and you believe it just because you read some news clippings? Get out of this house now, before I have you thrown out. Get out!'

'Well, that went well,' said May, stepping out into the pouring rain.

'I thought I'd discovered something new. I was sure Renalda was setting himself free from his past.'

'No, Arthur, you believed what you wanted to believe, no matter how demented the notion was. You squeezed the facts to fit your theory.'

Bryant was indignant. 'I did not!'

'Of course you did. That thing about the high note warning Miles Stone's mother. The flautist was late that day, remember? There was no high note from a flute, just somebody scraping a violin in the orchestra. And another thing. Edna bloody Wagstaff and her chatty cat. She couldn't have heard Dan Leno in the Palace, because he never came to the Palace. He died in 1904 without once performing there. She's just a crazy, lonely old woman. Andreas Renalda's story appealed to your romantic notions of classical literature and myths, that's all. Maybe Biddle was right when he asked to leave. You don't share information and you don't listen to reason. I'm not sure I'm cut out for the unit any more than he is.'

'What are you talking about?'

'You, Arthur. I'll never get used to working like this. Just sitting in your room is enough, all those volumes on clairvoyants, astrologers, white witches, spiritualism, covens. While everyone else is reading the *Daily Mail,* you're studying the *Apocryphal Books of the Dead.* All the stories they laugh about over at Bow Street while you look for a vampire that preys on foreigners in Leicester Square. Running down alleyways in the dead of night, trying to catch some kind of shapeshifting wraith that sucks the blood out of Norwegians. How do you talk people into believing stuff like that? Why did DS Forthright spend her New Year's Eve in a King's Cross goods yard waiting for a priest to mark out crucifix patterns in holy water? And did you ever catch him? According to her, you're the only one who saw him dash into that cul-de-sac. He must have run up the wall, you told her, they can do that in moments of stress. You have us all mesmerized under the spell of your insanity.

'Well, no more. I've just not got that turn of mind. It's the effect you have on people, you mean well but you get everyone caught up in these ridiculous fantasies. Why can't you just face the truth and admit you've not got the right experience for the job? You should be curating in a museum or something, lecturing on ghosts and goblins, digging out Egyptian tombs. It was good enough for Howard Carter, he didn't decide to be a policeman, did he?'

'May I remind you,' said Bryant, trying to muster some dignity, 'that this is called the Peculiar Crimes Unit?'

'The day we met, you told me that their definition of peculiar and yours were different. You just didn't warn me how different. I know you're a bit older than me, but I'd like a chance to handle things another way, before Davenport hears what you've done and nails boards across the entrance to the office. I should have put my foot down when you brought in the clairvoyant, then perhaps none of this would have happened. Why don't you take a break, go and give the ARP boys a hand, make use of yourself, and try not to think so much?'

'I'll admit that as a team we've been having a few teething troubles.'

'*Teething troubles?* You just accused a man who has the ear of the Home Office of practising witchcraft! Christ on a bike.'

'John, at least let's leave it until the morning,' Bryant pleaded. 'You might feel differently then.'

John raised his hands defiantly. 'No, because in the morning you'll try to convince me that Renalda is part of a satanic sect, or that the theatre is built on an ancient Saxon burial ground. Besides, it has nothing to do with me. Renalda—and Biddle, come to think of it—will be on the phone to Davenport right now, and he'll have taken you off the case before dawn. I'm prepared to go a long way with you, Arthur. I even see some demented sense in what you say. The killer is a psychopath driven by desperation, fine, yes, I agree with that. But Muses, curses, protective spells? That's where we part company.'

He stopped when he realized that his partner was no longer following him. Looking back, he saw Bryant standing in the rain, his head dropped forward onto his chest. He looked close to tears, but May knew he couldn't be because nothing ever seemed to up-set him.

'Where are you going now?' asked May.

'I promised my mother I'd look in on her,' Bryant replied miserably.

'I'll drive you. There won't be any buses running at this hour. Then you must try to get some sleep. At least it's a quiet night. I'll go back to the theatre and make sure Forthright has everything she needs.'

'You're right,' Bryant said softly. 'I thought it was—I don't know what I thought. I'm so sorry.'

'Don't be, just get some rest. Leave it to me. You won't have to do anything. I'll sort everything out with Davenport. Just accept that things didn't work out with us, that's all.'

Bryant suddenly looked so pale and fragile that May felt a rush of pity for him.

He drove his distraught partner slowly back through the smouldering ruins of Hackney and Bow, past a makeshift hospital set up on the broken pavements. There were patients lying on brass beds outside McFisheries and Woolworths. A woman was sitting on the steps of a church with her head in her hands. When a nurse tried to comfort her, she pushed her away.

As they drove on, the devastation grew. The house where Bryant asked to be dropped was in a bomb-scarred terrace of slum dwellings long due for demolition. May was shocked to find that his partner hailed from such a rough neighbourhood.

Embarrassed by the events of the night and by his own impoverished circumstances, Bryant stood awkwardly in the entrance to the alley beside his mother's house and waited until the Wolseley had pulled out into the deserted road, its tail-lights fading in the thickening drizzle.

As he watched John May drive away, he knew that the unit's last chance for survival was leaving with him.

52

TAKING LEAVE

Early on Sunday morning Londoners once more awoke to the drone of the bombers, but the drizzle had persisted through the night, and only a few aircraft had managed to drop their loads. Several fires were started, and their smoke added to the city's dawning pallor of eye-watering gloom. After the RAF released two thousand bombs on Hamburg as a reprisal for Coventry, Germany turned its attention to the Southampton docks, steadily bombing them for the rest of the day. Attack, reprisal; the process continued in a depressing rhythm of retaliation.

Sidney Biddle sat on the bench near the tea stall with his hands stuffed deep in his overcoat, watching the oily water surge back and forth around the barricaded pillars of Waterloo Bridge like the action of some vast diseased lung. Daylight had begun to creep across the sky, and now he could see the silver barrage balloons following the shoreline. One of them was tied to the top of Bank power station's chimney. Another had partially deflated, and hung amorphously over the river like a creature in a Salvador Dalí painting. Biddle's foot was throbbing, but it was strapped up with splints and bandages and he was able to walk with the aid of a crutch.

'Your char's getting cold, love,' said Gladys Forthright, churning the contents of her mug with the end of a pencil. 'They never leave enough chain on the teaspoon to give you a good stir, do they?'

Neither of them had slept. Biddle was angry and confused, but invigorated by the action of the night before, newly hooked on the case and on the unit. 'I mean, you outrank him,' he said finally. 'Can't you do something?'

'It may have escaped your notice, Sidney, but although I have the rank, I'm still a woman. Davenport won't even talk to me. He acts as if I'm not there. My appointment was approved because women have to be drafted into the force. We're fine for driving fire engines and ambulances, tracking aircraft and manning switchboards, but they don't want to give us jobs that involve strategic decisions. You won't find policewomen in positions of power. The men want to keep those for themselves.'

Biddle took a sip of his tea. 'Why does Bryant always come here? PC Crowhurst told me he sits at this spot nearly every day at sunset.'

So that's it, thought Forthright, he wants to understand.

'You don't know the story?' she asked, surprised. 'I thought someone would have told you by now. I know it's hard to believe, but our Mr Bryant was once a man in love. Back then he was still training out of Bramshill on a one-year intensive. So many were pushed through the courses because of the approaching war. He was very young, of course. Boys leave school at fourteen in the East End, and they marry early. By the time I came up from Hendon as a DC he had met the love of his life and become engaged to her.'

'Bryant had a fiancée?'

'Nathalie was from France, Marseille, I think. She was dark and rather beautiful. Not easy, mind you—very independent. When they met, she was working in ground command, co-ordinating air-support units. There were so many rehearsals for war that I was relieved when it finally happened.'

Forthright warmed her hands round her enamel mug. 'This is where she died, on the evening of her eighteenth birthday, May nineteen thirty-seven. She fell from the bridge, just in front of us. She'd climbed up onto the balustrade and was walking along it. They'd been out drinking, celebrating, and were both a bit tipsy. He'd asked her to marry him. She would probably have been fine, but at that moment a bus horn sounded behind them, and it made her start. She lost her balance, and when he turned round to grab her, she'd gone. Arthur jumped into the water and tried to save her, but the tide was going out, and the current was too strong. He was wearing his overcoat and hobnailed police boots. He nearly drowned as well. Underwater search teams dragged the river for weeks, but they never did find her body. The river widens here. There's nothing between us and the sea.'

She rested the mug on her strong, shapely knees and sighed. 'He was taken very bad for a while, tried to enlist when war was declared, but the War Office looked at his mental health record and wouldn't take him. They marked him down as unstable. He was training to spend his life helping others but hadn't found a way to save the girl he loved. She was the point of his life, the one he felt fated to be with for ever.

'That was three years ago, and although he never talks about her, he never looks at anyone else either, not in a serious way. Oh, he thought he'd fallen in love with me for a while, but I could see it was just a crush, and put him straight. As far as he's concerned, he was given his chance for happiness and buggered it up. It's something he'll never find a way to make amends for. That's why none of this touches him.'

'I wish someone had told me.'

'We all have our private tragedies. You can't change the past. You keep going.'

Biddle swallowed from his mug. 'I'm not part of your past. You all seem suited to each other. I don't think I'm the right person for your kind of operation.'

'That's where you're wrong. We're all so different. They say all the good men have gone to war, that only the unemployables are left. That's why we were lucky to find Mr May. He's practical, he'll give Arthur the grounding he needs. We've no permanent staff over the age of twenty-five. I'm the oldest person in the unit. The Home Office will close us down as soon as the war ends. Davenport hates us, thinks we're a bunch of academic pansies. Now he's got all the ammunition he needs.'

'I don't see what I can do.'

'You've got Davenport's ear. You can protect us if you stay.'

'I already told Bryant I was going.'

'Then eat your words. No one will think less of you. Tell him you'll stay.' Forthright followed his gaze to the river beyond the railing. 'I came back, didn't I? Swallowed my pride. I was supposed to get married. I could have kept away, but I didn't.'

Biddle looked at her. 'Why not?'

'Mr Bryant needs me.' She checked her watch. 'God, I can't remember the last time I ate. You must be starving.'

'There's a decent workman's café near Coin Street.'

'I need sausages. You're allowed a hearty breakfast on the morning of your execution, aren't you? I'm in charge of the unit's petty cash, and you won't shop me, will you? You can tell me more about this monster you saw in the rafters.'

They passed a skinny brown nag drinking noisily from a corporation horse trough. Forthright paused to give its milkman a cigarette. The poor man looked on his uppers, as thin as his horse and the empty wire crates on his cart. It was the first animal she had seen in days; she wondered if they were being taken out of the city.

Biddle waited for her, then they resumed walking in comfortable silence through the miasmic mist that ebbed over the Embankment, down to the roads where daylight and life were returning to the city.

Arthur Bryant gently placed the framed photograph of Nathalie, the one he had taken by the river that terrible afternoon, into a cardboard box, added his carved Tibetan skull, tossed in some incense sticks, some mystical diagrams of Solomon's Temple, several beeswax candles, a gramophone record of Sir Arthur Sullivan's *Te Deum*, two volumes of criminal records from Newgate Gaol, a three-dimensional bronze model of the Kabalistic Pentagram of the Absolute, a rare limited edition of Seymour's *British Witchcraft and Demonology* and a paperback copy of *RAF Slang Made Easy*, then closed the lid and bound it with thick brown tape. Set beside each other, the three crates contained almost everything he owned. It's not a lot to show for my life so far, he thought gloomily.

He propped the letter of resignation, addressed to Davenport, against May's desk lamp. He wanted to leave before his partner arrived. He felt that he had passed the point beyond which no amount of apology and retraction could return him, and he did not wish to place John in the embarrassing situation of having to defend him to their superior.

Perhaps it was for the best. He wasn't cut out to be a politician. It was clear now that the unit was little more than a public relations exercise. For a while he had believed that the old-money occupants of the HO could be superseded by a new breed of experimentalists for whom the past held no loyalties, that brave new rules would operate throughout British government, from the lowliest town council to the offices of Whitehall. Now he doubted that the war would make any difference to government at all.

Bryant loved London. He had been born in Whitechapel, in the lowliest of circumstances, and had grown up on the streets of Wapping and Borough and Mile End. He was proud of having got this far. But now the city was changing. Its sense of good cheer was being chipped away by bombardment in a war that Neville Chamberlain had insisted would never happen.

He was going to load the boxes into a cab if he could find one, but remembered that he had packed some hefty mementos, including a paving stone that held the burned-in handprint of Jack the Ripper, and decided to have them delivered instead.

There was no place for his arcane studies in the police force of the future. He thought of his friends in the Camden Town Coven, and their arch-rivals, the Southwark Supernaturals. He gathered together the scrawled addresses of the Mystic Savoyards and the Prometheus League, the emergency numbers of the Insomnia Squad's sleepless academics, the diary that contained lists of assorted primitives, paranormalists, idiot savants, mind-readers and madmen, all available to the unit if someone only trusted him enough to use them wisely.

All for the best, he told himself. John was young and bright. He might be able to modernize the unit and bring fresh technology into their casework once Bryant himself was out of the way. They were clearly doing something wrong if they couldn't keep lads like Sidney Biddle interested enough to stay on.

He unclipped a small glass case of poisonous caterpillars from the wall behind his desk and emptied it into the bin. There was a time when he would have taken them out of their case and dropped them in Oswald Finch's teapot, but the spirit had gone out of him.

Bryant saw now that he had willed a culprit into existence because he wanted to be challenged. The real solution would doubtless prove to be rather ordinary, not peculiar or paradoxical at all, a disgruntled employee, a youth filled with such directionless anger that he could equally have decided to attack the staff of a bus depot or an insurance office. Grey crimes for a grey nation.

It was the second time he had failed. Overcoming his guilt about Nathalie's death had been tough, and just when the world was starting to make sense again he saw that he hadn't made sense of it at all. He knew he would have to write a formal apology to Renalda.

He looked about the desktop to see if there was anything he had forgotten, and saw that the drawing of the statue he had deciphered as the key to a mythological conundrum was just another memento. He carefully folded it into a square, tucked it into his tattered briefcase and snapped the lock shut.

Pausing in the doorway, he took one last look around the room he and May had shared for the past few days, and wondered about the cases they might have solved together.

Then he quietly pulled the door shut behind him.

53

TOUCHING THE TORTOISE

Mementos and conundrums, all the cases we solved together, thought May. It was always Bryant who had set the puzzles. He himself had just been the faithful sidekick, an anchor of reason to his partner's flights of fancy. We solved our first case together. I'll solve our last one if it kills me.

His bandaged leg was swollen and sore. He looked along the crowded platform of the tube station, unpleasantly sweaty even though the day was cold, and waited for the approaching train. He felt his coat pockets. The tortoise; he had left the damned shell in Maggie's flat, but he wasn't going back for it now. I'm old, I'm tired and I've been stabbed by a ghost, he thought angrily.

Not that he remotely believed in such things. The breadboard had fallen, hitting the handle of the knife. More accidents happened at home than anywhere else. Besides, even if he was a believer it would have made no sense. Why would his best friend return from the grave to hurt him? The only person who could do that now was very much alive.

Except that it wasn't him ... unless he had grown fangs ...

And then he saw the error he had made. He saw how badly he had misread the situation, just as Arthur had all those years before. How guilty he had been of jumping to the same mistaken conclusion.

May pushed his way back up the stairs of Camden Town tube

station, fighting the onrushing flow of travellers. He needed to obtain a signal for his mobile. Outside, wedged into a litter-strewn corner, he punched out Alma Sorrowbridge's number. He waited for fourteen rings, but there was no answer. The shadow of the buildings opposite had begun to reach this side of the street. He looked at the keypad of his mobile, and was about to try her again when it rang.

'Grandad, is that you?'

'April?'

His granddaughter couldn't have picked a worse time to call, but it was good to hear her voice.

'I've been meaning to ring you for days. I was so sorry to hear about Mr Bryant. He was always nice to me. You must be—'

'Listen,' May cut across her, 'I'm more sorry than you could ever be. Arthur asked me to call you and I didn't. I've been too wrapped up in my own problems. How are you? Have you been able to get out at all?'

'A little. It's tough. Open spaces still do my head in, but I'm handling it.'

'Remember what the doctor said, one step at a time.'

'I know, but I want to go back to work,' April complained. 'I've seen enough of these walls to last a lifetime. I could do with some advice.'

'Sure. I'll come and see you.'

He wanted to tell her he was ashamed, that he would make up the time they had lost. Instead he could only promise to ring her again in a day or so. It wasn't much, but it was a start.

'It's funny speaking to you at this hour. It's the time I always think of you.'

May was puzzled. 'Why?' he asked.

'Oh, you know. You always took a walk with Mr Bryant at sunset. It was the only real ritual you had.'

'I suppose it was a ritual, wasn't it?' May was amazed he hadn't thought of it earlier. 'I'll call you tomorrow, sweetheart. There's something I have to put right.'

And he was off along the pavement, moving around the crowds and into the road, the pain in his leg forgotten, breaking into a run as he speed-dialled Janice Longbright's number, praying that she would pick up the phone.

54

FULL DARK HOUSE

'There's nothing to report that a layman can't see with a cursory examination of the body,' said young Oswald Finch, rinsing his hands at the deep ceramic sink. The remains of Valerie Marchmont, Public Opinion, lay under an ordinary bedsheet; the army had requisitioned the pathology unit's entire supply of rubberized covers.

'It's the same as the others. There are no second-agent marks on the skin or clothing, just a few fragments of corroded metal at the contact point. I presume the iron rod that passed through her head was slightly rusted. Some of the rust was scraped off by the edges of the skull. Not much point in making a toxicological examination, but I'll do one if you want. The damage is consistent with what you'd expect to find in an accident of this kind. You see wounds like this all over London these days.'

'Dr Runcorn has been over the stage equipment but he's come up with nothing,' said May, leaning against the sink with his hands thrust into his pockets. 'The skycloth came down a fraction later and slightly further over to centre stage than it was supposed to, and the revolve stuck for a moment. The stagehands reckon they oiled the revolve before the performance but say it still judders occasionally.'

'An unfortunate combination of factors. Although I daresay young Mr Bryant would have us believe something different if he was here.' Finch rubbed a lotion into his fingers that was supposed to remove the smell of chemicals. 'To be honest, it surprises me that Bryant could be so *completely* wrong. I mean, we've had our disagreements, and he's certainly going to make mistakes during a time like this when you can't get your hands on basic equipment, but there's usually something vaguely right about his thinking. Are we having a farewell party?'

'I don't think any of us could stand it,' said May despondently. 'His landlady hasn't seen him, only his boxes. He's not been home for a change of clothes. It's been two days now. I wondered if he might have gone to stay with relatives.'

'He could be at his mother's in Bethnal Green Road. Forthright tells me the house next door to Mrs Bryant's got bombed out and she's worried about her walls falling in. I know he wanted to help her move somewhere safer. She's not on the telephone but I daresay someone in the local nick could run round.' Finch leaned back on a stool and administered drops to his right pupil. The atmosphere of formaldehyde left him with perpetually red-rimmed eyelids.

'Do you think Davenport will keep us open with Bryant gone?' asked May.

'That's a tough one, seeing as he set you chaps up in the first place. It could be construed as failure on his part. He'll probably merge you with one of the other divisions: fraud or this special squad that's been set up to deal with looters. At least it'll keep you afloat. Did Forthright mention that your Mr Biddle has had a change of heart? He's decided to stay on after all.'

'That's good,' May said. 'Arthur thought he might come round. What happened to the tree he gave you?'

'Bit of a sore point, that. It was too big for the bureau so I took it home, and now the wife won't talk to me.'

'Why?'

'Her cat ate one of the leaves and died. She tried to chop it down with a kitchen knife and it leaked some kind of poisonous sap on her. The doctor reckons her arm should stay bandaged for at least a week, which is inconvenient because she plays the organ. I have a suspicion,' he said, blinking the drops from his left eye, 'that it was one of Bryant's pranks. He really was the most impossible man.'

'He's not dead,' said May.

'Well, he is missing,' responded Finch, dabbing his eyes on a flannel and blinking.

May was surprised by the way his partner had responded to failure, but his first duty was to the case. 'He'll turn up,' he said unsurely. 'You might try liaising a little more with Dr Runcorn rather than telling me you can't find anything. Four dead, one vanished, a few near misses. I need physical proof fast, or we'll all be out of a job. A couple of heel marks, no fingerprints, no real murder weapons to speak of, it's not much to go on. You'd think we were dealing with someone who doesn't exist in the real world.'

The annoying thing was that, although he had not believed Bryant's explanation, his partner was still the only one to come up with any suggestions at all.

He looked in on Forthright and Biddle, who were continuing to check customs information from air, sea and freight terminals for the whereabouts of Jan Petrovic. At dusk he walked through brown smoke billowing across Lincoln's Inn Fields, searching the darkness of the unsettled trees as he tried to work out how they had gone so wrong. Crows called loudly from the lower branches as he passed beneath them, their old eyes glittering between the leaves. An elderly man was hoeing a muddy trough through an allotment, one of many that had been dug across the once-perfect lawns.

Just when he was free to follow traditional procedures, May tried to imagine how Bryant would consider the evidence. Minos Renalda was dead, and with him died a motive for revenge. Forthright had confirmed that Andreas was a witness to his brother's burial. The body had also been identified by close friends and relatives.

But what of Elissa Renalda? Her body had been too long in the water for proper identification. Suppose it hadn't been her, and she had survived somehow? What if she had returned and disguised herself as a member of the cast, and was trying to destroy her husband for—what? Failing to save her from his brother? May angrily kicked a stone into the bushes. That was the trouble with thinking like Bryant, it made absolutely no sense.

When he reached his aunt's house in Camden Town, he opened his briefcase and pulled out a stack of the unit's files. Bryant had perversely embedded his private notes into illustrated cryptograms representing Offenbach's theatre posters. To provide the reader with clues, he had painted sections of the posters in the wrong colours to their originals. He had taken Davenport's precautionary measures to a ludicrous degree, without disobeying his orders. Codes, encryptions, puzzles, everything was a game to him, thought May as he began to sort through the material, wondering if Bryant, wherever he might be, was thinking of the files and chuckling at his partner's confusion.

He sat on the candlewick bedspread and laid the posters before him, trying to plot a new direction through the details of the case. He could hear his aunt on the landing outside, polishing the lino for the third time in a week. Perhaps as a response to the chaos outside, she had become obsessed with keeping the house immaculate. She made her own cleaning fluid from Castile soap, saltpetre and ammonia, and mixed up polishes and liniments from turpentine and vinegar until the entire house stank. He felt trapped in the dark little terrace, too broke to be able to take a girl anywhere, unable to get away from the blighted city, unwilling to knock mugs with the sanctimonious doomsayers and patriots who gathered around the piano in the corner pub.

His best bet, he knew, was to sort out the mess at the Palace and get a recommendation out of the unit. He thought of the way he had arrived at Bow Street the previous Monday, full of expectation for the days ahead. Instead he felt lost and abandoned. Arthur Bryant was the most annoying man he had ever met, but at least he was fun to be around. May lacked the confidence to continue without him. Now all he saw in the days ahead was failure and shame.

The door of Helena's office burst open, and Harry ran in. 'Can you come quickly?' he gasped. 'The Phantom, we've got him cornered.' It was the middle of Monday morning, and the first rehearsal after the start of the run was in as good a shape as could be expected. Reviews were in, a combination of outrage and ecstasy in equal measure. Sandwiched between cheering articles about opera singers becoming train drivers and church wardens who had narrowly missed being hit by bombs were the sexy photographs that Helena Parole had approved for use. The scantily clothed chorus girls were already being nicknamed 'Dante's Infernettes', and had prompted outraged calls to the Public Morality Council. This august body already had its in-trays full, thanks to the problem of 'undesirable women' approaching servicemen in the West End, and had formally asked the Provost Marshal for military police to help close London's illegal gambling and drinking dens. Without the Lord Chamberlain to back them, the council could only acknowledge complaints against the theatre and suggest that it was carrying out investigations into the matter of public indecency.

Harry excitedly led Helena up the central staircase and down through the upper circle. 'Look over there,' he cried, pointing up into the gantry that ran along the right side of the stage. 'One of the profile spots came loose and fell onto the stage, missed Eve by inches. Luckily she'd just been called back by Ben Woolf.'

'What was he doing up onstage?'

'I don't know, giving her some kind of legal advice, I think. The stagehands saw someone up on the rear gantry, moving about by the lights. He's trapped against that far wall.' A dark shape could be discerned caught in the crossbeams of torches.

'He's making weird noises,' said Harry. 'Nobody's had the nerve to go and challenge him because the walkspace is very narrow, and the rails are low.'

'Can't you get more light on him?' asked John May, beckoning to Biddle.

'We can put the house lights up and all the backstage ones, but it'll take a few minutes. Half the areas near the top of the house will still be in darkness,' warned Biddle.

'All right, let me think. Sidney, how's your foot?'

'I can be pretty sharp on it if I have to be.'

'Then you can give me a hand. Get Crowhurst off the stage door. You go up to the balcony.'

Sidney hobbled forward as the others approached the figure behind the torchlights.

'I know who it is,' Harry announced as they stepped onto the gantry. 'It's that rude critic who wrote about us being cursed and snored through the second half on opening night. He trod on my foot at the intermission, rushing to get to the bar, without so much as a by your leave.'

'Gilbert Riley?' asked Helena Parole. 'Are you sure? What's he doing up here? Mr Riley, is that you?'

'Dear lady,' called a wavering voice. 'I was making some notes, but I'm stuck. My trousers are caught on something.' His arrogant tone had vanished. As more torch beams pinpointed him, they could see the goateed critic splayed above the stage like a Savile Row–suited barrage balloon.

'Sidney, see if you can get him free,' directed May.

'Maybe we should just leave him there.'

'Don't tempt me. What *are* you doing here, Mr Riley? You know it's off-limits.'

'That's the problem,' whined Riley. 'No one will talk to me about what's going on. I'm trying to do a feature and no one will tell me the truth. I'm doing your show a favour, bringing it the oxygen of publicity. The least anyone could do is return my calls.'

'So you thought you'd break in and nose around.'

'It's hardly breaking in. I know the boys on the stage door.'

'You mean you bribed them. And you nearly killed someone.'

The critic raised his hands in a gesture of horror. 'I leaned on one of the lights to get a better view and it came loose. Everything is held together with clips and ropes up here.'

'You're not supposed to be here at all, Riley,' said Biddle, reaching over and tugging at his trousers. 'There you go.' There was a tearing sound, and the critic fell forward with a yelp. The officers helped him back onto the balcony.

'For this I thank you, dear fellow,' said Riley shakily. He dusted down the knees of his trousers, regaining his composure. 'It was ghastly. There was someone else back there with me, breathing heavily through his nose. It sounded like he was wearing a gas mask. I could hear him moving around, jumping between the gantries. He stopped right in front of me, watching, then moved away.'

'You didn't get a good look at him?' asked May.

'Only enough to see that he was barely human, hulking and hunched over, a giant dwarf or some kind of large animal, great big teeth. I'm sure he meant to do me harm.'

'He's not alone there,' muttered Parole. 'And I'm not sure what you mean by a giant dwarf.'

'I think you should go down to the stalls and apologize to the cast for nearly wiping out the star of the show,' Biddle told him. 'Then we'll go and write up your report while Mr May decides what to charge you with.'

'Charge me?' Riley looked shocked.

'Unlawful entry and trespass,' agreed May, taking his cue from Biddle, 'circumstances of *actus reus,* some broken by-laws because this is a public building, several causation and situational offences, and anything else the lads can think of, the precedent of the Crown *v.* Woolmington nineteen thirty-five springs to mind. Then Miss Noriac will probably want to press charges for invasion of privacy and attempted assault, and sue you and your paper, assuming you were acting under its auspices, for causing her undue distress.'

'Please, no! Think of the publicity!' Riley wheezed.

'I imagine her attitude could be mitigated by the level of contrition you show her.'

'And you might want to pin yourself up, seeing as your arse is hanging out of your trousers and there are ladies below,' added Biddle, leading the horrified critic downstairs. Parole and May followed at a polite distance.

'Are you really going to press all those charges?' asked Helena as they descended to the stalls.

'No, I was talking absolute rubbish. So, another false alarm.'

'It's wearing down my cast. They're seeing things in every dark corner. We're all spooked, but of course nobody wants the show to close. I think I preferred it when there was just a murderer loose. Now all they talk about is this—creature.'

'You shouldn't believe everything you read in the papers,' said May.

'No, other people have seen things. Corinne says she glimpsed it again in the upper circle. Says it was running on its hands like a monkey. Madeline, my ASM, was understage and heard something hooting, or crying, near the orchestra. She reckons it sounded like an animal in pain. Your Betty still hasn't got over her nasty turn.'

That's a point, thought May. We were supposed to see each other at the weekend. He suddenly realized that he had been too preoccupied by the investigation to call her.

'They can't all be imagining things,' Helena continued, 'but what on earth could it be? It's not like anybody's keeping a noisy pet tucked away backstage. Stan Lowe was the only one in last night, and said he was just about to lock up when he saw the shadow of something swinging back and forth on the underside of the dress circle. I know they're very artistic people but this is a kind of collective madness. It's a dilemma: do we stay open for business and hope to catch this thing, or close and never discover the truth? Have you heard anything from the council?'

'Still no word from Westminster on the safety ruling,' said May, 'and the Lord Chamberlain's office is suspiciously silent, so I think it's safe to assume that Renalda nobbled them.'

Helena stopped as they reached the landing. 'I hear your partner accused Andreas of sabotaging his own production, and that he's been chucked off the case.' She smiled ominously at him. 'Don't look so surprised. Everyone talks around here. You should hear some of the rumours. I even heard that he was having an affair with poor Elspeth, but I know that's not true.'

'Why are you so sure?'

'Darling, she's a professional virgin. Married to the theatre. It takes some people like that. They get like nuns, very vocational.'

'What else are your cast discussing in their dressing rooms?'

'They're saying the Phantom will attack again tomorrow night, during the show. It's a gala charity benefit and we have a lot of celebrities attending, including Vera Lynn, half of the Crazy Gang and Mr Claude Rains, if you please, so if the Phantom does appear perhaps the two of them can have it out on one of the electroliers.'

'You don't sound very worried.'

'At this point, Eurydice would have to explode into flames and burn to death in front of a thousand people before anything could surprise me. Although of course poor old Valerie did get her brains knocked out in front of a full house.' Helena examined the end of her cigarette. 'And to think she was always so worried about being upstaged.'

55

ENGLISH CRUELTY

The front door was locked and barred with planks.

For added emphasis, a DO NOT ENTER poster had been glued across it. This was how May found the Peculiar Crimes Unit when he returned to it in the afternoon. He walked round to the Bow Street duty desk, where Sergeant Carfax could barely suppress the smile on his face.

'Ain't you heard?' he asked May. 'Davenport's closed you lot down, pending an official inquiry. You and your weedy book-reading chum are for the high jump, mate.'

May was shocked, but wasn't going to let Carfax see how upset he was.

'Then I'll set up a base at the theatre,' he told the sergeant. 'If Mr Davenport has anything to say to me, he can do it to my face.' There was a typewriter in the company office at the Palace, and a telephone. That was all he needed. With Bryant gone and Forthright's position hingeing on her undecided marriage, he was now in charge, and determined to make sure that everyone knew it.

At five P.M. the Westminster Council ruling came in. The envelope arrived by messenger and was taken to Andreas Renalda's office. The tycoon summoned May, who was in the process of taking up residence on the ground floor. May found Renalda sprawled on his leather couch, resting the steel calipers that caused him so much pain.

'We have been granted a stay of execution,' he said, indicating that May should pour whisky into a pair of glasses. 'You will join me? "The council was not presented with any proof that these deaths could have been avoided by better safety regulations within the theatre." I told you. Their inspectors found only minor infringements. We must open the second pass door to comply with fire regulations, then we get a clean bill of health. The exact word they use to describe recent events is "unfortunate". So we go on, and unless you can come up with any positive evidence for nightly turning away over one and a half thousand people, your job here is over.'

'I'll still be close by,' threatened May.

'Your partner behaved in an irresponsible manner.'

'Mr Bryant voluntarily tendered his resignation. Our director endorsed his decision for a transfer, and has closed down the unit. He'll probably take me off the case as soon as he can find me.'

'One would hope to discover friends in adversity, Mr May, but I suspect this makes us enemies.' Renalda smiled knowingly. 'Your people are famous for supporting each other against the rest of us, even when you're not in agreement.'

'I have no quarrel with you. I was trained to believe that the case is always greater than the officer.'

'Well, that is very diplomatic of you, but I come from a long line of grudge-bearers. I know how the world works. Business decisions are not made for the good of the people, but for the sake of profit, loyalty and expedience. Why do you think I am financing this production? You think I am honouring my wife, paying a debt to my Muses, giving something back to the world of theatre?'

'I imagine your motives are the same as anyone's in business.'

'I go where I see the money going next. There's no future in manufacturing during peacetime. Once we have rebuilt the cities, people will have more time on their hands. They'll have money to spend.'

'They're turning the theatres into boxing rings, Mr Renalda.'

'Only while the war lasts.' He knocked back the rest of his whisky. 'Afterwards they will pay fortunes to see spectacle. There will be many more young people. We are killing off the older generation. Shows like this are just the start. What humanity wants most is crude sensation.'

'Really? I thought what humanity wanted most was dignity.'

'He was a shrewd man,' May told his biographer decades later. 'But someone else beat him to his big idea. Two years after *Orpheus,* a play called *Oklahoma!* opened, spawning over thirty thousand different productions. It is one of the highest-earning entertainments of all time. Then popular television programmes arrived. Renalda hailed from a shipbuilding family, but he missed the boat. It's not enough to have vision, you need foresight. I often wonder what happened to him and his dream of entertaining the masses. He was in it for money, not pleasure. That was why success eluded him.'

'Let's get back to the murders,' said the biographer.

'Tell me something.' May turned to the tycoon, watching as Renalda's broad hands absently massaged the steel pins in his knees. 'Where did we go wrong?'

The magnate sipped his whisky. Drinking dulled the pain of his strapped-up legs. 'By looking for someone foreign,' he said at last. 'I suppose it's only natural during a time of war. You don't see it, do you? The English cruelty. That is what your crimes stink of. The culprit is English. You are a cold race. You don't beat your animals, you're subtler, less human. This killer does not think of others, he cares only about himself. You could not find him because you, too, are English.'

'It seems to me that you care only about your company, and the City's faith in it.'

'Faith is a fragile thing these days. A good businessman takes nothing personally. It is unfortunate that lives have been lost. This whole war is unfortunate.'

'Thank you for the advice,' said May, buttoning his coat. 'I'll see you this evening at the theatre, and I will bring the violence to an end. The unit may have been shut down, but it will not stop operating until justice has been served.'

He only wished he was as confident as he sounded.

He left Renalda's office and walked into the dimly lit corridor, where his eye was caught by the ornate gilt-framed wall mirror that stood there. The glass was cracked, and something had been scrawled across it with a blood-red stick of greasepaint. The letters were six inches high: GET OUT OF OUR HOUSE.

I'll get out, thought May grimly, but I'm taking you with me.

'I have a terrible feeling about tonight. He should be here,' said May fretfully. 'It doesn't seem right without him.'

'I understand how you feel, John, but you have to give him some breathing space.' Forthright hooked back the dusty brown drapery and studied the edge of the stage. 'They're running late again. The curtain should have gone up five minutes ago.'

'We're starting it late because the trains are disrupted again,' said Harry, listening for the backstage sounds that told him things were running to schedule. 'There's hardly any service from the east. A church steeple fell on the line outside Fenchurch Street. They reckon Winchester's going to cop it next, after Southampton. Trouble is, it's all getting back to Hitler.'

'What is?' asked Forthright.

'The air-raid damage reports. Franco gets them in code from the Spanish ambassador in Whitehall. That's what Lord Haw Haw reckons.'

'Things have come to a pretty pass if you're believing *him*,' said Forthright indignantly.

'There's a lot of coughing and sneezing in the audience this evening. My mum says it's because everyone stands around outside at night watching the planes circling. Right, there goes the signal.' Harry darted off through the narrow corridor leading to the left wing just as applause broke out across the auditorium. The conductor was taking his place at the podium.

'Where's Biddle?' May checked the area behind him. 'I thought I told him to keep in the backstage area. I have a suspicion he's rather enjoying his new role.' May had spread his constables around the theatre, but with tickets changing hands for high prices on the black market, they had been refused seat allocations and were forced to stand conspicuously at the rear of the stalls.

'He wanted to write up his report, so I gave him permission to use the company office. He said he's expecting some news.'

May sniffed the air and looked at the sergeant suspiciously. 'Are you wearing eau de Cologne?'

'Why, yes.' Forthright blushed. 'I thought, well, it's a night out at the theatre.'

'You're not worried about Davenport closing us down, then?'

'I have confidence in you, Mr May.' Her hand squeezed his shoulder. 'You'll see us through.'

'I wish I had your faith.'

'Oh, it comes from being around Arthur. It'll rub off on you, don't worry.'

The orchestra launched itself into an *allegro* version of Offenbach's overture, and May was forced to raise his voice. 'I don't know which area to watch first,' he confessed. 'A murderer operating in an area the size of a football pitch, and we can't find a damned thing.'

'More like eight football pitches, with all the other levels,' said Forthright. 'If someone wanted to stay hidden, what chance would you have of finding them?'

'Everyone backstage is signed for. It would have to be someone in the audience.' The music thundered to a crescendo. 'Or someone we haven't thought of,' mused May.

'I missed that,' shouted Forthright.

'Forget it.' He realized he was following the same mental patterns as Arthur Bryant. He'd been about to wonder if it could be someone they had dismissed as dead. But all the victims were accounted for. There was no one else.

Slowly the realization dawned. 'Blimey.'

'What is it?'

'We've overlooked something. You'd better come with me.'

A tidal wave of applause broke over the theatre as the conductor took his bow. May pushed Forthright back towards the right-hand pass door. 'I was thinking the other day—suppose she's not dead.'

'Who?' asked the sergeant, trying to keep up with him. 'What are you talking about?'

'Elissa Renalda. I've had a chance to go through some of the other clippings, and there's been a fair amount of speculation since her death. They never properly identified her body. What if she didn't drown? Suppose she *was* the gold-digger that Minos had always suspected her to be? She could have married Andreas for his money. Sources agree that Sirius liked her, she managed to wrap him round her little finger. But she lost everything when Minos warned her to get off the island. Imagine. She has to flee before dawn, while her husband is away. She has nothing but the clothes she's standing in, and maybe her passage on a fishing boat. Minos tells the police she accidentally drowned. He protects her memory for the sake of his brother. Only Andreas believes she was killed. Elissa comes back to England, her home country, and bitterly follows the business exploits of the Renaldas in the newspapers. She waits for an opportunity to exact revenge. She returns to Athens and tracks down Minos, who's killed in a car crash after a day of heavy drinking. But we don't know the details of that event.'

'So Minos is killed by Andreas's wife. For what motive?' asked Forthright.

'Elissa was in the line of succession, but her "death" cut her out of the will.'

'You realize you're sounding like Arthur.'

'I know,' May admitted. 'Once she was declared dead, she was free but penniless. Mere revenge isn't enough for the way she's been treated. She stages an attack on Renalda's empire, to ensure that his credibility is destroyed for ever. She'll back off, though, if he gives her a cut. Who is she? She could be anyone. None of us has even seen a decent picture of her. She could be operating here, inside the company.'

Forthright struggled with this new idea. 'You think Renalda knows who she is now?'

'I think he was lying the night Arthur accused him.'

'But why wouldn't he have told the truth?'

'Because...' May clutched at the air, trying to make sense of his idea, 'he would have been forced to admit that he was still married. If Elissa is alive, she's still an heir, and the case would have to go to court.'

They had reached the musty company office, where Sidney Biddle was working.

'Sidney, I need you to check whether there was another vehicle involved in the crash that killed Minos Renalda. If there was, find out whatever you can about who was driving. Bryant left all the relevant phone numbers in his work folder. I don't care who you have to disturb to do it.'

Biddle's smile broadened at the thought of upsetting people in the name of the law. 'Right away, sir,' he cried, only just resisting the temptation to salute.

Andreas Renalda was watching the performance from the sealed-off royal box. The divider between the two sections had been re-stored. In one half sat a group of noisily enthusiastic businessmen. On the other side of the brown partition, the millionaire sat in the shadows, absently chewing his thumb. When the door opened a crack it threw a shaft of light across his pale, angry face. 'You cannot possibly wish to see me now,' he hissed at May. 'The American investors are here. It is the time of Orpheus's big duet. We have the *Times* critic sitting in the front row.'

'Fine,' whispered May. 'I'll come in and tell you why I think your wife is in this theatre. Then you can try to convince me that you're not an accessory to murder.'

Even in the dim light of the box, he could see Renalda blanch. 'Help me up, damn it,' he hissed. May opened the door wider, ushering him out into the corridor. For the first time since they had met, Renalda looked unsure of himself. May wondered if he was deciding whether to lie again.

'Can we talk where your clients can't hear us?' May asked as he pulled the box door shut behind them.

'Here, this is the eviction staircase, nobody uses it any more.' Renalda unlocked a door on their right and led the way onto a concrete landing faced by damp-tainted ochre walls. 'What do you need to know about Elissa?'

'You could start by telling me how long you've known she's alive.'

The millionaire rubbed at his broad forehead, as if afflicted by a migraine. 'You're saying that—'

'Any delay now risks everything you've worked for.'

Renalda sighed heavily. 'She contacted me about eighteen months ago. A phone call out of the blue. At first I did not believe her.'

'But you arranged to see her.'

'We met for a drink at the Savoy. She told me that she had been ordered off the island by my brother. Minos had acted in good faith. It is the way of our family, to protect one another. She was very beautiful, very young, and I was blind, a cripple bewitched by a girl who tricked me into marriage. Minos scared her away for my sake. The police found the body of a drowned swimmer a month later, and after I spoke to them, they conveniently decided that it was my wife's. It suited us for her to appear dead. No loss of face, you understand.

'But she was alive. Elissa timed our meeting well. I was about to sign the deal with the theatre. She asked me to sign half of my holdings in Three Hundred International over to her. If I did not agree to do so, she said she would go to the press, tell everyone that she was still legally my wife, that I had conspired to have her killed and that she had survived the attempt. Me, who had only ever loved her! I could not allow an ugly court case, just when I was fighting to make a name for myself in London. I was not prepared to risk losing the confidence of our shareholders. But I would not sign over my father's empire. We drank, and I let her talk until she talked too much. She said she had heard about Minos's death.'

'She caused his accident, didn't she?'

'She was in the other car, the one that ran him off the road. I saw in her eyes that I had won. She had only one card to play, you see. Any accusation from her would bring a far more serious accusation from me. How the press would have loved that! We had reached an impasse.'

'So she followed you here, and the trouble began. Do you know where she is now?'

'Of course. She is here all the time, where I can keep an eye on her at every single performance.'

'Who is she?'

'Who do you think? That girl in the chorus, the one you spent the night with.'

May's jaw fell open. 'Betty Trammel?'

'Elissa. Elissabetta. Betty. You see? She is a little older and more experienced than she looks. What could I do, tell Helena not to hire her because she was my wife?'

'She's not only your wife, she's a murderess,' said May, horrified that he could have been such a poor judge of character.

'She followed Minos in a state of frustration and anger, and ran him off the road. She did not mean to kill him. And I don't think she's harmed anyone in this theatre.' Renalda gave a sour smile. 'Although she's broken a few hearts. I imagine she found it exciting to seduce a boy who could have her arrested.'

'Where is she now?'

'Backstage, I suppose, waiting to go on. She's a natural performer, as I'm sure you have discovered.'

Andreas Renalda pressed his hands against the sides of his calipers to steady himself. 'God spare me from the designs of angry women.'

56

A DEATH FORETOLD

If John was now thinking like Arthur, the reverse was also true.

Bryant was pursuing a more logical line of enquiry. Forget mythology, he told himself. Don't be misled by the intrigues of the Renalda family. The feud is a red herring. Start afresh, follow a new path. How, he asked himself, would a sensible, methodical man like John May interpret the facts?

After his humiliating experience at Renalda's house, the young detective had carefully rethought his strategy. Seated on his favourite bench by the river, as close as he could get to the memory of his fiancée, armed with the blue crystal fountain pen that Detective Sergeant Forthright had given him on his twenty-second birthday, he mapped out the personal details of the Palace's victims.

Immediately, one name separated itself from the others. One of the two key factors, he felt sure, was Jan Petrovic. Phyllis, her housemate, had told May that Petrovic wanted to leave the show because she wasn't up to the part. Two days later she had gone missing.

The other key was the fact that, however much you allowed for coincidence or fate, the deaths were patterned exactly on Renalda's family mythology. It followed that the murderer not only knew about his past, but was attempting to shift the focus of blame onto him. But why? To take revenge on him for some perceived slight? Possibly. Surely it was more likely to have been arranged out of convenience? The killer was going to commit acts of violence whatever happened, and it made sense to deflect suspicion by implicating an innocent man.

Bryant raised his head and looked across the sluggish brown river, out towards the open sea, the breeze lifting his fringe from his eyes. Two further possibilities presented themselves. Either the person he was looking for had read about Renalda's background—according to the tycoon, it wouldn't have been difficult—or Renalda himself had provided the information. Which meant that it was someone he trusted, somebody close to him in the production.

Petrovic's flatmate said she had lied her way into the job, and was unable to handle it. Suppose she had used the murders as a way of disappearing? She fitted Renalda's mythological beliefs perfectly—almost any chorus girl would have done so—and it was easy to fake her own abduction. But in her haste she had made a mistake, failing to allow her 'abductor' any method of entering the flat. The doors had been shut from the inside, and the neighbours had seen only Petrovic herself entering and leaving the house.

Bryant gently shook ink into the nib of the pen, and drew a series of connecting lines on his pad. Petrovic had wanted to break her contract. Her fellow performers at the Palace were mysteriously disappearing, so she used it as a chance to vanish, to set herself free from a contract she didn't feel capable of honouring. She couldn't provide a body, of course, just a few tiny drops of blood, and a smear of crimson nail polish when they didn't look enough. The rest was easy. When someone had a little money in their pocket and didn't want to be found, Bryant knew, it was difficult to track them down. With the war on, it seemed that everyone was on the move.

Bryant studied the missing section of his diagram. Who knew about Petrovic's problem, and had been able to provide her with a solution? Who told her about Andreas Renalda's Muses, and could explain how her own vanishing act might work?

It had to be the same person the tycoon had confided in. One person linked them both together. Bryant stared at the blue question mark he had scored on the pad, and pensively scratched at his unshaven chin.

What puzzled him most of all was why someone would go to so much trouble. Why was it in their interests to make it look as if Petrovic had also been attacked by the Palace Phantom?

He assumed he had been locked in the archive room by the killer, but at the very same moment Valerie Marchmont had been murdered onstage. How could her attacker have been in two places at once?

The odder pieces of the puzzle sharpened into focus. The picture of the statue in the archive room. The canopy that hung over the east face of the theatre. The reason why the murders had been made to look like accidents.

Actors, damned actors, covering up their secrets, hiding behind their masks.

He had been lied to, again and again and again. He was young and eager, blinded and sidetracked by the mythology of a famous family, all because their story so perfectly matched the opera they were presenting.

Bryant released a groan as he realized the truth. Something far simpler, far more apparent, something that had been staring him in the face for the past week. He needed to get back to the theatre, to check the paintwork on the other pass door—the door that Stan Lowe's boy was supposed to be jemmying open to comply with the safety regulations.

There was only an hour to go before the curtain went up on Monday night's performance of *Orpheus*. It took him nearly twenty minutes to locate a working telephone in the Aldwych, and then, in his haste to find someone who could help him, he managed to call the woman who was most likely to make his mission more difficult.

'Who is this?' shouted Maggie Armitage, practising white witch and founder member of the Camden Town Coven.

'Who have I called?' Bryant asked himself aloud.

'Don't you know, you silly man?' she shouted more loudly. 'If this is Trevor Bannister from the Southwark Bridge Supernaturals, I've already told you, we don't want your South London call-outs, thank you. Five shillings for spirit clearance, it's not worth the taxi fare. I'm not wiping up other people's ectoplasm for less than seven and six.'

'Maggie, I'm sorry, I seem to have dialled without concentrating...' Bryant had been staying with the spiritualist for the past two days. He had felt the need to be away from people who knew about the case, and his landlady was in daily contact with DS Forthright.

'Arthur? Is that you? Your dinner's ruined, I'd give it to the dog but turnips give him wind. I had a feeling you were going to call. It's about the Palace, isn't it? You think you know who's behind the murders.'

'I, er, ah...'

'Your timing is spot on, we just finished a séance. We were going to have a few madrigals, but my harpsichord has suffered some minor bomb damage. I used to be able to slice hardboiled eggs through the top chords, but of course it's all powdered stuff now. Do you want me down there? The auspices are very good tonight. Fog always helps the ectoplasmic manifestations. I hear the show is absolutely disgusting, can you get comps?'

'I'm on my way there. I think I'm going to make an arrest,' he foolishly admitted.

'I can do you a quick reading on the telephone if you like. I get the vibrations from the tone of your voice.'

'That's clever,' said Bryant. 'What do you know about fear of open spaces?'

'That's psychology, dear, not spiritualism. It can set in when a susceptible person doesn't get out of the house for a long time, especially if they're undergoing some kind of personal crisis. You think your murderer is agoraphobic?'

'I'm sure of it.'

'Be careful, though, won't you? Phobics can be very nasty when they get into a state of panic. Phobias are powerful vehicles for aggressive feelings. They condense anxiety. Intrusive phobias aren't part of general personalities, they just kick in at key moments. They're a defence against intense trauma, fear of intimacy, stuff like that.'

'You seem to know a lot about it.'

'I once performed an exorcism for a bonce doctor. He was broke and paid me off in therapy. Oh, I'm sensing something very dangerous.'

'In what way?'

'The war. An unexploded bomb. I'm seeing fire and screaming. An explosion, Arthur, a terrible explosion that I'm rather afraid causes the death of one of you.'

'Are you sure?'

'Absolutely, as sure as if it has already happened. In a way, of course, it already has. I don't think you should go to the theatre tonight.'

'I have no choice.'

With the witch's warning words ringing in his ears, Bryant hung up and ran grimly on towards the Palace. When he arrived there, he immediately headed for the right-hand backstage area.

He knew he would find the proof he needed on the lintel of the second pass door.

57

A LIFE IN THE THEATRE

'Because I need you to help us,' said Sergeant Forthright, pausing at the top of the stairs and making sure that the coast was clear.

'I don't know anything about detective work,' Alma Sorrowbridge complained. 'I'm a landlady, for heaven's sake. I'm better on beds.'

'Mr Bryant reckons that any respected person with common sense and an analytical mind could be recruited, so I'm recruiting you.'

'I thought you'd resigned.'

'I never technically left. Although I'm still hoping they'll throw me a party.'

'But why me?'

'Because you're the most enormous person we know. You weigh what, about seventeen stone, don't you?'

'Sixteen and a half. There's nothing wrong with my weight. It's my height, I'm too short.'

'The point is, Alma, you're strong.'

'I'm not that strong.'

'How do you clean behind your mangle?'

'I lift it out.'

'Exactly. What I want you to do is wait at the top of these stairs and don't let anyone—*anyone*—get past you.'

'What if the audience starts leaving? How can I stop them?'

'They won't be turning out for a while yet. I think you'd better have this, though.' The sergeant handed her Bryant's swordstick and showed her how to unscrew the pewter top.

'I've never used a sword before,' said Alma hopelessly. 'I'm more at home with a mop.'

'Hopefully you won't have to run anyone through.' Forthright struck a pose with the sword, then resheathed it. For a moment she looked like Douglas Fairbanks in drag. 'If anyone comes this way, just sort of—spread out. And scream blue murder. Someone will come to assist you.'

'This is beyond the call of my duties,' sighed Alma, practising with the stick. 'Wait a minute, how did you get this?'

'Arthur.' Forthright grinned. 'He's back.'

'You mean he's here?'

'Right here in the theatre. He's been staying up in North London with that mad girl from the Camden Town Coven, the one who came to dinner and got poltergeists everywhere. She insisted on saying grace, only she read from the wrong book and we had manifestations. She told him someone's going to die tonight in a UXB explosion. Mr Bryant reckons that whatever happens, he'll make an arrest before the end of the show.'

'Nice of him to tell me where he's been living. He didn't even take a change of underpants.'

'I'm sure Maggie Armitage has been taking good care of our boy.'

'Well, I never did.'

Forthright gave her an old-fashioned look. 'No, but you wish you had.'

'I've got a soft spot for him, that's all.' She waved the stick. 'OK, bring on this phantom of yours. I'm ready for anything.'

'What do you mean, he's here?' whispered May. He was wedged in his usual position at the side of the stage, in a black-painted brick inlet provided for quick changes. 'You're telling me he's back?'

'He's figured it all out and is going to make an arrest,' said Biddle excitedly. 'I can help. I was a boxing champion at school.' He took an experimental swing with his left fist. 'I put my geography teacher in the hospital. He shouted at me about alluvial deposits so I decked him.'

'Really? I'm seeing another side to you,' May replied, alarmed. 'I hope violence won't be necessary. We're the police, we don't thump people.'

'It's funny, isn't it? I thought I was more interested in the paper-work side of the job, but it turns out I much prefer the chase.'

'What does he want us to do?' asked May.

'Who?' Biddle took another practice swing.

'Mr Bryant, you idiot.'

'Oh. He said to go to the foyer of the theatre at exactly half past the hour.'

'What time do you make it?'

Biddle tilted his watch to the light. 'Twenty-nine minutes past.'

May shoved at him. 'Well, let's go, then!'

They filed through to the end of the corridor and dropped down to the pass door, making their way along the dark tiled halls to the front-of-house area.

'I don't suppose Bryant told you who he was planning to arrest, did he?'

'He didn't want anyone to know in advance.' Biddle hobbled on ahead. 'He told me to tell you no mythology this time. He said he needed our help because it wasn't one person.'

'What do you mean?' asked May.

Biddle shrugged. 'He said there are two of them.'

Arthur Bryant checked the buttons on his smart scarlet waistcoat and straightened his scarf. Forthright was bound to have put some constables in the auditorium. If things turned nasty, he hoped they would get here in time.

He checked his watch again. There could be no more mistakes. His nervousness receded as he walked confidently forward to the box-office window. His knock on the glass echoed in the eerily empty foyer.

Elspeth Wynter suddenly appeared from behind the counter. She was holding Nijinsky, her tortoise. 'Oh, it's you, Arthur.'

'I wonder if I could have a word with you, Elspeth.'

'Of course.' She smiled sadly, then set the tortoise back in its box. 'Look, Arthur, I know what you're going to say, and I'm flattered by the attention you've given me, but I don't think it would work out between us.'

For a moment Bryant was flummoxed. This wasn't what he had come to discuss.

'I thought you were—lonely.' He knew by the look on her face that he had chosen the wrong word.

'Whatever you thought we had in common, I don't—I mean to say, I'm not as free as you. I can't leave this place.'

'I realize that.'

'No. I mean I really can't leave.'

'Elspeth, I have to talk to you about Jan Petrovic.'

'Oh, I see.' He heard the relief in her voice. 'Have you found her?'

'No, but I have a good idea where she is.' Bryant tried to sound nonchalant.

'You do? Where is she? Is she safe?'

'She's fine. She's in Dublin.'

'Dublin? I don't understand.'

'Petrovic wanted to get out of the show but had an unbreakable contract, so someone suggested a way that she could escape. That was you, wasn't it?'

Her shoulders slumped wearily, and she placed a hand over her face. For a moment he thought she was going to cry.

'I know the truth, Elspeth. I'm sorry. I spoke to Phyllis, her flatmate. She told me Jan came to see you. She didn't think anything of it at the time, because Jan told her you worked at the theatre.'

Wynter raised her head and studied his eyes intently. 'I just suggested that with these murders going on, there was a way she could easily leave. I told her, it's just a bit of theatre, that's all. Break a window, give yourself a little nick on the thumb, leave a drop of blood and people will think that the Palace has claimed another victim. She's a Hungarian Jew, Arthur. Her parents are waiting for her in Ireland before the family heads for America. She desperately wanted to go and join them.'

'But why would you do that?' asked Bryant. 'Why would you give the police even more cause for concern?' He held her gaze steadily, and in that moment, she knew that he knew. 'I've never made an arrest before, Elspeth. I'm afraid you're going to be my first. You see, this time, I know I've got the right person. I know it's you.'

'Arthur, please—'

'I know you've spent your whole life in the theatre,' said Bryant quietly. 'Raising him and looking after yourself. I can't blame you for wanting to be free. But you chose the wrong way to do it.'

She unlocked the box-office door and closed it behind her with infinite care. 'So you really do know.'

'The other pass door,' he explained. 'There are no coats of paint holding it shut, just a lock. Nobody ever thought to check it. You told Stan it was sealed, and he told everyone else. I knew that if it could be opened, somebody must have a key. I found it in your tortoise box.'

'So you unlocked the door and discovered the room. I wonder if we could sit down.' She looked around, her hands knotted together.

'Of course.' Bryant ushered her to a small alcove with a velvet-covered bench seat.

'I thought we were fine,' Elspeth explained. 'It was such a big building, that was the thing. Nobody even knew he was there. Oh, one or two of the girls sat with him when he was small, but they all moved on. I hadn't even realized I was pregnant, Arthur. I was fifteen years old. Nobody told me the facts of life. A painful two-minute act in the dark of a dressing room with a man I had never seen out of villainous stage make-up. I was frightened out of my wits. The show closed and he left with it. I gave birth just as my grandmother had, here in the theatre. The difference was I was unmarried. There was no one I could go to for help.'

A look of overwhelming misery settled on her. 'I knew I would have to raise the boy alone. They wouldn't let me stay in my lodgings, not in my condition. It was a respectable boarding house. So I moved in here with him. Nobody knew—why would they? There are whole floors barely used. That's when I found the other storeroom behind the pass door. We slept there and were happy enough. My boy stayed quiet. He was as good as gold. There were members of staff in whom I confided. They all moved on. The shows came and went, just as they always had. We would still have been in lodgings, sharing a room. There was so much homelessness. You started to see people sleeping in the parks. We were better off here. Then my boy began to grow restive. He spent too much time alone. Something went wrong in his head.'

'What did you expect?' asked Bryant. 'You can't lock a child up, away from the real world, away from light and friends, no matter how much love you give him.'

Elspeth appeared not to have heard. 'He was always playing with the costumes and props, you see. Trying on the masks. He especially loved the Greek ones, but the comedy face got broken and he was left with the mask of tragedy. It got so I couldn't get him to take it off. He seemed happier behind it. We would eat together, and I would leave him playing or asleep while I went to work, just as always. But he kept the mask on more and more. I tried to pretend that things were normal. Then he became ill and started acting oddly, and I finally took the mask off.' She bit her knuckle, tears welling in her eyes. 'At first I couldn't remove it. He'd cut himself, you see, and the cut was infected. The mask was papier mâché. It was damp from his face all the time. It went rotten. It did something awful to his flesh. I treated it as best I could, but there were terrible scars. It was too late for a doctor. I knew they would send me to gaol. My poor boy. The skin dried all shiny and stretched. He started to remind me of men who'd been in the Great War, the ones who'd been burned, who stand on street corners selling matches. I didn't know what to do. I decided it was time to leave. This place had become our prison. But when I went to go—'

'You found you couldn't leave.'

'I couldn't even set a foot outside the door.' She shook the memory from her head. 'I looked up at the sky and felt sick. Had to sit on the step to stop myself from vomiting. The sun burned my eyes. The cars, the traffic, the noise. I didn't know there was a word for it.'

'Agoraphobia. It's hardly surprising, the amount of time you spent in this dimly lit building.'

'Then the war started. The blackouts. Everything went quiet. Everything was dark. I felt it more with each passing performance, the pressure to leave, it stalked me through the building like a living thing, daring me to go outside. I took my first steps out of the Palace in seventeen years, and was violently sick. Everyone else was in the shelters. The bombers passed overhead but they kept on going. You'll think this is strange, but it was so peaceful.' She exhaled sadly. 'Then they sounded the all-clear and people came out onto the streets again. But the lights stayed off. I knew that if I was ever going to get out of the Palace and back into the world, I would have to leave soon, before the war ended and all the lights came back on.'

She looked at Bryant pleadingly. 'But I couldn't go. How could I go? A new show starting, I'd never missed a performance, never let anyone down in my life. The rehearsals were beginning, they were relying on me. There was no one to take my place. I'm the only one who knows where everything is. There's Stan Lowe, of course, he's been here as long as me, but he's fond of a drink, the place could burn down and he wouldn't notice. So long as the show stays open, I have to be here.'

'So you decided to close the show.'

'It was my boy, Todd. I called him that after Todd Slaughter, the star of *Maria Marten—The Murders in the Red Barn*. That was the show his father had been in. Todd was growing up fast. He took a shine to Tanya Capistrania, watching her from the wings while she practised. I thought he might try to do something cruel, something bad. I thought, history's going to repeat itself if I don't do something, he'll become like his father, and I won't be able to control him. He's too big for me now. He's seventeen. He's already started to slip out during the air-raid warnings, moving under cover of the dark, while everyone's off the streets. I didn't want to see Tanya raped and left pregnant with some awful— I thought, if she dies, there'll be a scandal. They'll shut the place down and I'll have to go. I'll be forced out. It was the only way I'd ever be able to leave.

'No one liked her, no one was close. I didn't want her to suffer, so I poisoned her. I thought it would just put her to sleep. The hemlock was the easiest thing to get hold of. It grows on the bomb sites, you see. I put it in a sandwich and gave it to her. I thought she'd be able to tell if there was something funny about the flavour, so I got quail, something she'd never eaten before. She trusted me. Everyone trusts me. The hemlock made her fall down, but she wouldn't die. Todd saw she was sick and got very angry. He tried to pull her out of the lift, and, God forgive me, in my panic I pressed the call button.

'He went crazy when he saw what the lift did to her. He threw the severed parts out of the window in a rage. He wanted me to be caught. They rolled off the canopy and landed somewhere below. When I went to look for them they were gone. Tanya's body was discovered, and I thought the show would be shut down at once. But no, Mr Renalda kept it going. I'd met Mr Renalda at the start of rehearsals, and instantly disliked him. I read about his family in the papers, all that stuff about him being raised to believe in Greek myths, and I thought, this is perfect.

'A theatrical mind, you see. Plot mechanics. I see them every day of my life. Plots and puzzles and murder mysteries. Faking the way things look, it was second nature to me. I thought, I'll just keep going until they close us down and someone puts the blame on him. Todd had helped me once, so I got him to help me again. I'm his world, Arthur, he'd do anything for me. I told him to watch certain people and to look for opportunities, things he could do that would make everyone get out of our house.

'I made him wear gloves, the same gloves his father had worn on the stage in his role as a murderer. He knows the theatre better than anyone. He cut through the cable holding the globe, and he pushed the boy over the balcony, and he jammed the stage revolve so that Valerie Marchmont died. I knew if he acted during the raids, no outsiders could come into the theatre and discover him. But whatever he did, it seemed that everyone just became more determined to stay. The Blitz mentality, it's infected everything.'

'It was you who locked me in the archive room,' exclaimed Bryant. 'Why, because you wanted to keep me away from the site of Valerie Marchmont's murder?'

'No, I was just really annoyed with you.'

'Oh.'

'I thought I was leaving such an obvious pattern, using symbols of the Muses. You were supposed to go and arrest Mr Renalda. The show couldn't continue without him. But you made it so much more complicated. He slipped out of your hands, the show went on, and I was still *stuck* here, with Todd upstairs, threatening to expose us, becoming more disturbed with every passing hour.' She wiped her eyes with the sleeve of her cardigan. 'Now you'll have to take me out of here, won't you?'

'Yes,' Bryant admitted, 'but you'll be swapping one claustrophobic building for another, I'm afraid.' He looked at his watch. Half past eight. Biddle was supposed to have brought May here by now.

'Where is Todd?' he asked. 'What's planned for tonight?'

'He's under the stage right now,' said Wynter. 'You may already be too late.'

'Bryant! You're back! So Biddle wasn't pulling a fast one!' May rushed forward across the foyer, followed by Sidney. He clapped his partner on the shoulder, then looked at Elspeth Wynter and saw that she had been crying. 'What's going on?'

'Come with me,' said Bryant. 'There's not a moment to lose. Sidney, whatever you do, don't let Miss Wynter out of your sight.'

May fell into step as they headed off along the corridor. 'Where are we going?'

'Do you have a torch?'

'Yes, I always carry my Valiant.'

'Good,' said Bryant, pulling his scarf tighter. 'Where we're going, we'll need it.'

58

LIVING LEGEND

'What's going on?' asked Janice Longbright, trying to catch her breath. An absurdly long McDonald's truck had nearly run them down on the Strand. 'Where are we heading?'

'There's not a moment to lose,' May warned. Longbright strode beside him as they raced off along the pavement. May was forced to push his way through a slow-moving crowd of backpacked tourists, and for a moment the detective sergeant was worried that she would lose him.

'What have you got there?' She pointed at the bulky plastic Sony bag slung over May's shoulder.

'Something I thought we might need. Keep up with me, the sun's nearly set,' May called back. Lorries and vans chugged sluggishly onto the bridge, their exhaust fumes obscuring the kerbs with grey waste. Longbright caught up with her former boss as he waited for the pedestrian signal to change.

She pushed her hair out of her eyes, turning to face the stale breeze from the river. 'Tell me what happened. Did you have any luck with the dentist?'

'He's in Sydney, Australia. I woke him in the middle of the night. Arthur had an appointment with him just before he left. He'd cracked the top plate of his false teeth and wanted them replaced. The dentist didn't have time to cast new moulds before he left, and typically Arthur had lost the old mould he was supposed to keep safely stored away for just such an event, so he had to make do with a pair that didn't fit. They were far too big.'

'I don't understand,' said Longbright. 'Why does it matter how big his teeth were?'

'According to my next-door neighbour, the intruder who she thought was trying to break into my apartment had beady eyes and abnormally large teeth. Do you know anyone with beadier eyes than Arthur? Alma Sorrowbridge said that someone had been in Arthur's room, but the front-door lock hadn't been forced. There are few things more personal than your dental records. Who else would take them?'

'Wait a minute. You're telling me Arthur's alive?' shouted Longbright.

'Oh, he's alive all right, but I think he's suffering from amnesia. Over sixty years ago, Elspeth Wynter's deranged son climbed out of the well at the Palace via its drainage tunnel. Bryant recently tracked him down to the Wetherby clinic. He disturbed a forgotten history, even added a footnote to his memoir before changing his mind and hiding it. Todd followed him back to the unit with the intention of attacking him.

'I think Todd took some kind of explosive device along, but it went off at the wrong time, and Todd was killed. He was only five years younger than Bryant. We found the remains of Todd's body, and Bryant's old teeth. Bryant had been placed at the site, and we weren't looking for anyone else. I think he survived, but he's confused, or concussed or something. He went home, but didn't stay. He came to me, but couldn't get in. I've been stalked by Arthur, not Todd. And if there's anywhere in the world that he does still remember, it's here, on Waterloo Bridge at sunset, where he's walked every night for most of his life.' He pointed across the dual carriageway. A blood-red sun shimmered through exhaust fumes behind the Houses of Parliament. 'You take one side, I'll take the other.'

It was May who saw him first.

Bryant was standing at the spot where his fiancée had died, peering over the edge of the balustrade into the opalescent brown water. He was wearing his favourite gaberdine coat, several filthy scarves and a torn hat. He looked—and, as May got closer, smelled—like a very tired tramp.

'Arthur, it's you. It's really you. I thought you were dead.'

May grabbed his arm and twirled him round for a better look. Bryant had a raw-looking gash on his head which he had tried to bandage with an old tie. He was sporting a set of ridiculous ill-fitting teeth that looked as though they had been made for someone with a much bigger head.

'Look at me.' May grabbed his empty face and tilted it up. 'It's me, John May. You're here on the bridge, on Waterloo Bridge where we always go, where Nathalie died. You're Arthur Bryant of the Peculiar Crimes Unit and you're my best friend. Look at me.' He held Bryant's face steady in his strong hands, but the old detective's eyes remained impassive.

'For God's sake, Arthur,' May shouted, 'you'd remember Edna bloody Wagstaff well enough if she was still alive. Well, take a look at this.' He dumped the carrier bag on the pavement and pulled the stuffed cat from it. Time had not been kind to the Abyssinian. Most of its fur had been eaten away with mange, its remaining eye had fallen out and one of its back legs was missing.

'You remember Rothschild?' May thrust the deformed cat carcass in his partner's face. 'It was her familiar. Squadron Leader Smethwick used to send messages through it. Edna left it to Maggie Armitage in her will.'

It was the only thing he had been able to lay his hands on that Bryant might recognize. Rothschild had sat on his desk like a moulting familiar for over twenty years. Slowly, very slowly, the light of recognition began to return to the elderly detective's eyes. Finally, he opened his dry, cracked lips.

'John, what are you doing here?'

'It lives! It speaks!' He turned excitedly to Longbright, who had reached them. 'Look who this is—Janice is here!'

'Why are you talking to me as if I'm a child?' Bryant complained. 'Is there something wrong with you? Hello, Janice. Have you got anything to eat?'

Then he fainted.

May caught him and sat him against the balustrade while Longbright rang for an ambulance.

59

THE CRUELTY OF THE MOON

'Sergeant Forthright has got your landlady stationed across the stairs,' May explained.

'What on earth for?'

'She thought we might need reinforcements. We've only got Crowhurst and Atherton in the auditorium.'

'The White Witch of Camden gave me a warning about tonight,' Bryant cautioned. 'The killer can't go back to his lair because I took the key to his room out of the tortoise box.'

'I think it's this one.' May pointed out the brown door that led to the first of the understage areas. 'What's been going on?'

'Well, it struck me that if you removed Jan Petrovic from the victim list, all of the deaths took place in the theatre. Why? I asked myself, knowing there could only be one answer. They happened here because the murderer hardly ever leaves the building. Elspeth Wynter has been trying to close down the show because she needs to be free of this house. But she's become agoraphobic. I remember her sweating in the restaurant when we went out to lunch. She can't bear to be trapped in here any longer, but on that day she couldn't wait to get back. Hiding her boy all these years was easier than hiding her own feelings, but she managed that as well. Hardly surprising, seeing as she's spent her life in the theatre watching people fake emotions. In a way, she's more talented than any of them.'

Bryant pulled the door shut behind them and flicked on his

torch. Ahead lay a maze of bare wooden walls. Makeshift timber railings prevented them from falling to the lower levels.

'She couldn't have killed anyone,' May pointed out. 'You only have to look at her, she's tiny.'

'She staged the murders for her son to carry out. He's getting too big for her to take care of any longer, creeping around the theatre frightening the ladies in their dressing rooms. He's down here somewhere. Elspeth can never have a life, never be close to anyone, never ever leave so long as a production continues. She needs the show to close so she can finally escape. And now it's all too late.'

He led the way along the wooden bridge that ran round the central dark square. 'We're nearly under the orchestra. Look up.' Above them was the dust-caked wire mesh that indicated the start of the orchestra pit.

'So you were right, in a way. It was about the assassination of theatre gods—just not the ones you thought. Mind your head.' The corridor was lower now. They passed several rusted iron-rung ladders leading to the star traps, segmented doors through which an actor could be catapulted onto the stage under cover of smoke. At the downstage centre point stood the grave trap. Light from the spots above the dancers shone down through the grille.

'I don't like this, Arthur. He could be hiding anywhere.'

Bryant pulled something metallic from his pocket. The click of a ratchet sounded.

'Are you armed?' asked May.

'It's a service revolver that belonged to my brother.'

'I didn't know you had a brother. Do you know how to use it?'

'The principle's not hard to grasp. Trigger here, bullets come out of the end. It's my understanding that he kept it loaded. I don't think the boy is on this level.' Bryant peered over the side of the rickety balustrade and shone his torch into the darkness below. 'We're going to have to go further down.'

'I don't like this at all,' May complained, feeling for the steps ahead. From the stage above their heads came the sound of the orchestra launching into the show's grand finale set piece, the cancan.

The stamping of the dancers dislodged showers of dirt. Sawdust sifted past their faces. Bryant pulled out a handkerchief and discreetly coughed into it.

'Are you sure he's down here?' May shifted uncomfortably. He was starting to feel shut in.

'Listen.' They stopped as they reached the middle of the three floors constructed beneath the theatre. The music was distorted by the gurgling steam pipes that ran all around them. Bryant shone his torch beam over the walls. The shadows of the stage props, a dozen twisted demon heads, stretched and fell away. The giant eyes of Cerberus, the watchdog of Hell, gleamed wetly at them from a corner. Spiders and mice scuttled from the light. Ahead, just out of the beam, something moved.

'I think that's him.' Bryant's eyes widened. 'Stone the crows.'

The boy caught in the torchlight seemed more frightened than angry. His pale, fleshy face was cicatrized with the marks of a badly healed infection, the skin pulled taut and shiny across his skull, his right eye milky with cataracts. His chin was sunk into the bulky mass of his chest, so that he appeared to have no neck at all. Having never left the confines of the theatre, he had the typical deficiencies of a human deprived of sunlight and nutrition. His bones were twisted with the effects of rickets.

'The light's hurting his eyes, keep the torch trained on him,' Bryant called over his shoulder as they advanced.

'Go away from me. I know she sent you,' cried Todd suddenly, throwing his hands across his eyes and edging from the circle of brilliance cast by May's torch. The voice was as dry and dead as the air in the theatre, no louder than the rasp of a scrim sliding in its oiled wooden groove, and yet its tone was clear and cultured. He had spent his life listening to actors' declamations.

'Todd, we don't mean you any harm, we want to help you, but you'll have to come with us.' Bryant took a step closer.

'She intends to leave me here, all alone here.' The boy backed away with his arms still raised.

'No, she doesn't, your mother is going to take you with her,' Bryant promised.

'I've seen you, both of you. I did it for her, so we can get out. But I know she's not taking me.'

'Where did he get this idea from?' whispered May.

'I hear everything through the grilles and traps. I heard her telling you.' Todd thrust an accusing finger. 'You, the short one.'

'I'm not short,' said Bryant indignantly.

Todd suddenly broke free from the light and dropped down the wooden staircase leading to the lowest level of the theatre. The detectives were forced to move forward over the narrow footbridge, one behind the other. Far above them, thirty dancers bared their thighs and hammered out the steps of the cancan.

Beneath the three great turbine engines, the steam pipes and oiled cables that led to the flies, Todd darted along the open corridors, loping from side to side like an ape, dislodging props and items of clothing that hung along the walls, a half-wild creature at home in a penumbral world of brick and iron.

'Keep away from me.' They heard him before May could shift the torchlight onto his face. He was on the far side of the understage. The ground beneath the detectives' feet had turned from planks to stone and earth.

'Keep the torch trained on him, John.'

May picked out the boy's twisted features with his beam. Todd released a despairing bellow of pain as the light seared his eyes.

'All right, wait.' May moved the circle of light lower, over the boy's chest, until he had grown calmer.

'I didn't want to hurt her,' he called back, 'the dancer, she was so beautiful, but Mother poisoned her. Then she started the lift and it ruined everything. She wanted to shock the outsiders. Poor precious feet, I threw them from the window of the smoking salon, hoping someone would see. But outside was all black, there was no one about.'

'The air raid,' murmured Bryant. 'You weren't to know.'

'My mother says it is too dangerous to go outside, there are bombs falling from the sky. But I've been out. I know how to drive a bike.'

Todd reached down and picked up something that looked like a length of oak. May lowered the torch and saw that it was a sledge-hammer.

'She'll leave me, and I will have to stay here alone in Hell, with Eurydice.' He shifted his weight until he was standing astride something grey and heavy, and raised the sledgehammer in his broad fists.

'Don't go any closer, Arthur.' May's torch picked out the object at Todd's feet, an absurdly bomb-like thing with tail fins, spattered in white dust, in a round steel case as tall as a man, tapering to a point. How it had reached the basement was a mystery; the ceiling above it was intact.

May had seen enough photographs of unexploded bombs in the *Evening News,* with proud ARP men standing beside them. By the end of the war, fifty thousand would have been defused in streets, factories, shops and homes. Sixty years later, they would still be discovered and deactivated.

'We'll all go together, to the real Hell, not one made of paint and plaster,' said Todd sadly. 'It's for the best.' He raised the sledgehammer higher over his head.

'No'—Bryant threw up his hands—'don't do it, Todd. Remember all the girls above us, the young dancers, like the one you didn't want to hurt.'

'None of them will have me. Who would want me? I'm a man, not a child. I have no face. I have no life. Can't go. Can't stay. And now I am a murderer.'

'Todd, please.' A sense of dread flooded over Bryant. He was horribly aware of Maggie's warning, that death would come from an unexploded bomb. He held out his hands. 'Please,' he begged the boy again. May was standing right in its path.

The muscles in Todd's arms flexed, and he swung the sledgehammer down into the bomb with all his might. Bryant and May threw themselves down onto the floor.

The only sound that followed was a violent splintering of wood. May groped for the fallen torch and twisted its beam back towards the boy. The head of the sledgehammer was lodged firmly inside the bomb case.

'It's a prop, a bloody balsa-wood stage prop,' cried May.

'Blimey.' Bryant rose clumsily to his feet as May ran past him. He saw his partner wrestling with the boy, then watched as they fell with a crash that jolted aside the torch beam. Grunts and shouts filled the enveloping darkness. A few moments later came a terrible cry. Bryant thought of Maggie's death warning again.

'John!' he shouted, but there was no reply. Nothing but silence in the turgid claustrophobia of the darkened underworld.

60

THE MOON IN A BOX

Biddle pulled a Woodbine from behind his ear and kept his eyes on Elspeth Wynter as he dug around for a light. He didn't like the look of her. Panic was flickering in her eyes. She was searching for a way out. From the street outside came the familiar whine of the siren mounted on the roof of St Anne's Church. For a moment he thought she was going to drop in her tracks.

'It's all right, Mrs Wynter, our lads will find your son. Everything's going to be fine.' It was the reassurance everyone gave each other throughout the war.

'He's very strong,' she warned. 'I feel a little faint. Do you mind if I sit down over there, where it's cooler?'

'Here.' He took her arm and helped her to the stool in the box-office booth. 'They timed the raid well tonight. The show's just turning out.'

Behind them, the ushers opened the auditorium doors as the sound of applause billowed into the foyer. Moments later, they were engulfed by members of the audience, leaving quickly to obey the warning of the air-raid siren. Biddle took his eyes off her for only a second. When he looked back at the booth, Elspeth Wynter had gone.

'John, where are you?' called Bryant. 'Shine your torch.' He heard a strangled grunt in the dark. Water was dripping somewhere.

'Over here.' May was coughing, trying to catch his breath. He grappled for the Valiant and pointed its beam up once more. Bryant saw that he was sitting beside the mouth of the artesian well. He limped over and joined May at the glistening ring of stone.

'Down there.' May shone the torch over the side and saw Todd hanging by one claw-like hand from the slippery green brickwork.

'Good Lord, look how deep it is.' Bryant got onto his knees and leaned as far over the well mouth as he dared. 'Todd, give us your hand. We can get you out of there.' He turned to May. 'You're taller than me, you can reach further.'

The boy was shaking his head rhythmically, scraping the damaged skin of his forehead along the brickwork until a dark caul of blood veiled his eyes. 'No,' he called up. 'I come from deep inside the Palace. This is where I belong. I see the stars from the skylight, lying up on the grid, just under the roof. The moon is always in a box, and the box is only full of tricks. I want something to be real. Death is real.'

As the detectives cried out in unison, Todd opened the fingers of his left hand and dropped down the centre of the well, a fall of almost seventy feet before he hit the black water below. There was nothing either of them could do. For a moment they lost him from view. Then they turned the torch on the distant oily surface until it settled once more into an unbroken mirror, the remaining effect of a vanishing act.

Biddle pushed through the crowds, shoving his way out of the congested theatre foyer. His one chance to make good, to do something positive, and he had messed up. He threw his cigarette aside and looked around desperately as the theatregoers began making their way towards the shelters. There was no sense of urgency on the street, no rush or panic. Couples crowded the narrow pavement outside the Palace as ARP wardens directed them to the nearest shelter. He couldn't see her. There were people everywhere. As Biddle searched the faces, the detectives arrived beside him.

'Where's Elspeth?' asked Bryant, wheezing badly. 'What have you done with her?'

'It's my fault,' Biddle admitted. 'She ran out as the stalls started emptying into the hall. My eyes were off her only for a second.' He looked at Bryant's dirt-covered clothes. 'What happened to you?'

'We have to find her, Sidney.'

'She can't have got far. Here, give us a hand up.' Biddle leaned on the detective's shoulders and hoisted himself onto the edge of a stone horse trough. On the other side of Cambridge Circus he saw the back of a woman in a brown cardigan and skirt, fleeing in the direction of the British Museum. 'I can see her. Come on.'

The detectives lost precious seconds extricating themselves from the crowds. When they managed to catch sight of Elspeth Wynter again, she was running blindly across the intersection beside the Shaftesbury Theatre.

'Where's she heading?' asked Biddle.

From somewhere near the river came the dull drone of a bomber squadron.

'Out,' said Bryant, 'just out into the open, away from the theatre, but the more open it gets, the more frightened she'll be.'

They were fifty yards behind her when she turned into Museum Street and froze, standing in the middle of the road, looking up.

Overhead, the thick grey clouds had parted to reveal a midnight-blue sky glittering with stars as bright and sharp as knives. As the gap grew larger, the oval of the moon appeared, flooding the street with silvered light.

Bryant, May and Biddle came to a stop some way back, amazed by the sight of the buildings' dark recesses melting away beneath the lunar brightness. 'She's reached it,' said Bryant, 'she's reached the light. If she can survive this, she'll be free.'

'She's still going to gaol,' said Biddle indignantly.

'Freedom will be inside her head.'

They could hear Elspeth sobbing in awe and relief as she looked up, transfixed by the quiescence of the moon. The droning of the bombers was fading now, growing quieter and quieter until the four of them were standing in unshadowed silence.

Bryant knew he could not compete with the world that beckoned to her. He watched as she took a faltering step away from him, then another. Part of him wanted Elspeth to run and keep on running, until she was liberated from the city's life-crushing influence, free to live a normal life. Go, he thought, don't look back. Whatever you do, keep going.

'Look, are we just going to stand here and let her get away?' asked Biddle impatiently.

'No, I suppose not,' said Bryant with a sigh as they walked forward. 'Elspeth,' he called gently. 'Please. Let us help you.'

She stopped in her tracks and looked back over her shoulder with sad deliberation. She saw Bryant and held his eye, unable to move any further, and in that moment she was lost.

Up ahead there was a muffled thump, and the road vibrated sharply beneath their feet.

'What the bloody hell was that?' asked Biddle.

Elspeth had heard the noise too.

'Oh no,' was all Bryant managed to say before the two-storey front of the antiquarian bookshop lazily divorced itself from the rest of the terrace and fell forward in an explosion of dust and bricks.

As the airborne sediment settled, they saw the neat rooms inside the bookshop exposed like a child's cutaway drawing. The building's frontage lay collapsed across the road, virtually unbroken. As a fresh wind picked up, the entire street was scattered with the pages of rare books. Colour plates of herons, butterflies, monkeys, warriors and emperors drifted lazily past them. There were diamond shards of glass everywhere. The detectives' clothes were pincushioned with sparkling slivers.

'Bloody hell,' said Biddle, scratching his head in wonder.

Of Elspeth Wynter, there was no sign at all.

61

SPIRITS OF THE CITY

Margaret Armitage sipped the glass of vervain tea made from leaves she had specially shipped to her from a French necromancer in the town of Carcassonne. Beside her, Arthur Bryant and John May dangled their legs over the ancient wall of the riverbank, nursing foamy pint mugs of bitter. Above the pub door was a large blackboard that read: HITLER WILL SEND NO WARNING—ALWAYS CARRY YOUR GAS MASK.

The waitress of the Anchor had looked at Maggie as if she was mad when she asked for a glass of freshly boiled water. It did not help that the teenage leader of the Camden Town Coven, an organization that had counted Sir Arthur Conan Doyle and Edgar Allan Poe among its members, was wearing a purple and gold kaftan belonging to an African tribal chief, topped with a peacock-feather hat and half a dozen amber necklaces inscribed with carvings representing the souls of the dead.

'I'm a bit disappointed about there not being an actual phantom at the Palace, just a poor tortured boy,' said Maggie, looking out across the placid grey water at the bend in the river, where it widened to the docks. 'Let me get under your overcoat, it's big enough.'

'Yes, that was rather an intriguing aspect,' Bryant agreed as he extended his gaberdine. 'Of course, Todd Wynter was never at Jan Petrovic's house, so there were no walls to walk through, so to speak. But when he vanished from the top-floor corridor, and again from the roof, he had me fooled for a while. John, you remember I asked you about the wind that night?'

'Yes, I wondered what you were on about.'

'We found Todd's jacket,' he told Maggie. 'The one his mother had made for him, just a hood and cloak stitched out of blackout curtain, but it was absolutely huge, rolled up like a sheet. When I ran after him, I imagine he simply remained still at the end of the passageway and unfurled the cloak. It was too dark for me to see him. An old magician's trick; he'd witnessed plenty of those at the Palace. He threw it off the roof when he was finished with it, and waited until he could return to his private quarters. We found it hanging from the steeple of St Anne's Church in Dean Street. The wind had carried it like a sail.'

'What a pity,' said Maggie. 'I had hoped you might be able to give us proof of the spirit world.'

'Oh, I've no doubt Andreas Renalda is possessed, but he's possessed by the spirits of his childhood.' Bryant swallowed some of his bitter, savouring the pungent taste of hops. 'In her own way, so was Elspeth Wynter. Her life was shaped by the ghosts of the theatre. She was a woman forced to survive in a world of harmful magic.'

'That's what witches are. Do you think she was a witch?'

'Well, someone dropped a house on her,' said Bryant, 'so she might have been.'

'You can't fool me. You were keen on her.'

'I was only ever keen, as you quaintly put it, on one girl. Once you've met the one, all the others are just phantasms.'

Maggie lightly stroked his hand. 'Perhaps it's time to let her memory go, Arthur.'

Bryant looked out at a pair of swans settling on the oily water. 'It's not a matter of choice. I have to wait for her to do that.' He took a ruminative swig of beer. The evening's chill had blanched his cheeks and knuckles.

'Did you hear about your landlady?' May was anxious to change the mood. 'She stabbed the editor of *Country Life* in the foot with your swordstick.'

'Serves him right,' said Bryant, cheering up. 'He has no business being in London.'

'And Davenport's very pleased. He came into the unit this morning and wandered around for a while, shifting pieces of paper about, looking into drawers, fiddling with things. Turned out he'd come to congratulate us formally, and was having trouble uttering the words.'

'Perhaps he could jot it on a postcard,' offered Bryant. 'He means well but he's such an awful clot. Fancy ordering our front door to be barred.'

'I think he was a bit embarrassed about that. You should have seen his face when Biddle stood up for you. He looked as if he'd been stabbed in the back.'

'I don't suppose Davenport's good mood will last. The Lord Chamberlain has changed his mind about the show. Says it's indecent and has to come off. I think somebody higher up must have had a word with him.'

'So all of Elspeth Wynter's efforts were wasted. The production would have closed anyway. How sad. God, we're such a lot of hypocritical prudes.'

'You didn't sleep with her, did you?' asked Maggie. 'You didn't get your conkers polished by a murderess?'

Bryant looked horrified. 'No I did not, thank you,' he said, as though the thought had never even occurred to him. 'For a spiritualist, you can be very crude.' He suddenly brightened. 'Mind you, *he* did, our Mr May, he made love to a murderess.' He pointed at John May.

'Unproven,' said May hastily. 'I mean Betty's involvement in the death of Minos Renalda. There's nothing on record, only the conversation I had with Andreas.'

'I thought her real name was Elissa.'

'That's right, abbreviated to Betty. She has a sister in the Wrens. I should introduce you.'

'I don't think so. Once bitten and so on.' Bryant raised his trilby and shook out his floppy auburn fringe.

'I should be going.' Maggie Armitage set down her tea glass. 'I'll be late.'

'What have you got tonight?' asked May. 'Druid ceremony? Séance? Psychic materialization?'

'No, Tommy Handley on the radio at eight thirty. I never miss him.' She thrust a lethal-looking pin through her hat. 'I was listening when Bruce Belfrage got bombed. We hadn't laughed so much in ages.' Belfrage was a BBC news announcer who became a national hero after carrying on his live radio broadcast even though the studio had received a direct hit and several people were killed. 'I actually think I'm going to miss the war when it's over.'

'Don't be obscene, Margaret,' said Bryant hotly, swinging his legs down from the weed-riven embankment wall. 'Death is stalking the streets, death made terrifying by its utter lack of meaning.'

'The closer you are to death, the more attached you become to life,' the coven leader reminded him. 'The city is filled with strengthening spirits.'

'The city is filled with brave people, that's all,' said May, and took a long drink of his beer.

'If people ever stop thinking about the ones they leave behind, Mr May, your job will cease to exist. All that you see—all this,' she gestured around her, 'is about generations yet to be born.'

'Don't take her too seriously,' Bryant warned his partner. 'You were wrong about one of us dying in an explosion, Maggie.'

'It's never a dead cert, otherwise I'd make my fortune on the gee-gees instead of helping the police with their inquiries,' she snapped at him, stung.

'You told me you once copped a monkey on a nag called Suffragette racing at Kempton Park because he was possessed by the spirit of Emmeline Pankhurst,' complained Bryant.

Maggie saw more than she ever dared to tell anyone. Time compressing, days blurring into nights, speeding skies, great buildings whirling into life, wheels of steel and circles of glass. She saw a girl her age but half a century away, a girl too afraid of life to leave her house.

She saw the future of John May's grandchild.

'I'm sorry,' she apologized suddenly. 'I have to go. Don't be downhearted, Mr May. And don't worry about the future. Things have a way of working out. The song of the city will live on, so long as there is someone to sing it.'

'Well, I wonder what got into her?' exclaimed Bryant. The detectives watched as she walked off down the street, pausing to stroke a tortoiseshell cat on a doorstep, listening to it for a moment, then moving on.

'You know some very peculiar people, Arthur,' May pointed out.

'Oh, you haven't seen the half of it. I intend to bring many more of them into the unit. I have a friend who can read people's minds by observing insects. He'd be useful. And I know a girl who's a ventophonist.'

'What's that?'

'She can throw her voice down the phone.'

'Now you're teasing me.'

'Our work is far from finished. I think I've finally found a purpose to my life. Something I can dedicate myself to. Thanks to you.'

Bryant looked over at his partner and grinned as the sun came out above them, transforming the river into a shining ribbon of light. He rubbed his hands together briskly.

'But where to start? We have yet to discover the lair of the Leicester Square Vampire. He's still got my shoes, you know. And that poor girl he snatched, buried alive with all those rabid bats and someone else's head. There are other cases starting to come in. We've got a twenty-one-year-old Hurricane pilot accused of a brutal stabbing in Argyll Street, several witnesses, his bloody fingerprints on the body, and a cast-iron alibi that places him in the middle of Regent's Park, tied to the back of a cow. He's one of the Channel heroes, so it's in everyone's interests to exonerate him, but how? No, our labours here are only just beginning. This city is a veritable repository of the wonderful and the extraordinary. Isn't that right, Mr May?'

'I couldn't agree with you more, Mr Bryant,' replied May with a lift of his glass, and this time he really meant it.

Bryant looked over his friend's shoulder, in the direction of Waterloo Bridge. Something drew his eye to the centre of the bridge. There was a coruscating flash of dark sunlight, a spear of greenish yellow, and for the briefest moment two elderly men could be seen leaning on the white stone parapet. Then the light settled, and they were gone.

Far above them, the silver-grey barrage balloons that protected the city turned lazily in the early evening air, like old whales searching for the spawning grounds of their youth.

62

SLEIGHT OF HAND

'What time is it?'

'Almost sunset.' May came away from the hospital window. 'You can see the river from here.'

'Look, John, I've still got the mobile phone you bought me.' Arthur Bryant pulled the silver Nokia out from under the bedclothes and waved it at his visitor, waiting for a compliment. The hospital room was awash with garish flowers and get-well cards.

'I thought you'd lost it,' said May, tearing off a grape and eating it.

'No, I'd accidentally switched it with the television remote. Every time Alma changed channels to watch QVC she speed-dialled the Berlin headquarters of Interpol.'

'Well, why didn't you use the speed-dial to call me?'

'I wasn't thinking very clearly. I'd been hit on the head,' Bryant complained.

'How is the old noggin?' May peered at the top of his partner's skull. A row of neat stitches extended from his right ear to the middle of his left eyebrow. 'You're going to have a scar there. Can you remember what happened that night after I left you?'

'Only bits,' Bryant admitted. 'I went downstairs to get my paper-weight back.'

'What paperweight?'

'The one I threw at the lads from Holmes Road when they came by to make fun of me. It must have been around six in the morning when I went out. I thought I'd better get the thing back because it was a souvenir from the war. I was just coming up the stairs when I saw him. The top door was wide open, and Elspeth Wynter's son was standing there. He had a green metal cylinder in his fist. He started accusing me of persecuting him, and said he was going to kill me. I should never have sought him out at the Wetherby. I'd up-set him when I reminded him how his mother had died. It's funny the way little things can trigger memories. Give me those, for God's sake.' He reached forward and emptied grape pips from May's cupped palm. 'Ow.' He clutched at the top of his head and fell back onto the pillow.

'You shouldn't move about,' warned May. 'The nurse says you have to lie still for a few days. What happened after you saw Todd standing there at the unit?'

'What do you think? He hit me, and there was an explosion. I'd just nipped out in my shirt sleeves, I had no ID on me, no wallet. I woke up in a hostel off the Charing Cross Road. A very nice lady kept feeding me mushroom soup. I went back home but my teeth were hurting, so I picked up my dental records.'

'You also took the blueprints covered with your notes from the Palace.'

'Yes, but I couldn't remember why I'd taken them. I went to see you but I couldn't get in, so I thought I'd wait. Some hideous monkey-like woman appeared from nowhere and started screaming at me.'

'You missed your own funeral.'

'Was it a good turnout?'

'Excellent, lots of wailing and gnashing of teeth, really miserable. You'd have loved it.'

'How did you figure out what had happened?'

'I must admit you had me going for a while. Maggie suggested we try to get in touch with you on the other side—'

'Don't tell me you've become a believer,' interrupted Bryant.

'—and she needed something you'd touched, so I took her Nijinsky's shell. She reached the person who'd been killed in the ex-plosion, just as she'd promised. But she'd made contact with Todd, not you. He'd touched the tortoise too. It had probably been his only childhood friend.' May tucked the blanket around his partner's pyjama'd chest. 'I think you'd better come and stay with me for a while, just until you're a hundred per cent.'

'God, no, you have the television on all the time, it would drive me mad. This one's bad enough.' He pointed to the wall-mounted TV, tuned to a silent news broadcast.

'We'll discuss it later. What would you most like to do when you're better?'

'Oh, I don't know, take tango lessons, do a bit of sky-diving, the usual stuff.' He thought for a moment and smiled. 'Or perhaps we could just go to the river and watch the tide going out.'

'Why not?' May agreed. 'There aren't too many of the old rituals left. It seems a pity to break this one. We'd better get your choppers sorted out as well.' He looked at the bedside table, where Bryant's gruesomely enormous false teeth sat grinning at him. 'If it wasn't for those horrible things I'd never have thought of searching for you.'

'Then I'd like you to keep them.' Bryant grinned toothlessly, then the smile faded. 'He'd not had much of a life, you know, Elspeth's son. In and out of institutions and halfway houses. He was registered under his mother's name, Wynter. Yet he seemed not to remember her when we spoke.'

'He remembered enough to follow you back to the unit and wait there until the next night. We were wondering where he got the incendiary device from.'

'Ah, um, I'm rather afraid that was my fault.' Bryant looked sheepish.

'What do you mean?'

'It was mine. I'd kept it as a souvenir from the war.'

'Kept it, all this time? Where?'

'On my desk.'

'I don't remember anything like that on your desk.'

'The paperweight, the one I chucked at the lads from Holmes Road that night.'

'You're telling me that was a *bomb*?'

'I thought it had been defused. I painted it yellow in the sixties—it was the sort of thing you did back then. I must have destabilized it when I threw it out of the window. I got back to the room and found Todd there. He threatened me.'

'So this green metal cylinder he was carrying wasn't a bomb?'

'No, it was his thermos flask. He hit me over the head with it.' Bryant gingerly touched his scar. 'That's how I got this. He was trying to kill me. I didn't know what to do, but the paperweight was still in my hand so I chucked it at him. I didn't expect it to explode.'

May buried his face in his hands. 'I can't believe you blew us up. We thought you were the victim, not the bomber.'

'Try to look on the positive side,' said Bryant brightly. 'Maybe now they'll give us some decent offices.'

'We are in so much trouble,' moaned May. 'Do you realize we've buried someone else in your grave? Why can't you be like regular old people and put irresponsibility behind you?'

'I know there have been some inconsistencies in my past behaviour, John, but from now on I'll try to be exactly the same.' Bryant's watery blue eyes looked hopefully towards a more certain future.

'Oh, before I forget,' said May, emptying the contents of his nylon backpack onto the end of the bed, 'I know how much you hate staying in bed and I thought you might like something to occupy your mind while you're lying here, so I brought you the job applications Sam Biddle forwarded to the unit. You can go through them and select a few of these "ordinary civilians" for interviews.'

Bryant eyed the pile of letters suspiciously. 'Do I get paid for working overtime?'

'You merely receive the thanks of a grateful nation.'

'Huh.' He lifted the letters up by their corners, examining them as though they were dead animals. When he reached one handwritten envelope, his brow furrowed even more deeply than usual. He opened its flap with a theatrical flourish.

'Hmmp.' He waved at his bifocals. 'Pass me those, would you?' He unfolded the letter. 'Aha. Hmph.'

'I assume you are making those cartoonish noises to attract my attention,' said May wearily.

Bryant tossed the letter at him. 'How about this one? We'll give her an interview, shall we?'

May read for a moment, then raised his eyes. 'This is a formal application to join the unit from April, my granddaughter.'

'And you thought there wasn't anyone in your family willing to carry on the tradition.' Bryant smirked. 'Shows how much you know about people.'

'Wait, did you put her up to this?' asked May.

Bryant's eyes widened with indignant surprise.

'No, of course you didn't. You couldn't have, because when I told you last week that the Chief Association of Police Officers was inviting non-professionals to train alongside detectives, you acted as though you didn't know anything about it.'

'Oh, well then, I don't. You ought to see her, though.' He licked his lips. 'Blimey, I'm starving. It must be nearly time for them to bring the mince trolley round. You'd better be off before it arrives.'

As May slipped the note back in its envelope, he couldn't keep himself from grinning. 'Perhaps I should get Longbright to fix up an appointment.'

'I think you'll find she already has. Next Tuesday at eleven.'

He was going to ask how Bryant could possibly know, but his partner was already starting to feign sleep.

'You missed your vocation, Arthur,' he said softly. 'You really should have been on the stage.'

'The city is my theatre,' murmured Bryant. 'I never want to leave it.' He closed his eyes and allowed himself to sink into vast white pillows. 'The war.' His voice became a faint whisper. 'How little we knew about people then. How little we ever really learn.'

Above the foot of the bed, the silent television replayed footage of guns and men, and a distant battle that could never be won.

Appendix

NOTATIONS MADE BY MR ARTHUR BRYANT IN AN ACCOUNT OF HIS FIRST CASE WITH MR JOHN MAY

Abyssinians, uses of when stuffed
  For purposes of ventriloquism
  Possession of by squadron leaders

Actors, unreliable behaviour of

Agoraphobia, dangers of

Airships, German, poor performance of

Amateurs, abilities of encouraged by Home Office

Architect, incomprehensible explanation by

Armitage, Maggie
  Psychic powers of
  Price charges for ectoplasm clearance
  Link between horseracing and women's suffrage

Ability to use harpsichord as boiled-egg slicer

Astaire, Fred, appearance at Palace

Bananas, as weapon against Hitler

BBC, hilarity caused by bombing of

Bengal tiger, as shameless plug for other published Bryant and May cases

Betts, Corinne, as murder witness
    As stand-up comic

Biddle, Sidney
    Bovine addiction to law and order
    Enjoyment of complicated paperwork
    Pleasure derived from hitting geography teacher

Bombs, used in destruction of police stations
    Falling on London like jellyfish
    Exploding in tube stations
    For use as stage props

Bridge, Waterloo, as conduit for rumination
    Psychic phenomena on

Bryant, Arthur, displays of temperament against constables
    Addiction to illegal narcotics
    Insensitivity
    Rudeness
    Uselessness with opposite sex
    Poor dress sense of
    Comparison to tortoise
    Inability to read flags

Love of tachygraphy
Hopelessness with technology
Association with tontine, Savoyards, butterfly-covered corpse etc.
Possibility of being mistaken for mental patient
Preference for wood carving to having sex
Unflattering description of

Capistrania, Tanya, thankless role in tale as unloved murder victim

Carfax, Sergeant, similarity of wife's face to witch doctor's rattle

Caterpillars, poisonous, use of in teapots

Cats, ginger, arrival through kebab shop windows of
  Stuffed, as conduit for dead squadron leader

Cheese, see Skittles

Chorus girls, unlikeliness of wearing knickers

Davenport, Farley, highly unflattering description of
  Emotional constipation of

Dental records, pertinence in murder investigations
  Likelihood of use in identifying werewolves

Dwarves, gigantism amongst

Finch, Oswald, inflexibility in humorous situations
  As butt of cruel practical jokes
  Under attack by dangerous vegetation

Forthright, Gladys, desire for assonance of
  Peculiar taste in role models
  Unsuitability of choices where men are concerned

Ginger people, use of by Germans during blackouts

Greeks, shipbuilding and theatrical enterprises

Incendiary devices, inadvisability of using as paperweights
    Mistaken for thermos flasks

Jack the Ripper, ability to melt pavement slabs

Landladies, unlikely swordsmanship abilities of

Lift, as device for removing feet

Lithuanian botanists, incidence of vampirism amongst

London, bus standing on end in

Matthews, Jesse, eerie power to drive men mad

May, John, predictability of female dinner dates
    Peculiar ability to turn women's knees to jelly
    Last chance to have sex of
    Stoic qualities of
    Claustrophobia suffered by

Memory, lost

Memory, regained

Memory, revived

Muses, as template for murder spree

Norwegian painter, similarity to medical officer

Norwegians, anaemic condition of

Offenbach, Jacques
    As progenitor of Gilbert and Sullivan
    As inspiration for deranged serial killer

Opinion, Public, violent death of

Orpheus mythology, as motive for murder

Palace Theatre, resemblance of to Borley Rectory

Paperweight, use of for incendiary purposes

Parole, Helena
    Heartlessness of
    Alcoholism of
    Medusa-like qualities of

Pepys, Samuel, talent for tachygraphy

Petri dishes, mysterious existence of under Bryant's bed

Phantoms, ability of to walk through walls
    Likelihood of picking a fight with Claude Rains

Planet, as symbol of Freemasonry
    As murder weapon

Plants, tropical, propensity for sickening cats, wives etc.

Poltergeist, dangers of intrusions by while saying grace

Pope, violation of with roofing tiles
    As condom spokesman

Pork, as substitute for human feet

Senechal, Charles, clouted by planet

Skittles, as a boring esoteric hobby for aged detectives

Statuary, as esoteric clue in criminal investigation

Stone, Miles, unfortunate choice of pseudonym by
    Inability to be faithful with women

Technology, peculiar backfiring of when confronted by technophobes

Teeth, as clue in criminal investigations, see Dental records

Theatre critics, climbing abilities of

Thwaite, Olivia, floral solution to prominent nipples by

Tortoises, life-threatening habits of
    Uses of in spiritualist rituals

Trammel, Betty, mysterious true identity of

Traps, grave

Traps, star

Turk, body parts found in chestnut brazier by

Varisich, Anton, orchestra conductor forced to work with buskers

Wagstaff, Edna, psychic sensitivity of with dead pets

Whittaker, Geoffrey, unorthodox sexual arrangements of